Bridging the Gap:
African Traditional Religion and Bible Translation

United Bible Societies
Monograph Series

1. Sociolinguistics and Communication

2. The Cultural Factor in Bible Translation

3. Issues in Bible Translation

4. Bridging the Gap: AfricanTraditional Religion
   and Bible Translation

5. Meaningful Translation: Its Implications for the
   Reader

6. The Apocrypha in Ecumenical Perspective

UBS Monograph Series, No. 4

Bridging the Gap:
African Traditional Religion and Bible Translation

Philip C. Stine and Ernst R. Wendland, Editors

UNITED BIBLE SOCIETIES
Reading, UK
New York

) 8

UBS Monograph 4
© United Bible Societies 1990
ABS-1992-400-800-CM-2-104643
ISBN 0-8267-0454-9
Printed in the United States of America

CONTENTS

Introduction

Deciding on a title for this book has been perhaps the most difficult part of the project. One working title was *African Religions: Problems in Translation.* But what do we mean when we speak of religion in an African context? As all the papers make abundantly clear, religion in Africa is not something that can be easily isolated and studied as is done in a Western context. Then, what general statements can be made about Africa, a region with such incredible diversity? All who have lived and worked there can attest that the more we learn the less likely we are to generalize.

What we were interested in doing as we began this project was to look at several different languages in Africa and consider the problems Bible translators face in dealing with religious concepts and in rendering words which relate to the spiritual realm: "God," "Holy Spirit," "Devil," "unclean spirit," and others. As these papers show, such studies are not so much linguistic as cultural, for that segment of behavior which we in the West call "religion," in Africa is part of the very warp and woof of all of daily life. To quote Colin Turnbull, "The practical role that religion plays in African society can be seen in almost every sphere of life" (Turnbull 1976, p. 74). In fact, even to speak of "religion" in discussing African cultures is to impose a foreign concept; the word itself is one of the most difficult to translate. Van der Jagt appropriately cautions against interpreting African religions in Western theological terms.

As we moved from linguistic to cultural considerations, there was a parallel expansion of the notion of spiritual to include the cosmological, as the terms we were interested in could only be understood in that wider world-view.

No one should come to these studies expecting to find descriptions of traditional religions of long ago. Since our interest is in translating for readers of today, we were concerned to examine indigenous religion as it is now practiced, with all the influences of modernization and major world religions which have shaped it.

In addition to describing African religion, Turnbull has also struggled with the matter of what generalizations can be made about Africa. In *The Lonely African*, published in 1962, he presents a series of life sketches which illustrate the diversity that exists, and it is only with great caution that he draws a few general conclusions. In *Man in Africa* (1976), however, he attempts to describe "a vital unity underlying the cultural diversity" which he finds in the "*conscious* (author's emphasis) dependence of the African upon his environment" (p. xiii). Unlike cultures which have developed an industrial technology in an effort to dominate the environment, African cultures, according to Turnbull, have been shaped by attempts to adapt themselves to the world around them, and the diversity of cultural types there relates directly to the diversity of environments.

In fact, it is from the realm of the cultural practices and beliefs which relate to this accommodation to the environment that much of the vocabulary is drawn for translating the "spiritual" or religious terms. The other major domain is human relationships, although this in many ways depends on the environment; people's understanding of their own identities and of their relationships with others is conditioned by their environment, or at least by their understanding of the environment and what they must do to accommodate themselves to it and be in harmony with it.

The papers here are a little like Africa itself: there is much which unites them, and yet they exhibit great diversity. The cultures the authors discuss are from Central, East, and West Africa; the authors themselves have training in different disciplines, namely African literature, linguistics, philosophy of language, anthropology, and biblical studies; and they followed different approaches and theoretical models.

But they do share an understanding of religion as an inseparable element of life in Africa. Wendland defines it as "dynamic application of the world-view to human character and conduct in their totality," and Zogbo states "There is no dividing line between spiritual and human entities; the combination of all these elements constitutes reality."

The authors also share the belief that understanding the religion of a culture entails understanding what constitutes "reality." As Mojola says when discussing "Holy Spirit" and *Roho* in Luo, "this is not just a translational problem, but an existential one as well."

How religion, including its concerns with the transcendent, is so totally a part of African life is discussed by Ernst Wendland in his study of the Chewa and Tonga peoples of Malawi and Zambia respectively. In chapters 1 and 2 he outlines a model of culture and world-view which provides a coherent and contextually sensitive theoretical framework against which the many interlocking religious themes can be analyzed (chapter 3). In particular he looks at those themes which enable people to deal with their environment and the unexpected events which impinge on their lives. He outlines seven principles which account for a traditionalist's notion of reality, its relation to the practice of religion, and also for the ways in which such a person would tend to perceive the content of the Bible and of Christianity itself.

Another recurring topic which unites the papers is the impact of modernization and culture change on traditional belief. But as Philip Noss demonstrates, the new does not replace the old; rather "The new mat is woven over the old." These papers give several examples of this process as it is now taking place.

There is also an implicit assumption that all languages and cultures are fit (or equally unfit) vehicles of the biblical message. If not, how could "God" be rendered by local terms such as *Akuj* in Turkana or *Nyasaye* in Luo? In fact, these writers assume, as Lamin Sanneh has recently pointed out (see, for example, *Translating the Message*, 1989), that for people to understand God's word it is not necessary they learn a new language, since God reveals himself to them through their own language and culture. He will subsequently transform these, just as he will enter the individual's life and transform it. After the Bible is translated, the understanding people have of *Akuj* and *Nyasaye* will change as the characteristics of God which are revealed in the Bible will supplant or transform those which people understood before.

How to choose the terms in the receptor languages which will best permit this communication and transformation is the purpose of four of these studies. In chapter 4, van der Jagt presents the world view of the Turkana of northern Kenya, and shows the kinds of mismatch in concept and terminology which Bible translators there must deal with.

Another East African language is Luo. In chapter 5, Aloo Mojola uses two fascinating recent events in Kenya, one involving a case which went to the Supreme Court, to illustrate what happens when traditional Luo practices encounter and adapt to the present realities of modernization. As he turns to the translation task of bridging the gap between the biblical and Luo cultures, he shows how difficult it is to avoid using one cultural framework to understand and interpret the other. When this does happen, one result is misunderstanding, and another is erecting a barrier to God's transforming activity in that language and culture.

Lynell Marchese Zogbo's paper, chapter 6, could well serve as a model for other analysts and translators. First she presents the religious world of the Godie people in the Ivory Coast, and then, term by term, discusses the theoretical and practical problems a Bible translator faces. Translators must understand the belief systems of the source and receptor cultures, not only to choose the most effective vocabulary, but also to prepare Scripture portions and selections which will most effectively correct, supplement, and transform the knowledge a people have of God.

In chapter 7 Philip Noss raises the question of changes in the symbols of faith of the Gbaya of Cameroon. As the traditional encounters a changed world, translators and theologians alike struggle to find those symbols and metaphors which will communicate most effectively the Good News, not only today but tomorrow as well.

What the authors have done, then, is present the nature and extent of the gap that must be bridged when the Bible is translated into African languages, and to offer as well both theory and models which will help others who are undertaking this same task.

BIBLIOGRAPHY

Sanneh, Lamin. 1989. *Translating the Message: The Missionary Impact on Culture*. Maryknoll, NY: Orbis Books.

Turnbull, Colin M. 1962. *The Lonely African*. New York: Simon and Schuster.

———. 1976. *Man in Africa*. Garden City, NY: Anchor Press/Doubleday & Company.

PART I: Traditional Central African Religion
Ernst R. Wendland

Chapter 1

TRADITIONAL CENTRAL AFRICAN RELIGION TODAY: A SOCIOCULTURAL APPROACH

In this chapter we will present a broad overview of some of the chief aspects of indigenous religion in Central Africa, using a modified structure-functional method of analysis. We begin with an effort to delimit this vast topic by providing a general definition of the object of our study, traditional religion, within the sociocultural context of a Central African world-view, and more specifically, from the ethnic perspective of the Chewa and Tonga peoples of Malawi and Zambia respectively. This preliminary orientation is followed in the next chapter by a survey of several models, or structural analogies, which will be useful in both a descriptive and an explanatory capacity as we carry our investigation further into the traditional religious matrix of the target area. The strictly functional component of our approach will be modified by identifying several of the important disfunctional features of this complex, culturally focal phenomenon as well as by a consideration of certain crucial elements of its operation as a varied and variable symbolic system in Central African society.

The more theoretical discussion of these two chapters serves as a necessary background for the third, in which practical application is made to a number of key facets of the average traditionalist's notion of reality, particularly as this concerns the manifold religious dimension of life. The theoretical models will be employed as a conceptual framework for a partial exposition of some of the salient features of the people's belief and value system as these may be presumed to interact in the composition of a Central African (Chewa/Tonga) world- and life-view. Seven basic principles are outlined and exemplified with a special focus upon their relation to the practice of indigenous religion. In other words, an attempt is made to provide a coherent, contextually-sensitive setting for analyzing the many interlocking religious themes that give substance and meaning to some of the unexpected and otherwise unexplainable events that intrude upon the lives of individuals as well as entire communities.

As part of our overall presentation in these three chapters, an informal comparison with some of the chief premises of a Western (American) world-view will be carried out. This differential approach will serve to highlight the importance of obtaining a clear understanding of and appreciation for a local religious perspective before attempting to engage in the language-specific, cross-cultural communication of the biblical message. A number of instances will be cited to demonstrate the critical influence that ancient traditional beliefs have upon the contemporary interpretation and application of the Christian Scriptures in Central Africa.

What Is Traditional About Tradition?

A tradition refers to certain thoughts, words, and/or actions which have been handed down from one generation to the next either orally, in written form, or by visible demonstration. Usually such items are combined to constitute a recognized corpus of material which serves to guide the thinking and behavior of a significant portion of individuals in a contemporary society. But traditions are never static; they normally change, or rather, are modified by the current generation, whether deliberately or as an almost imperceptible product of the passage of time, in response to various alterations in their environment and way of life. Often such shifts occur due to contact with other peoples and their cultures, through trade, education, warfare, colonial domination, travel, and so forth. Certain components of culture are altered more rapidly than others—customs of dress, for example, as opposed to important religious ceremonies. Similarly, some segments of a population, such as well-educated urban residents, will give evidence of greater adaptability than others when it comes to their traditions, despite the possession of a common language and unification under a single political system. Isolated pretechnological rural folk, on the other hand, people who practice a subsistence economy and form a more closed, undifferentiated kinship-oriented society, tend to be much more rigid and defensive with respect to their beliefs, customs, and life-style.

In reality, therefore, there is no such thing as a discrete and uniform body of "traditional Central African (or even 'Chewa' or 'Tonga') religion." There does appear to be a common substratum, or deep structure, of belief, but its surface manifestation in the form of associated precepts and ritual practices may vary considerably depending on the particular area concerned, the parties involved, and the specific life-situation which they are in. In many respects, then, religion appears to be as disparate a phenomenon as it is prevalent.

Furthermore, it is also becoming increasingly vulnerable to some of the same influences leading to stagnation and decay with respect to theology, the cult, and an enveloping organizational structure which have rendered certain world religions in some areas, Western Christianity in particular, more or less impotent as a meaningful force in society at large; e.g., institutionalization, the concretization of dogma, a routinization of symbolic communication as in the liturgy, and a general tendency to succumb to the various forces of secularization—desacralization, rationalization, relativism, and so forth (cp. O'Dea, 1983, ch.5).

Nevertheless, compared with the situation in the Western nations of Europe and America, which are composed of a complex mixture of cultures and subcultures, the peoples and hence traditions of Central Africa are considerably more homogeneous in nature and conservative in outlook. Thus, for the majority of the population, religious beliefs and values also tend to manifest a certain resiliency in the face of some strong pressures for change as well as an underlying structural similarity and a significant degree of functional correspondence. Like the familiar chameleon, which is also a prominent figure in many local myths of origin, African religion has the capacity to adapt to the external situation and in many cases to blend in so completely with its surroundings that it is virtually unnoticeable. Its overt forms (i.e., pertaining to ritual observance and the practice of worship) may be quite different from one area to the next, and the cultus of Christianity may even largely displace them. As a discrete entity, however, the basic belief system of the past remains essentially unchanged.

The description and analysis which follows is based upon a large collection of popular as well as scholarly ethnographic studies, dating from both the pre- and post-independence eras, supplemented by numerous recent personal interviews and discussions (mostly in the vernacular) with men and women of many different backgrounds and walks of life. This wide corpus of data, coupled with a specific focus upon the Chewa and Tonga peoples, made it possible with the invaluable help of several national participant-observers to synthesize what appear to be a number of relevant conclusions which provide one with a fairly accurate picture of some of the principal tenets of traditional religion as believed and practiced today in distinction from pre-Christian times (for some important historical surveys, see Schoffeleers, 1979). Two different kinship-oriented, matrilineal societies were selected, namely Chewa, matrilocal and agricultural, and Tonga, patrilocal, cattle-culture, in order to offer a more varied perspective and a somewhat fuller delineation of the object of our investigation, which is directed towards a selective description of the current nature and influence of the "faith of the fathers" in Central Africa.

A Chewa Folk Tale

As we attempt an overview of some of the principal constituents of Central African traditional religion, it is first necessary to define as closely as possible the main subject under consideration. This is not easy to do in an African setting, since the commonly recognized boundaries between what we might term "religion" and other important elements of culture are not very clearly distinguished, if at all. In the West, religion as a social institution is considerably more sharply defined, both officially from the point of view of the government for instance, and also intuitively by the population at large. But that is not the case in Africa, where religion in one form or another permeates virtually all of a community's interpersonal interaction, both on the individual level and that of society as a whole.

By way of introduction, then, we will examine the following account, which is an English summary of a Chewa drama by Mr. Julius Chongo that was broadcast on Radio Zambia in 1973 (Wendland, 1979, 1760-1773). This narrative illustrates certain facets of traditional religious belief and behavior as they would typically be manifested in a rural sociocultural setting. It includes a number of legendary motifs which reflect a more ancient stratum of oral literature. The story serves as a background for our attempt to specify the scope of the present study, namely, the dimensions of natural religion as practiced in diverse forms in Central Africa. The synopsis below will necessarily emphasize only what one might tentatively consider to be the potentially religious implications of this radio tale.

- - - - - - - - - - - - - - - - - - - -

The Dog-Child

An elderly barren woman named Lumbiwe has made fervent supplications to God (Chauta) for a child all her married life. In her latter years the prayers get more bitter as the miserable woman complains about God's unfair treatment of her: "Alas! what have I done to offend Mlengi the Creator seeing that he has deprived us of offspring? I am tired of going to medicine men for help—woe is me!" By now even her husband, Mcekeni, has given up all hope: "Lumbiwe, it is time you quit complaining. You must realize that it is Chauta, the Owner of all, who determines how to distribute the gift of life. You cannot say that because he has given such and so to others he must also do the same for me. It is up to him alone!"

One day Lumbiwe unexpectedly becomes pregnant, and as one might suppose she suddenly becomes the talk of the whole village: "What kind of an evil omen is this, that an aged person should become pregnant?!" Mcekeni, too, joins in the general reproach: "Lumbiwe, you had to persist in grumbling about a child! Perhaps God has simply granted your request so he can rest from your complaints. Surely you have been lamenting too loudly—all day long: 'God has refused to give me a child!' Now he is angry; he has given you a pregnancy after you've passed the proper age!" Others became even more sinister in their disparaging remarks: "Hah! she has obtained some really powerful medicine! If this isn't witchcraft now! How is it that a person covered with grey hair should still desire a child?!" Others observed that it would not be a genuine baby that Lumbiwe would give birth to. Rather, it must be the spirit of someone else's child—one whom Lumbiwe had bewitched!

Thus it was no real surprise that when Lumbiwe finally came to term and delivered, she gave birth to a live puppy! At daybreak the news spread like a bush fire that Lumbiwe had delivered a dog. What could she have expected, people concluded, from becoming pregnant so late in life, when she was already too old. Most of the women who had come to witness the event fled from the birthing hut when they saw what had happened. Only her close relatives remained, and they urged Lumbiwe to get rid of the dog since it was not human. "Surely this is an evil omen," they complained. Lumbiwe adamantly refused, however, and replied in tears, "You people, I have been praying for a child ever since I was a young girl. But then when I became pregnant, some evil persons practiced their sorcery on me so that I would give birth to an animal. I cannot throw this creature away! Whether this is the result of black magic or comes from God, it makes no difference. I will raise this dog!" And since Lumbiwe believed that some worthless people had put a magical spell upon her, she named her puppy "Worthless."

When Worthless was fully grown, Lumbiwe became pregnant again, but this time she gave birth to a real human being—a male child! She named it Tembo after its "brother" ("Tembo" being the name of the "dog" clan). Tembo and Worthless became close friends, and when Tembo reached marriageable age, according to custom it was up to Worthless as the elder brother to assist him in finding a wife. They journeyed together to a distant land where Worthless helped Tembo to kill a ferocious ten-headed monster bird which had been terrorizing the village of Gonondo. As a reward, the chief gave Tembo the choice of all the maidens in his kingdom for a wife. Tembo married and settled down. He became famous throughout the country because of his fierce hunting dog which kept everyone supplied with an abundance of game meat.

After some years, Tembo decided to return home to his own village. The greedy, and by now quite lazy, men of Gonondo did not want to see their source of fresh meat depart, so they decided to kill Tembo in order to steal his dog and present it to their chief. One day, while out in the bush on a hunt, they lured Worthless away and secretly speared Tembo to death. When Worthless returned and discovered what had happened, he went mad and killed each one of the murderers. He then raced back to the village and wiped out all of the inhabitants. Afterwards Worthless the dog was transformed into the original lion on earth. It is for this reason that lions and human beings are such bitter enemies—all because of the ingratitude and deceit of the "worthless" people of Gonondo!

- - - - - - - - - - - - - - - - - - -

Beneath the surface of this action-packed radio drama we find expressed in outline form the basic conceptual framework that organizes the Central African indigenous belief system. We start with a human being, *munthu* (male or female), which constitutes the heart of the traditional religious perspective. This person is never considered in isolation, however, but he/she is always regarded as part of a family or clan—Tembo, for example, the lineage- preserving son of Mcekeni and Lumbiwe. These are all of "one blood." In addition an individual is normally related to other people of "alien blood," first of all by marriage, such as that contracted by Tembo to the maiden given to him by the chief of Gonondo. Many additional associations of mutual dependency (to varying degrees) are established within any healthy society. Man is also linked to a host of nonhuman beings throughout his earthly cycle of existence, to superhuman personages on the one hand, like God the Life-Giver, and on the other, to the subhuman creatures of the world of nature. The character of the dog, Worthless, illustrates how close this latter relationship is conceived of. It is, in fact, only one world of fully integrated participants and props, both animate and inanimate, which furnish the stage upon which the drama of human experience is played.

Each of these four principal types of interpersonal connection can involve attitudes and actions that are either favorable or unfavorable with respect to a given individual, and hence his/her entire extended family as well. The helpful members of the cast of "The Dog-Child" in relation to Tembo are notably only those of the immediate nuclear family. In addition the narrative presents a number of hostile personages; for example, relatives, such as Lumbiwe's skeptical kinspersons; nonrelatives, such as the envious inhabitants of Gonondo village; superhuman ones, such as malevolent spirits (responsible for the inauspicious birth of "Worthless"); subhuman beings, for example the fierce ten-headed bird monster. These various interrelationships, whether positive or negative, might be visualized as follows:

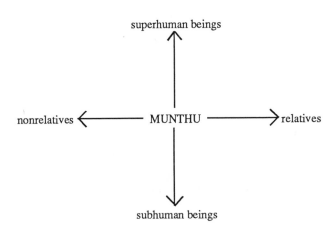

This thematic scheme of personal interplay, which depicts all of the possible character sets of the "Dog-Child" drama above, also summarizes the essence of participant interaction that is manifested in the dogma and practice of traditional religion. It will be explored more fully in our discussion of several conceptual models in the following chapter.

Key Aspects of Culture

Before one can produce a satisfactory exposition of religion, one must first consider the wider context in which this phenomenon is conceived of and practiced, namely, its cultural setting. The concept of culture is itself open to a variety of definitions, but the following will suit our present purpose:

> *Culture* refers to the sum total of a people's system of beliefs and associated attitudinal as well as behavioral attributes—both verbal and

nonverbal, symbolic and nonsymbolic, institutionalized and customary, material and immaterial—all of which are shared to a greater or lesser degree by all of the members of a given society and passed on from one generation to the next by means of explicit as well as implicit learning experiences.

There are two primary focal points in this view of culture, which is always people- or group-specific. These pertain to: (a) their way of thinking, or *world-view*, and (b) their way of behaving, or *life-style*. These two aspects are, of course, very closely connected: thought gives rise to action, but these same actions, in turn, may have a subtle influence upon the conceptual system that originated them, especially over a period of time. This is particularly true in cases where modifications in a people's way of life are made necessary due to the operation of culture change and other external pressures in one or more spheres of social organization.

The world-view has four major dimensions which are thoroughly interrelated with one another within the context of the particular human society in which they are realized. At its core we find the underlying *belief system* of a people. This refers to their key principles, presuppositions, and perspectives on life in relation to their basic *needs* (i.e., material, physical, psychological, social, esthetic, and ethical) as they conceive of and experience them in their everyday cycle of existence (birth, maturation, marriage, reproduction, death). For most people this set of beliefs is an abstraction in the sense that individuals are not consciously aware of them. However, these crucial notions are generally embodied at a more apparent level within the surface structure of culture in the form of an elaborate system of symbols which represent the group's time-honored perception of reality and philosophy of life. Often they are simply taken for granted until one or another is called into question in a time of conflict or crisis when they must either be reinforced in resistance to the forces of transformation or altered to accommodate sociocultural change through the processes of addition, deletion, substitution, and/or permutation (Nida, 1971, 244-245; see also Kraft, 1974, 306).

Illustrated in the preceding narrative, for example, we find specifically religious beliefs such as these: there is a personal Supreme Being; this all-powerful God controls human destiny by either granting or withholding life; other forces in the cosmos may be directed to influence one's personal destiny; the boundary between man and nature or between what is natural and the supernatural is not rigidly defined; human or superhuman agents of evil can mystically subvert God's beneficial purposes for a particular person or clan. The basic belief in the benevolence of God is questioned at the beginning of the account, but such doubt occurs, at least in this story, only on an individual level. God comes through at last to grant an urgent request; it is man who fails the test of uprightness and fidelity.

Integrally attached to these fundamental beliefs and felt needs are a number of key *values*, both positive and negative in orientation, which serve to fix the norms and standards of popular thought and behavior. These values and value clusters comprise the dynamic nucleus of a given culture, for they determine how all of reality and human experience are to be evaluated and in turn responded to, particularly in relation to the fulfillment of a people's primary goals in life (Nida, ibid., 251). In most, if not all, African societies, religion is the principal factor that establishes and continually influences their system of values, and hence it also plays an important role in governing the pace and direction of culture change. In the Dog-Child story, the value of life is emphasized: the biological life of parents is bestowed to their children; the spiritual life and well-being of parents is in turn dependent upon their offspring; furthermore, the preservation of life in both body and soul (or spirit) depends on the maintenance of mutual fidelity in interpersonal relationships, within the clan as well as in society as a whole.

A community's system of values is normally associated with a corresponding set of personal *affections*: feelings, attitudes, biases, esthetic tastes, preferences, and so forth. When persistent and widespread, these also serve to modify the accustomed manner of thinking and acting of a particular group or subgroup within the larger social unit. Events that are unexpected and/or extraordinary in an African setting are always unwelcome and usually feared; consequently they are normally attributed to the activity of malicious personal beings. Thus, when Lumbiwe finally becomes pregnant after many years, people come to the conclusion that she has been practicing witchcraft. They were naturally upset by such antihuman behavior. Similarly, when she gives birth then to a deformed child (characterized by a lowly dog in this narrative genre of the fantastic), she bitterly accuses those who were jealous of her good fortune, stating that they had employed sorcery against her.

This culturally-specific complex of beliefs, values, and affections is crystalized into an implicit hierarchy of desired objectives or *goals*. Thought, or mind-set, transforms into action as the world-view reveals itself, as it were, by motivating a person/people's characteristic way of living—their visible culture. Such influence may take the form of either broad patterns of popular convention (their customs; e.g., for a childless woman to seek magical means to promote pregnancy) or more rigid rules of decorum (e.g., applying the law of the levirate in case of the death of a spouse of child-bearing age). Such tradition-governed activity is organized with respect to seven major areas of concern within human society, i.e., the social institutions of art, kinship, education, economics, government, medicine, and religion, each of which covers a variable and partially overlapping range of communal belief and behavior. The primary need-value-goal component of a people's world-view to a large extent also determines the material objects and artifacts which they produce in order to carry out their accustomed way of life in their chosen environment and according to these seven institutions as they have been socially constituted. A simple diagram of the mutually interactive nature of these essential relationships is shown below:

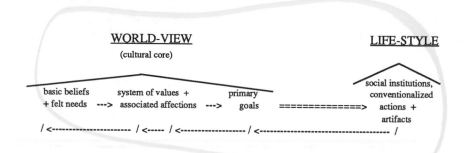

The Components of Culture

Now when we speak about cultural behavior, we are not thinking of just any sort of action or artifact. Rather, we are especially concerned with those objects, words, and deeds which function as *signs* in the society at hand. That is, people (normally the majority of the group) automatically attach a certain shared meaning, feeling, and/or significance to the appearance or use of such signs, whether they occur in isolation or combined and ordered with other signs within a particular social context. Most signs in common currency within a given culture, whether pertaining to food, dress, business, recreation, or whatever, are quite arbitrary in nature. That is to say, there is no special relationship between the sign and what it signifies; for example, between the actual sound of a particular word and the concept that it happens to refer to (e.g., *beth* [Hebrew], *oikos* [Greek], *domus* [Latin], *nyumba* [Chewa], *ng'anda* [Tonga], *house* [English] to designate "a building for people to live in"). The connection between the image and the idea which it evokes is simply one of popular convention within the language concerned. Similarly, with nonverbal signs, sometimes misleadingly referred to as "representational symbols" (Livingston, 1989, 70), there is no natural linkage between the object or event serving as the sign (e.g., a green traffic light) and its significance (i.e., vehicles should proceed). It is a matter of established custom, habitual practice, or common consent—in the case of a traffic light, one that is made obligatory through incorporation into a legal code.

In the case of other signs, however, notably those concerned with a people's religious beliefs and practices, there is a certain specifiable relationship which does link the image, whether verbal or nonverbal, and its referent. Such signs, which are normally selected from the immediate world of nature, whether animate or inanimate, and human experience, are frequently termed *symbols*. In other words, the concrete symbol (entity, activity) bears certain crucial associations that serve to forge a link between two distinct areas or aspects of reality as people generally perceive it. Furthermore, some definite connection with the cycle of nature, the human life-cycle and/or the structure and functioning of human society is inevitably involved in this process of symbolization. In a Central African context, symbolic communication is of utmost importance because it is always connected somehow with the phenomena of life and death or power and impotence.

For instance, if a Chewa villager notices an owl sitting on the rooftop of his house at night, he fearfully interprets this as an evil omen: somebody in the family is about to come under the spell of a witch, become sick or have an accident, and probably die. This is an example of a symbol based upon some conventional association, i.e., an *index* (cp. Nida, et al., 1983, 87). In fact, there are usually several levels of signification which interact in any instance of symbolic communication; e.g., within the conjoined ideational complex of nighttime/darkness/evil: OWL ---[agent of]---> WITCH ---[agent of]---> DEATH. Such conceptual and emotive connections may of course vary in different situationally-defined social and spatial settings, or culture frames. Thus, if an urban pastor would happen to see that same owl sitting high in the bell tower of his church building, he would probably not give it a second thought.

Another important type of symbol, called an *icon* (ibid., 86), is based more specifically upon the similarity in either form or function between a given sign and its referent. Most types of graphic art, such as a painting, carving, or molding, illustrate this principle. In the religious sphere, iconic, or analogical, symbolism is involved in the basic concept of giving libations and offerings to the ancestral spirits. The latter, as living extensions of the human community, continue to be regarded largely in anthropomorphic terms, and thus they, too, need food and drink for their essential maintenance. The spirits, in turn, symbolically indicate their acceptance of man's gifts in ways that correspond to the imagery being utilized. For example:

When offering a cow, they would cut off a piece and offer it at the village shrine. The remainder would be used in a feast. In the morning, then, if they should see the ants MBWEE!—all over the place, they would rejoice in knowing that the ancestors had received their offering (*Mtunda*, 11; translation from the original Chewa).

Many of the rites and practices connected with the traditional sacrificial system, divination, the preparation and application of magical substances, sorcery and witchcraft, and so forth, integrate symbols of both an iconic and an indexical nature. Among the Chewa people, the antelope "horn" (*nyanga*) is a prominent instance of this: it symbolically represents the person as well as the activity of the "diviner-doctor" (*sing'anga*) or conversely the "sorcerer- witch" (*mfiti*), for it is used as a container for magical preparations, either benevolent or malevolent in intent, some of which are actually made from pulverized animal horns. A magically-treated horn may also be employed as an instrumental device either to draw out from or to inject mystical forces into the human body of a patient or victim. We note that in the Old Testament the image of a horn, the primary means of defense of many of the local animals, conveys a rather different symbolic significance, namely, that of physical strength (1 Kg 22:11) and/or personal honor (Ps 75:10).

So it is that these symbolic forms and symbol systems, whether verbal, behavioral/social, or objectified in the form of some natural or man-made object(s), are typically quite culture-specific. That is to say, though commonly recognized and reacted to in a similar way by most, if not all, of the members of a particular human community, they may be expected to elicit, stimulate, or signal different meanings across cultural boundaries. This is because the respective user groups are frequently motivated and guided by alternative ways of perceiving the world and interpreting their experience in it. An ordinary Western male, for example, has undoubtedly been exposed to myriads of colors ever since he was old enough to distinguish them. Consequently the different shades have relatively little meaning for him, except that he may prefer some more than others. His wife would tend to pay more attention to the use of color combinations in different situations, such as for items of dress or decorating her house, but the significance even for her will usually go little further than what preferences have been determined by popular taste.

The basic color scheme of Central African peoples, on the other hand, is considerably reduced in scope, and consequently the individual concepts represented are more significant in their overall meaning and symbolic import. They generally function in a closely integrated basic set of three: black, representing darkness, of course, and by association also storm clouds and rain, has a positive value attached to it in the context of religious ritual; white suggests clear skies (no rain) and is also linked to the notion of purity and the ancestral spirits; red, on the other hand, signifies danger, for it reflects the color of blood, and where blood is being emitted, whether naturally (e.g., menstruation) or unnaturally (e.g., a cut), the affected body must be experiencing a serious loss of physical life.

The essential symbolism of the Chewa, Tonga, and many other ethnic groups in Central Africa revolves around a closely related set of four nuclear concepts, all of which reflect in some way upon the central notions of *fertility* and *life* or, by implication, their opposites, namely *sterility* and *death*. These are, together with their basic color connections: fire (red, but produces black smoke and coals); water (white, or "clear"); blood (red, but turns black after drying); and semen (white). The interaction of these four is very intricate and their associations manifold; for example:

FIRE: figures the sexual act (or the desire for it), which results in "heat"—physical, emotional, and ritual; also symbolizes life and the presence of superhuman power, either benevolent or malevolent;

BLOOD: the most powerful symbol of life and one's lineage, thus it also represents the ancestors—the "living dead"; during her monthly period a woman loses some of her vital force and becomes ritually "cold," hence sexual relations are forbidden;

SEMEN: when emitted, it typically produces "heat" and transmits life from the blood of the man (an alien ancestral line) to the woman; it consists of "seeds" and can itself therefore be represented symbolically by various grain products and beer; the latter in turn is also associated with—

WATER: as distinct from the preceding three, water "cools" and thus is the principal element in rites of purification and renewal; it, too, is associated with life and its preservation, and so it can also be utilized in offerings to the ancestors.

Due to their vital symbolic import, fire, blood, semen, and water (or their figurative substitutes, such as beer or white maize meal) play an essential role in virtually all ritual activity, whether integrative (e.g., initiation) or disjunctive (e.g., exorcism) in nature. In addition one or the other is always involved in the operation of any taboo, the basic function of which is to sustain and safeguard the life-giving fertility of the clan and the moral purity of a well-ordered human society.

Since symbols communicate on such a fundamental interpersonal level—often by a psychological identification with the higher reality which they would seem only to represent—they must never be ignored in any consideration of a people's religious system. Symbols are not mere signs and interchangeable at will. Rather, each is to a greater or lesser extent unique in form, function, and effect, for each active symbol possesses a certain inherent potential to bring about either stability or change, as the case may be, in its context of use. Their true meaning and significance, which is conveyed both verbally and nonverbally, lies much deeper in the human consciousness, and their social as well as spiritual implications are much broader in scope. As a result, their very presence as well as their importance is frequently missed by analysts who cling too closely to the surface of the anthropological phenomena which they are seeking to investigate. Symbol systems may differ just as radically as the distinct linguistic codes that can separate any two ethnic groups. Therefore the process of communication is in equally as great a danger of failure on this crucial level of message transmission, where the most basic concepts of a people's world-view are being dealt with in issues that vitally pertain to the central aspects of their everyday life and future well-being.

Now in some instances a certain measure of correspondence between two different systems of symbolic organization may be found, such as the significance for the Chewa or Tonga of Christian baptism as a ritual event which unites a performatory utterance and the cleansing/renewing power of water to effect a sacred act of initiation, incorporation, and/or rebirth. But more often than not, some serious clashes or divergences in perspective may be expected—as we observe in the sacrament of the Lord's Supper, for example, which features a mystical, metamorphic, or simply a representative (depending on one's theological persuasion) manifestation of the sacred-supernatural, in this case the body and blood of Jesus Christ, as a salutary, participatory act of fellowship. But from an indigenous Central African point of view, no person—let alone a savior—could have any real power left once he had been thus eaten as in the manner of witchcraft. Only the witch, who has partaken of such a human meal, would be expected to derive any benefit—and that for a totally diabolical purpose!

Notice that even within the same culture, a single sign may have different symbolic meanings and associations as a result of its use in varied social and linguistic situations. Take the concept "black," for instance. When applied in reference to one's physical appearance, the term can have a favorable connotation: "black is beautiful" is also true in a traditional Central African context. But when "black" is used to designate one's psychological condition or some prevailing personal interrelationship, it carries distinctly negative overtones; e.g., Chewa: "They were black with respect to (i.e., hated) one another"; "I am black in the eyes today" (i.e., completely at a loss for what to do); "She is black in the heart (i.e., very worried about) her son." Similarly, with reference to the weather in general, the color black may be desirable, as mentioned above; but in connection with the daily cycle of human activity, it definitely is not. Death and the various events which may precipitate it, such as witchcraft, are believed to take place as a rule during the darkness of night, when the heavens are black and the evil deeds of men cannot easily be seen or detected.

To give another, more complex example: the concept of "medicine" (Chewa: *mankhwala*; Tonga: *musamu*) is one that evokes a host of cultural associations, most of these implicitly connected in some way with the notion of mystical power—the capacity to alter, through nonempirical means, one's current situation or condition in life. This is considerably different from the corresponding, but much more limited, Western idea of a commercially prepared chemical substance that is employed, usually in a rather perfunctory manner, to relieve the symptoms of some generally minor bodily ache or ailment. At its deepest level in an African context, however, medicine pertains to the people's fundamental belief and value system, since it refers to a physical (natural) material which has been empowered with magical (supernatural) properties by a traditional specialist, i.e., a "medicine man/doctor" (*si-ng'anga*). It functions, through the precise manipulation of a concrete symbolism connected with the motivating force of a personal will, either to enhance or to inhibit one's "life force" (or "soul power," see below) with regard to a particular area of human existence, e.g., the ability to reproduce, maintain health, ward off the agents of evil, promote prosperity, increase one's attractiveness, popularity, and so forth.

The Central African concept is thus inherently a dynamic one; that is, medicine exists only as the result of and directed towards some specific human desire/objective—to be used in the interests of preserving one's selfhood and enhancing one's well-being. It therefore ranks relatively high on the average individual's scale of values because it is very closely connected with his/her efforts to maintain life in a world that is filled with so many hostile forces which are bent upon either controlling or even extinguishing it. The emotive associations that one has about medicine—the connotations which the word evokes when one speaks or hears it—may then be either positive or negative, depending on the situation and/or circumstances of use.

For example, a particular application of magical substances, such as those combined within a charm, might be utilized beneficially to protect a child from the attacks of witches. To illustrate the opposing notion, it may be diagnosed by a diviner that a certain potion administered to a man's food is responsible for his present illness. Finally, a person's beliefs, values, and feelings in relation to the symbolic complex of "medicine" will converge to establish and maintain a particular goal or set of goals that will motivate his/her own behavior regarding these substances; e.g., to obtain a specific type of magical material in order to accomplish a certain objective in life; to acquire some countermedicine (or antidote) to defend oneself from another person employing it against him/her; or to avoid such local concoctions altogether, since their use may be seen to conflict with another, more strongly felt belief/value/affection/goal system, such as that instilled by Christian indoctrination.

The importance of such seemingly intellectual concerns becomes more apparent when we consider the complexity of the evangelistic endeavor: a message encoded from the perspective of one (the biblical) ethos needs to be communicated within the cultural matrix of another, significantly different (receptor) way of looking at things. A certain mismatch of meaning, both designative and associative, is bound to occur no matter how hard one tries to maintain conceptual equivalence. Take, for example, the notion of the "medicine" practitioner (*sing'anga*) referred to above. Christ's observation that "it is not the healthy who need a *doctor*, but the sick" (Mt 9:12), has quite a different impact upon a Chewa hearer, as distinct from an American hearer. For the latter, the statement sounds almost like a truism, even in this context where it is applied to the religious relationship between Christ and the Pharisees on the one hand, the publicans on the other. But for someone with a traditional Chewa background, the sense would not be quite so obvious; in fact, these words could be rather misleading. This is because in a typical rural setting the services of a medicine man are normally required by people of both categories—by those who are "strong" (as the original Greek term implies) in order to preserve their good fortune, and of course by the "sick" as well to provide the necessary cure, or more likely, a magical preparation that will confound the evil medicine that has been applied against them by a sorcerer. The traditional "doctor" deals with the whole of life in all of its physical and psychological dimensions—and conversely with the various possible causes of death. His practice is not limited to the diagnosis and treatment of sickness per se, as it is in a Western setting.

Turning to the overt, behavioral end of our dual notion of culture (i.e., world-view interelating with life-style), we note that the same form of conduct, on a superficial level, as practiced by two individuals may well be the product of a completely different cultural perspective on the nature of things. For example, both the atheistic Western university professor, doing some sociological research in the Gwembe Valley of southern Zambia, as well as the deeply religious but nonliterate Tonga subsistence farmer who lives there are likely to carefully avoid any illicit casual sexual encounters. For his part, the professor will not want to risk the chance of contracting AIDS, that rather mysterious incurable disease which he has been told infects (at least with antibodies) a relatively large proportion of the female population in Central Africa. He believes the medical reports he has read, places a high value on preserving his life, shrinks with horror at what AIDS can do to the human body, and therefore alters what may for him under different circumstances be a familiar, uninhibited lifestyle.

In the same way, the typical Tonga resident will tend to shun such activity, but for quite different reasons, ones which stem from a more mystical, and at the same time more personal, belief concerning the source of the danger to his health and life. He abstains from indiscriminant sexual relations because he is afraid of falling under the curse of his partner's husband, a curse known locally as *lukanko* 'seizure' or 'trembling'. There are different degrees of this malady, only one of them life-threatening. As Daniel Mwale explains:

> There is *Lukanko* from the Cobra, the most fatal and from which victims die on the spot. There is also one which forces victims not to feel comfortable and have splitting headaches unless constantly under a shower, and another type leaves the victim trembling and shaking after sleeping with a woman who has had such a spell cast on her. . . . Ever heard of the usually disbelieved stories that a couple failed to separate after making love? That is reportedly another form of *Lukanko* ("The *Lukanko* Weapon—How Men of the Valley Cast Love Curses on Their Wives," Times of Zambia, July 11, 1982).

The practice of *lukanko*, and the set of beliefs associated with it, apparently had its origin in earlier days when warriors had to protect their wives while they were away from home fighting tribal wars. Later on in history the same function was performed when men often migrated to the industrialized regions of southern Africa in search of cash employment. As regards any protection from such sexually-transmitted affliction for the venturesome, the Tonga man is considerably better off than the university professor. Whereas no AIDS vaccine has as yet been successfully tested, there is a rather brisk business in anti-*lukanko* charms (termed *tsanga*) being conducted in the Gwembe Valley!

Toward a Contextually-Oriented Understanding of Religion

Scholars have tried a number of different approaches in their study of religion: sociological, philosophical, psychological, functional, and structural, to mention several of the major categories (Nida, 1960, 97-98; 1971, 243-244). Not surprisingly, a wide assortment of rather diverse definitions have been proposed. Generally, these vary according to where they place their emphasis in relation to a series of possible componential pairings: thought—behavior, supernatural—natural, personal—impersonal, individual—social, structure—function, sacred—profane, among others, in various combinations. The following list of definitions is a representative sample of the range which one encounters; it is given merely to illustrate how the preceding distinctions may be applied to give a general indication of the nature of the particular approach being considered:

Folk
Religion

X

X

[Religion is] any system of belief, worship, conduct, etc. [that is directed towards] a divine or superhuman power or powers, often involving a code of ethics and a philosophy (adapted from Webster: conceptual, behavioral, supernatural).

Religion is a system of symbols which acts to establish powerful, persuasive, and long-lasting moods and motivations in men, by formulating conceptions of a general order of existence, and clothing these conceptions with such an aura of factuality that the moods and motivations seem uniquely realistic (Geertz, 1966, 4: ideational, natural, individual).

[Religion is] a unified system of beliefs and practices relative to sacred things, i.e., things set apart and forbidden—beliefs and practices which unite into one single moral community, called a Church, all those who adhere to them. . . . [It is] the soul of society (Durkheim, quoted in Moore, 157; and in Shorter, 1973, 44: sacred, social, structural).

[Religion is] a concern of man in society with basic human ends and standards of value, seen in relation to nonhuman entities and powers (Firth, quoted in White, 1961, xvii: supernatural, social, functional).

Religion . . . is the human, socioreligious response to the divine (Hennig, 1964, 48: behavioral, supernatural, personal).

Religion [is] . . . the manipulation of nonempirical or supraempirical means for nonempirical or supraempirical ends (O'Dea and Aviad, 1983, 7: supernatural, impersonal, functional).

Now these are not necessarily the best definitions of religion in print, but they do demonstrate the point that, before embarking upon an analysis of the subject, an investigator needs to indicate clearly the particular perspective that he/she has

etic definitions; Wendland argues for emic context embedded approach

adopted. That is what we hope to accomplish in the remainder of this as well as in the subsequent chapter. We will begin with a brief outline of the sociocultural setting within which the indigenous religious system is realized in Central Africa. This essential background information will help us to derive an understanding of our field of study which is more contextually oriented and hence one that is also more relevant and useful as a guide in our efforts both to describe the nature of traditional religion and to explain how it operates in Bantu society.

Religion, like any of the principal organizational complexes of culture (such as the systems of kinship, politics, economics, education, and art), has its own distinct set of beliefs, values, affections, and goals. The extent to which the religious inventory happens to correspond with the composition and configuration that is displayed by the other social institutions varies according to the culture concerned. Different peoples place differing emphases on these institutional constituents. In Africa generally and Central Africa in particular, religion is supreme. Thus one observes that the boundaries between religion and the other foundational organs of society are not clearly defined at all. This is because in such so-called "natural" religious communities, there is little differentiation between religion and the general sociocultural life of the people. Thus it is not psychologically and socially compartmentalized as it tends to be in the West, where individualistic, "founded" religions prevail (Livingston, 1989, 133). Rather, it is diffused throughout all of the diverse manifestations of human life and acts as an integral part of each of the other major cultural components. As Geertz observes:

> . . . sacred symbols [i.e., religion] function to synthesize a people's ethos, the tone, character and quality of their life, its moral and esthetic style and mood, and their world-view . . . their most comprehensive ideas of order (quoted in Flatt, 1973, 336).

Moreover, indigenous African religion is not an abstract philosophical system. On the contrary, it involves a dynamic application of the world-view to human character and conduct in their totality. A useful analogy here is to compare the manifold realizations of religion in a traditional African setting to the hub of a spoked wheel: the hub is not only at the center of things, it also directs the forward motion of the whole system. In short, African natural religion penetrates and propels all of life. It is thus a much more vital component in the overall organization and operation of culture than it is in the West, where religion has been relegated by the rise of science, technology, and the influence of various naturalistic and secularized philosophies to a rather peripheral and subsidiary position on the "wheel of life." We might illustrate the Central African viewpoint as follows:

```
                        social structure
        medical practices        didactic lore
        ethical concerns    \  | /    agriculture
        rites of passage   \ \ | / /   music and dance
        land and property    — RELIGION—    oral literature
        kinship relations    / | \ \   annual festivals
        decorative arts     / | \    natural environment
            chieftainship      trades/crafts
                    herding/hunting
```

Of special note on the above diagram, which depicts only a representative selection of features, is the natural environment, both animate and inanimate. This item is included because according to traditional thinking, any feature of the ecosystem that man comes into contact with is part of his culture—his world-view and his way of life.

Complementing the preceding synchronic display of religion in relation to a given cultural world, is the following illustration which depicts the pervasive influence of religion on the diachronic level. This may be organized according to the seven key stages of an individual's life cycle, each of which are accompanied by various socioreligious rites of passage that both confirm and safeguard a person as he or she undergoes such a potentially dangerous transitional experience:

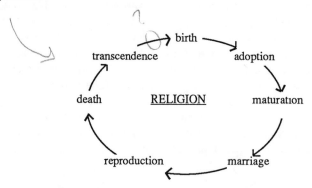

```
                          birth
        transcendence            adoption

        death        RELIGION        maturation

           reproduction        marriage
```

"Birth" is placed at the start of the cycle, since, from a religious perspective, that is most crucial. Birth means new life, an extension and reinforcement of the lineal cord which extends from the tribe's earliest ancestors and which must be continued in one's own children and their descendants. Each of the subsequent rites of passage is essentially a "death" and "rebirth" to a new level in the evolving social structure, one which entails a new role and its attendant communal responsibilities. The apparent anomaly of physical death is neutralized, as it were, by incorporating it into the circle of life, notably at "transcendence," when the family of a deceased member "canonize" him/her as an ancestral spirit by means of an elaborate set of rituals and ceremonies; and again at "adoption," when such a departed relative reestablishes a personal relationship with a living descendant, and the clan as a whole, through the process of "naming" (nominal reincarnation) or mediumship (spirit possession).

So what religion has in common with the other facets of culture is, in general, a corpus of beliefs and an associated value system (that is, assumptions about "the way things are" and "what is important" in life) which interacts with a corresponding set of behavioral patterns and social institutions. What links the two—mind-set and way of life—is the practice of religion, the cultus. Thus, for peoples whose outlook is largely governed by a religious orientation, liturgical behavior mediates between belief and life, the structure and function of society in particular; it embodies, in symbolic form, the culture-specific set of presuppositions by which human experience is ordered and controlled (Douglas, 1966, 128). The varied manifestation of what one believes in the form of specialized types of ritual action, whether engaged in consciously and deliberately or automatically out of pure habit, both reinforces those beliefs on the one hand and also affects one's daily habits of living and relating to the surrounding world, whether animate or inanimate.

In order to get at the underlying organization of needs, beliefs, values, and goals in a natural religious community, therefore, the investigator must first delineate and analyze the people's total behavioral system in terms of their major social institutions, especially those diverse elements which relate to the practice of their religion. These surface relationships, whether overtly expressed and displayed or simply assumed, can be linked in turn to their deep-level conceptual framework in a way which seems to best account for the various symbolic and ritual phenomena that have been observed as these pertain to either personal or communal concerns (i.e., life-cycle and afflictive crises versus agricultural/seasonal and mythic/historical events).

What is it, then, that distinguishes religion from the rest? After all, religion, as has been emphasized, is closely integrated with all the other aspects of African culture. Religious beliefs are more than just a mirror for the social man, or as Douglas puts it: an "expression of society's awareness of itself" (ibid., 101). Its diagnostic feature seems to be that this belief/behavioral system has reference to what is sometimes termed the "transcendent" in human experience, namely, an all-encompassing but invisible *complex of forces*, personal as well as impersonal, consecrating and corrupting, which both constitutes the universe and controls man's presence within it. In other words, Central African traditional religion has the distinct function of enabling man, the individual and society as a whole, to relate to the diverse hierarchy of helpful and hostile powers which comprise his sphere of knowledge and realm of experience—past, present, and future.

This life-giving/preserving process of interaction, whether viewed as a means of conformity, coexistence, manipulation, or mastery, involves various levels and modes of *communication*, which are carried out for diverse purposes: protection, purification, propitiation, thanksgiving, peace keeping, chastisement, and so forth. The result of this communicative activity—whether overt or covert, deliberate or spontaneous, ritualized or informal, physical or mental—is the establishment of a dynamic relationship between the participants or entities concerned, namely, the devotee and the object of his religious devotion. The latter functional and relational orientation is expressed by the usual indigenous terms that are offered as a translation of "religion," which lacks a generic equivalent in the languages of Central Africa, e.g., Chewa: *kupembedza* 'to entreat submissively,' *kupemphera* 'to pray for something,' or *kuyamika* 'to magnify, praise'. Notice also the predominantly active orientation of such words. Religion is action; it is a way of life. The belief system must normally be realized in specialized ritual activity as well as in everyday personal conduct in order for it to be valid and effective.

Thus, religion in a Central African sociocultural setting may be partially defined as man's efforts to orientate and integrate, that is, to *contextualize*, himself in both word (e.g., mythic charter) and deed (e.g., symbolic rite) with regard to the diverse human and nonhuman forces, both sacred and profane, that permeate his natural environment. To be sure, the Supreme Being, "God," is a recognized and important part of this unified program of personal and impersonal interplay, which is normally expressed by an elaborate system of symbolical representation. But so are magic, witchcraft, and the assortment of spirits which inhabit man's world. The latter influences are actually a great deal more important to human society in daily life than the deity, as will be shown as we turn to a consideration of the heuristic application of several models to our study. These will help us to explore more fully the various elements involved in the practice of religion in its sociocultural setting—participants, events, relationships, objectives, plus the many emotive connotations with which these are associated in the human experience of the divine and the unseen powers which complement, control, or confound the different facets of one's everyday existence.

Chapter 2

MODELS AND MATRIX: CONTEXTUALIZING THE STUDY OF CENTRAL AFRICAN TRADITIONAL RELIGION

In the preceding chapter we were able to approach the concept of religion in Central Africa in a preliminary sort of way. Perhaps we might further develop the implications of the ideas presented there and the issues which they raise by viewing the subject of our investigation in terms of a model, or better, as a set of related models. A model is simply a formalized and/or conventionalized analogy. More specifically, it is an analytical tool which gives one a simplified representation of some complex reality, one that pertains either to the universe of nature or to some aspect(s) of human thought and behavior. It provides a convenient perspective or framework for understanding, probing, explaining, and evaluating a multifaceted set of phenomena (persons, objects, events, qualities, etc.). A model helps the researcher to organize the facts of life--to reduce the maze of everyday existence and the world of experience to more manageable proportions so that a relevant and perceptive description or prediction might be constructed on that basis. Thus, just as religion itself is both a "model of" and a "model for" reality (Geertz, 1966, 93-4), so also other partial models may be usefully employed to elucidate certain aspects of the religious prototype.

An "etic" model, however, which starts from an outsider's or a universal perspective, always needs to be continually tested for reliability and validity against the diversity of concrete data which it seeks to explain, in particular the "emic" or insider's point of view. It must therefore be modified or corrected where it does not conform to that indigenous reality. It may then be further supplemented—generally by different models and specific methods, such as "key term analysis" (cp. van der Jagt, this volume)—where it is deficient in accounting for the local framework of interpretation, that is, what naive, native informants perceive and believe on the basis of their own experience. This emic viewpoint includes all local models of the cosmos and the human condition, such as the common Central African "hot—cold" [i.e., dangerous/potent/strong —vulnerable/incapable/weak] metaphoric explanation of illness in terms of prohibited interpersonal relationships and sociological circumstances. Such an internal outlook, on the other hand, often needs to be systematized, abstracted, and/or generalized to a certain extent so that it may be presented in a manner that is both comprehensible to the outside world and expressed in terms that are comparable with (yet not conformed to) the descriptions and analyses of other human philosophical systems. It is with such cautions in mind that we offer the three models below, each of which complements the others in offering a conceptual grid that will help us to understand something more of the dynamic, pervasive nature of religious thought and practice in Central Africa.

A Power Model

This is a simple dual-axis model which provides one way of looking at the manner in which religion, defined generally in the preceding chapter as a specific form of communication, is related to the social network of a particular community or an entire ethnic group. It is based on an organic analogy which employs a structure-functional approach and a holistic framework to investigate the phenomena under consideration. Thus society is viewed as being a system of interrelated parts in vibrant interplay, much like the human body. The various parts, or organs (since each may be regarded as a system in its own right), normally interact in cooperation to keep the whole intact and in balance, while any changes in the system, whether in response to some internal conflict or external crisis, are effected with the purpose of restoring stability, or homeostasis, to the whole.

But things do not always work so smoothly in a person's body, even when the members need to be acting together to ward off some alien force or antagonistic influence. The auto-immune system may shut down, for example, leaving one exposed to a host of bacterial-type infections; cancerous tissue may take over a principal organ, causing it to fail in carrying out its vital physiological function; a chemical imbalance in the brain may result in some serious mental disorder. Similarly not all, or even most, conflicts or crises that arise in a given social body or community are satisfactorily resolved, either temporarily or permanently, in a manner which is advantageous to the whole. A good model may therefore be used to elucidate such pathological conditions and to suggest a possible remedy. It may also be employed to describe, though not necessarily to explain, the situation where opposing powers coexist in an active state of mutual tension, each endeavoring to neutralize, absorb, overcome, or eliminate the other. The analogical method may therefore be utilized to give one a general idea of the intricate organization and vigorous operation of religion within the particular sociocultural context in which it is found.

Let us consider the culturally critical notion of power. In traditional Central African thought, every *created* being (the assumption is that God created everything in the universe) is believed to possess a certain force or vitality (*moyo* in Chewa, *muuya* in Tonga) which enables it to exist in the first place and then to interact with all other beings/forces that are present in the environment (cp. Tempels, 1959, passim; Douglas, 1966, 82; Nyamiti, 1977, 19,53; Maimela, 1985, 67). This force waxes (with life) and wanes (toward death) in intensity, and certain beings demonstrate more of it than others. Thus, we can posit a hierarchy which extends from the lower limits where we find creatures with an insignificant degree of power (as viewed from man's perspective), such as most living things, including plants, animals, and birds, to those that are associated with an appreciable amount of it, such as the larger, more long-living, and/or dangerous creatures, e.g., elephant, python, lion, or huge trees. The continuum proceeds through human society, which exhibits various power distinctions involving authority, prestige, and rank. Furthermore, the life force of individual human beings manifests itself in their relative physical strength and health, number of offspring, size of their herds or gardens, the skills or crafts which they excel at, their social standing in the community, and the interpersonal loyalties which they command. At the upper levels of the ladder, then, we have a significant progression from the nearest ancestral spirits to those which have been forgotten, to the great founders of the tribe and the clan totems, and on up to the Deity himself, who is the Creator-Source and Sustainer of all such forces in the universe.

Since a hierarchy is involved, we might visualize this personalized power continuum, which we will designate as *status*, as extending along a vertical scale from top to bottom. The relationship which then links any being on the ladder of forces with one situated on a higher rung is typically that of client (servant/vassal) and patron (protector/benefactor) respectively. And the more individuals who are either directly or indirectly obligated or subordinated to another, the higher is the status level of that particular being. But it is important to recognize the fact that ideally at least these unique forces are all mutually interdependent. A higher personal power exists to oversee and protect those under him/her/it, while the latter function to venerate and serve their superiors.

The attribute of power in any society is both evaluated according to, and exercised in relation to, one or more of five principal dimensions: strength, whether biological (e.g., body size) or mechanical (e.g., force of arms); skill, whether physical (e.g., sports figure) or mental (e.g., computer expert); knowledge, whether innate (i.e., wisdom) or acquired (e.g., by schooling or experience); wealth, whether in possessions (e.g., herds) or property (i.e., land holdings); and position, whether ascribed (e.g., royalty) or achieved (e.g., political). Societies therefore differ from one another with respect to the relative ranking of these five features as a manifestation of the lines of power-control within their respective communities; e.g., traditional Central African [TCA] versus midwestern rural American [MRA]:

TCA:	1. knowledge	2. position	3. skill	4. strength	5.wealth
MRA:	1. wealth	2. skill	3. strength	4. position	5. knowledge

Thus, in many parts of Zambia the specialist in knowledge (i.e., the diviner-doctor) is the most powerful individual in society, at least when it comes to matters of life and death. The accumulator of wealth, on the other hand, is at the bottom of the scale, for he becomes the inevitable object of witchcraft accusations. In a small farming town in Iowa, however, it is likely that these positions would be just reversed: the rich banker is in control while a local college professor, though having a certain amount of influence upon those whom he instructs, is not really a power figure in the community at large. Notice that one finds it increasingly more difficult to generalize in terms of such broad categories, the more complex and diversified a society becomes.

In order to correctly explain and interpret Central African religion (and, indeed, the culture as a whole), one must posit, in addition to the factor of status, a diverse range of social forces which increase or decrease in relation to a particular individual along a horizontal, or interhuman, axis. This we might designate the degree of cohesion, or solidarity which people manifest with respect to one another in the community, with those ties involving a blood relationship (consanguine) generally being the closest, or strongest, in intensity. Those linking persons related by marriage (affine) are somewhat weaker, and finally, those between individuals who are unrelated but somehow associated, whether by past experience or on a continual, day-to-day basis are the weakest. These cohesive relations contribute a great deal to general feelings of identification, belonging, and harmony within the group. Indeed, they are essential if society is to function effectively at all. However, such variable linkages and loyalties can also be a source of tension, suspicion, and conflict when things go wrong and a guilty party must be found. Where a case of witchcraft is concerned, for example, the closest relatives are frequently the most likely to be considered as suspects.

Thus the most prominent and socially most significant bonds in Central Africa are formed between a person and the members of his/her matriclan. The nucleus of this kinship group consists of those in the immediate family, including his/her maternal uncles and aunts (or ritual "fathers" and "mothers"). This force of attraction—and an attendant degree of responsibility, whether positive or negative—extends in ever widening circles of decreasing intensity to encompass finally all those who manifest any sort of blood relationship with him/her. The importance of ties forged by marriage between a person (more correctly, his/her entire family) and another kinship group is often marked by strict customs of prohibition (e.g., in-law avoidance taboos) and prescription (e.g., levirate or sororate marriage). Then there are also many essential connections which join an individual with people who are in some way associated with him in the wider community. These may, in the case of a chief, for example, be broad enough to span the entire tribe—beginning, in relative order of strength, with the members of his age-group and/or closest advisers and confidants, then all his friends, neighbors, acquaintances, petitioners, and so forth. The relationships on this level of communal organization are typically of a reciprocal or a contractual variety. These distinct cohesive—or divisive—forces (depending on the situation), though also dyadic in nature, are nevertheless different from those pertaining to status referred to above. But since the two types are so closely integrated in religious as well as social thought and practice, it is useful to consider them together.

Now the most important being from a traditional perspective on the vertical vector of the socioreligious scale of status is not God, but man (*munthu*). Indeed, it is clear from the study of typical patterns of behavior within the established structures of social organization as well as from various types of oral testimony, whether formally or informally rendered, that man himself forms the heart and core of this natural religious system (and others like it all over the world). We might depict this anthropocentric relationship involving humanity, religion, society, culture, and the enveloping cosmos, both natural and supernatural, as follows:

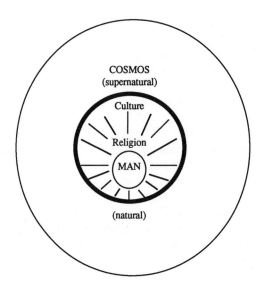

Thus a man is defined and situated in life, both objectively and subjectively, only by virtue of his relationship to others—to his own family first of all, and then to the human community at large. The universe, in turn, is completely humanized, that is, the beings and forces of which it is comprised are perceived, interpreted, and reacted to largely in anthropomorphic terms. The interaction of these two dimensions of power, namely, status and solidarity, as manifested by the structure of interpersonal relations in human society, is illustrated on the diagram below (cp. Nida, in Louw, ed., 1986, p.9):

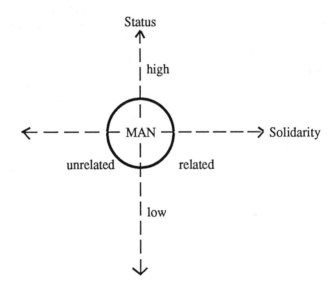

Model of Forces

This dichotomy clearly reflects two of the principal values of African life. On the one hand the power hierarchy of *status* in which every member of the group has a recognized place and an associated role to play gives each individual, no matter how lowly in the eyes of an outsider, an important sense of *security*. On the other hand, the cohesive force of solidarity, which focuses more on the group as a whole, creates a feeling of *harmony* that is crucial to the preservation of such a closely-knit community.

The similarity between the abstract schema above and the one presented in the preceding chapter as a summary of the chief religious elements in the account of the "Dog-Child" is obvious. The dramatic events of that story were played out largely on the horizontal plane of interpersonal relations and the tensions resulting from a conflict of interests between those related by blood or marriage and outsiders. We observed an apparent inversion of status, as God and the ancestral spirits seemed almost powerless to control the prevailing state of affairs, and thus it was left to a normally despised representative of the bestial world of nature (i.e., a dog) to resolve things in the end. It was certainly a shocking conclusion as the ultimate solution to disorder in the community (i.e., jealousy and greed leading to the abuse of status and a betrayal of solidarity) turned out to be complete annihilation. Perhaps it is this implicit warning which constitutes the tale's central message, as the narrator makes his incisive comment on the human condition: look what happens when the proper roles and relations among fellow human beings are not maintained!

Central African religion is thus strongly homocentric in orientation and humanized in operation, and one must understand it in these terms in order to properly appreciate its important functions within society even today, and also to correctly explain the pervading extent of its influence upon all types of interpersonal behavior. This crucial principle, which will be considered further in the next chapter, needs to be emphasized specifically with regard to four concepts pertaining to power and solidarity that surface time and again in any thorough consideration of traditional as well as modern religious notions, namely, spiritism, magic, wizardry, and witchcraft.

Upon considering the preceding diagram of forces, we might correctly conclude that the area of most concentrated religious (as defined above) thought and action would be found right in the middle, surrounding man himself, at the intersection of the horizontal and vertical vectors. It is here where the various helpful or hostile powers that envelop a person in his everyday existence converge to interact with his own personal life force, whether for good or for evil. It is here, too, where the process of communication is initiated as an individual seeks through various means to relate to these different personal and impersonal forces in order to preserve himself in a state of animated equilibrium with respect to his total environment. This man- centered focus may be viewed as extending along each of the two planes of power manifestation and on several distinct levels, to delineate the principal aspects of religion as it is realized in Central Africa.

There are two familiar negative, or detrimental, dimensions of this phenomenon. These primarily concern the medial or horizontal axis of solidarity, where we find a distinctly human/interpersonal perversion of religious symbolism. First there is "witchcraft" (*ufiti* in Chewa), which in its most dangerous or lethal form, among the Chewa at least, is typically thought to be practiced immediately or telepathically, through pure psychically controlled energy, by women against those who are related by blood. "Wizardry" (or "sorcery"; *zanyanga* in Chewa), on the other hand, is applied mediately, through various magical means, mainly by males and largely against those who are unrelated to them, but including affines (cp. Marwick, 1965, 98-103).

In popular thinking, however, especially in more recent times, the distinction between these two antisocial types of behavior is often blurred, and they are frequently linked in some sort of generic-specific relationship. In other words, though the characteristics of the pure witch (*mfiti yeniyeni*) and the practitioner of so-called "black magic" are recognized and applied in specific cases, all such hostile action is commonly referred to in general terms simply as "witchcraft" (*ufiti*). But depending on the situation of use, a more specific designation may be used, i.e., with reference to someone who is trying to advance himself at the expense of others through magical means (e.g., *mpheranjiru* 'the one who kills out of malicious envy'). In any case we are dealing with only a partially differentiated continuum of adverse, highly feared mystical activities which work insidiously to destroy cohesion, cooperation, and concord in the community. They weaken the internal fabric of a group, whether the members happen to be related or not, by exacerbating the feelings of mistrust, suspicion, fear, jealousy, and hatred that arise from repressed social tensions, particularly in periods of rapid or pronounced culture change and external calamity.

Some investigators have analyzed witchcraft and/or sorcery as being beneficial to a community by providing a psychological safety valve, as it were, for the release and externalization of interpersonal conflict in society. This may be true to some extent, but such behavior is certainly not viewed in a positive light by the people themselves. Furthermore, any release or reprieve that comes after one set of accusations erupts is in effect only temporarily maintained, for the antagonistic attitudes which these practices generate never completely die. Instead, the malignant feelings simply feed upon themselves, simmering beneath the surface of community awareness until another combination of suspicious and provocative circumstances appears to bring them out in the open again. Thus, if they are not checked and totally eliminated by a decided shift in world-view, they continue to reproduce a hostile social environment where divisions, arguments, fights, separation, and even murder (i.e., of the unjustly accused) recur with debilitating regularity.

The individual, however, has recourse to two potentially positive, beneficial forces, both personal and impersonal, which can give him protection against the many malicious agents seeking to control, corrupt, and consume his life. These are present on the vertical scale of status. Thus a plaintiff may appeal to those with increased rank in terms of power and influence, namely, the ancestral spirits—in particular, his own personal guardian spirit and the ones who are most closely related to him—to defend him from his adversaries and/or to take vengeance upon them. We might term this religious activity "spiritism." It is the sacred duty of these ancestors to uphold the moral order of society and to preserve its ancient traditions. In some cases this will involve a chastisement in the form of an accident or illness, but such misfortune will always be seen (i.e., through divination) as having the constructive purpose of correcting some human failing or fault in the community. Of course, there are also certain alien (as opposed to ancestral) and malevolent spirits which can harm or even kill a person, but these are invariably instigated or originated by an actual physical (e.g., murder) or psychological (e.g., hatred) transgression on the part of man, including the very practice of sorcery/witchcraft.

On the other hand, a person might turn to impersonal means and white magic to provide him with the desired protection or to retaliate against supposed enemies. The effectiveness of such "medicine" (*mankhwala* in Chewa, as discussed earlier) is believed to be dependent upon the correct manipulation of certain symbolic media and a utilization of the natural potency inherent in these select substances of the material environment. The powers concerned are lower on the status/vitality scale, but they are augmented by the force of human will (faith??) in order to either defend or develop one's own life force (the source of physical and spiritual well-being in life). In practice, therefore, magic turns out to be a connotatively ambiguous source of strength from the point of view of a given individual. He (or she) requires it in various forms and on different occasions throughout life in order to counteract its antagonistic use by others, i.e., sorcerers. From the opposite perspective, however, magical practice, either with or without the involvement of inimical spiritual agencies, may also be employed egocentrically to enhance a person's individual public standing and material well-being in the community. But inevitably this happens at the expense of someone else's status, and hence it is considered to be antisocial action that is strongly condemned by tradition as well as the present generation. These key religious concepts/practices, which invariably impinge upon the everyday life of every traditionally-minded individual, fit into the preceding diagram of forces as shown on the following page:

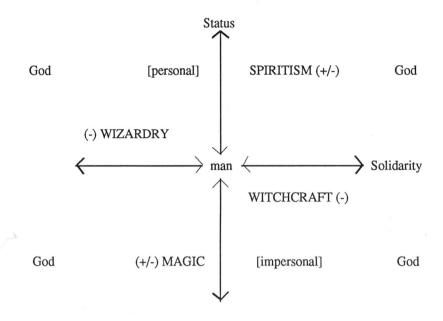

Positive-Negative Vectors of Dynamism in Religion

Any discussion of the *impersonal* forces unlocked through the application of various magical practices must at some point consider the operation of taboos in society. A *taboo* is a socially oriented and sanctioned rule, usually a prohibition—against incest, for example—which entails a clearly specified and automatically enforced punishment in the event of its transgression. While an overt violation of such a stricture may result in ostracization by the family or larger community, a consequence that is feared much more is a certain mystical affliction which sooner or later is believed to occur, such as a particular sickness, deformity, or even death, that strikes either the offender him/herself or, more frequently, a close relative. For example, a man who commits adultery when his wife is pregnant will automatically cause her to abort the fetus and even die when he returns and crosses the threshold. He is thus said to have "cut" (-*dula*) his wife by violating a taboo of the same name, i.e., *mdulo* "cutting." Many believe that the ancestral spirits are involved in such adversity, at least in a passive way, by allowing it to happen as punishment for the grave offense which was committed.

Taboos form an important part of the religious tradition of all Central African ethnic groups. They act as the proscriptive and prescriptive glue that holds the basic structure of traditional beliefs together. They also serve to define the so-called boundaries formed by the many different social categories and relationships which are found within the total circumscribing framework of status and solidarity as outlined above. In particular, such interdictions separate the sacred from the profane (e.g., during the offering of a sacrifice to the ancestors); they prevent ritual pollution by not allowing mutually antagonistic categories to mix (e.g., a man who is sexually "hot" from his wife who is ritually "cold" due to menstruation); and they help people avoid the dangerous consequences of contact with anomalous, disordered conditions (e.g., an abortion or deformed child) and marginal or transitional states (e.g., periods of initiation).

Rites of purification, therefore, such as those performed to exorcise a defiling spirit or to cleanse a woman who has just experienced a miscarriage, are intended to counteract the adverse effects of any negative taboo. They serve to renew the victim's "power," i.e., life force, and also to restore his/her solidarity within either the community at large or, more vitally, within the domestic unit (e.g., enabling a resumption of normal sexual relations). Conversely, the violation of a certain taboo (e.g., if a menstruating woman should season her family's stew with salt) results in a release of polluting energy which can act as a destructive force that proves injurious or even fatal (i.e., *mdulo*, a 'cutting') to anyone who happens to come into contact with it. Thus taboo restrictions function to maintain social equilibrium and the balance of nature by keeping the ritually pure separate from the impure, and the mystically powerful away from the impotent.

To be sure, the practice of religion in Central Africa most certainly involves man's diverse attempts to maintain a positive, beneficial relationship, i.e., solidarity, with personal beings whose power and status he recognizes as considerably greater than his own. A much more critical objective, however, is rather negative or, we might say, evasive, in nature. In other words, an overriding concern of the average individual is to defend himself from the host of hostile entities with which he shares his environment. The several major categories of misfortune—death, illness, infertility, crop failure, loss of a job, and so forth—to which one might at any unguarded moment fall prey are indicated on the diagram below. In most cases, especially the serious ones, the specific cause of the problem would be determined by divination of one sort or another. Notice that these coincide with the principal components of religious belief as mentioned in the preceding paragraphs:

Aspects of Misfortune

Type	Cause	Remedy
deserved	-provoke ancestral spirit -violate ancient taboo	sacrifice +/- compensation [same]
undeserved	-mystical attack by witch -magical attack by sorcerer	counter-magic... defensive or offensive

Of course most people, with the help of the local medicine man, take a variety of precautionary and prophylactic measures to try and insulate themselves from such pressing everyday calamities. It is not difficult to see that the practice of religion, albeit in this inferior, self/man-centered form, requires a great deal of time, effort, commitment, and expense. Simply put, it is a matter of power (Who is in control here?) and solidarity (With whom do I need to be allied to give me security in life?). Unfortunately the intellectual, dogmatic brand of Christianity that many have been exposed to—or have misinterpreted—all too often fails to provide the necessary and relevant answers to practical and pressing issues such as these.

A considerable amount of interaction occurs among these diverse applications of power in different socioreligious contexts, e.g., the involvement of both witches and sorcerers in the use of magic as well as in the manipulation of evil spirits. Various aspects of this dynamic interplay will be explored more fully in the next chapter, as we relate our three models to the basic presuppositions of a Central African world-view, and also in subsequent chapters with respect to a number of other distinct ethnic groups in Africa. It is important to take note of the reasons for our inclusion of such impious and often seemingly impersonal practices as magic and witchcraft together with the sacred rites associated with man's contacts with supernatural beings. As will be pointed out below, each of these activities may be analyzed in terms of a single comprehensive process, namely, that of communication with a transcendent entity, while at the same time they all reflect a coherent underlying viewpoint regarding the composition and functioning of these diverse forces in the universe of man's experience. In the apt words of Mary Douglas: "We shall not expect to understand religion if we confine ourselves to considering belief in spiritual beings" (1966, 28).

As indicated on the diagram above, "God," the Supreme Being (*Mulungu* in Chewa, *Leza* in Tonga), is not extraneous to this closed system of antagonistic forces. He has simply removed himself to the periphery, in sacred isolation, as it were, from the more mundane mechanics of its ordinary operation in everyday affairs. To be sure, the Deity set things in motion in the beginning. That is, he is firmly believed to be the Creator of the hierarchy of potency which animates life in all of its facets and regulates the mutual interrelationships among the diverse constituent forces. God is also seen as the paramount Force who continues to initiate, maintain, order, and stabilize the manifestation of all others. But now, though accessible to everyone (cp. Lumbiwe's pleas for a child), he now generally reveals his presence only in certain crisis situations, when the very course of human existence is threatened and society has reached its last resort, e.g., as the result of a drought, plague, pestilence, or infertility.

It is also interesting to observe that for many African Christians today, this same dynamic nucleus of traditional beliefs remains very much alive at the center of their thoughts and lives. The distinctive faith and practice of their respective denominations may be reflected quite strongly on the outside, especially when the going is good. But when times get tough, no matter how much modern sophistication a person might exhibit otherwise, there is a great, almost overwhelming, temptation for him to revert back to the religious tenets of the past—to spiritism, magic, wizardry, and witchcraft in particular. This is so because, as far as Western theology (and medicine) is concerned, such beliefs have no basis in empirical fact. Theoretically, then, since they do not really exist, there is no way in principle to deal with the life-threatening problems which they raise, except perhaps to perfunctorily ascribe them to the works of the Devil and his demonic agents.

This vital core of the hierarchy of forces represents what Hiebert terms "the excluded middle" (1982, 43) that stands between the visible natural world and the unseen realm of God, nonhuman spiritual beings (angels, demons), and the impersonal mystical powers of the universe. For all practical purposes, like God in the typical secularized, scientifically-oriented Western world-view, orthodox denominational Christianity in an African context often remains, when religion really counts in life, on the outside looking in! It remains then for one of the semi-Christian syncretistic sects to provide an acceptable bridge between the solutions offered by indigenous beliefs and the life-death crises that individuals as well as entire communities encounter in the contemporary world.

A Communication Model

The organic power model presented above, though dealing with the different mutually-opposing forces which can either bond or break society, would still be classified as falling into the category of a static system. That is to say, it gives us an overview of the principal aspects of what we have defined as traditional African religion and how these relate to one another in terms of the parameters of power (status) and solidarity (cohesion). This model, then, offers us an insight into the "what"—the content of the system, the primary elements of its structure or composition at least. But it does not give us much information about the "how" or the "why" of the system's performance. For that we require a more *dynamic* model, that is, one which deals with processes and the way in which the activities involving spiritism, magic, witchcraft, sorcery, and taboo actually function in Central African society. How do these operate both individually and in conjunction with one another (whether mutually reinforcing or in conflict) within the wider cultural context? Coupled with this, for a complete and accurate picture of the operational system, we need to know the symbolic value of each of the objects, places, roles, activities, and states that comprise the practice of religion in the different forms in which it is manifested. Here we are referring to the philosophy of life, or world-view, which underlies the overt behavior of the various individuals of society as they interact with one another for good or evil. The model that best serves this purpose is based on the process of communication (cp. Nida, 1968, ch.2; Shaw, 1987, 25-26), the main components of which are shown on the diagram below:

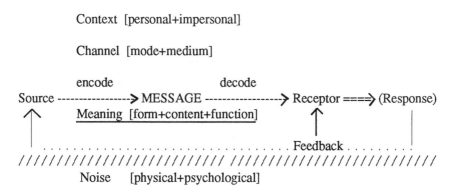

A Simple Model of Communication

In this cyclical, cause-effect, action-oriented model, the *source* (we will be considering only human/personal agents in this process) transmits a specific message to his intended *receptor(s)* via a particular channel. The *message* is comprised of a set of signs (or symbols) which, when appropriately arranged and encoded in the context at hand, convey a certain *meaning*, that is, a complex of content (*what* is conveyed, consisting of information, emotions, evaluations, and motivations), form (*how* the content is conveyed in terms of macro- and microstructure), and function (*why* the content is conveyed, i.e., the communicative intention/purpose of the source). In addition to the primary message, a verbal text for example, the source frequently also transmits one or more secondary messages nonverbally, e.g., gestures, facial expressions, tone of voice, body stance and posture. Such *paramessages* may either confirm or contradict the primary intention of the source, for example: reinforcement—drumming, singing, or clapping to encourage the dancing (i.e., medium and message combined) of a spirit-possessed person; reduction—use of a deformed or sickly animal when making a sacrifice to God (cp. Mal 1:13).

The *channel* involves both a sensory mode (sight and sound being the most important, but not the only ones available to the source, e.g., smell, touch) as well as a medium (i.e., the particular form of the mode, e.g., sight: television, book, newspaper, hand signals). The process of decoding the meaning of a message, which is never perfect, will normally provoke or elicit a *response* from the receptor, one which may or may not correspond in detail to that intended by the source. Note that even silence may be a relevant reaction, perhaps signalling shame, anger, rejection, or no comprehension. This receptor response in turn acts as the *feedback*, or a reverse message, which indicates to the source how well (or poorly) his intended meaning is getting across, and what he has to do to make the transmission more effective. Various kinds of *noise* may distort or even block the message, or at least certain aspects of it, at any stage in the process, e.g., physical: loud sounds in the background, a blurry print job; and/or psychological: negative feelings of the receptor regarding the source, e.g., hatred, suspicion, doubt, or lack of respect, or the message itself, e.g., a Muslim's reaction to the claim that Jesus is the Son of God.

Finally, it is important to recognize the fact that every act of communication takes place within a specific *context*. This may be personal (i.e., the social setting—who is speaking to whom under what circumstances) or impersonal (i.e., the external environment, e.g., an empty room, a packed cathedral, under a tree, during a thunderstorm). The context, from which the different types of noise arise, always affects the process of communication in one way or another, especially the form of the message. A goat sacrificed in a time of drought must be black (to attract the dark rain clouds), while during a period of flooding it will be white (to symbolize the sun and clear skies).

The application of a communication model enables an investigator to interpret effectively a broad range of diverse religious phenomena within a unified theoretical framework by following a similar set of principles. The use of this type of approach is particularly appropriate since, as was noted earlier, any religion, no matter how elaborate, may be defined as essentially a form of communication—or, as it is figuratively expressed in a Bemba saying: *ipupo lulimi* 'prayer [is] a tongue,' i.e., by metonymy: religion is a system of communication. It involves the transmission of messages to, from, and by means of extra human powers, the overtly impersonal (e.g., a magical charm) as well as the obviously personal (e.g., a departed chief). In the practice of traditional African or any other form of religion, diverse messages, for the most part very elaborate and highly symbolic in composition, are both encoded for and also decoded from the supernatural (cp. Nida, 1960, 101).

An understanding of the cult, the ritual process, in all of its different manifestations, is therefore indispensable in any analysis of a group's religious system. By means of the symbolic actions and objects of ancient rituals, people dramatize their important experiences and expectations in life, especially in times of personal or corporate transition (e.g., puberty), unexpected crisis (e.g., physical affliction), or seasonal focus (e.g., planting the new crop). The predominantly representational forms of cultic activity reiterate and reinforce the validity of a community's major institutions as well as its governing set of social values, including those pertaining to right and wrong on the interpersonal (human/superhuman) level. The latter concern thus presupposes an essential association with the sacred, namely, the divinities (great spirits) and Deity upon which all of life and the well-being of the cosmos depend. Religious ritual action, involving the three distinct stages of separation, [status] reversal, and reincorporation, serves to reinforce the spiritual bond between God and man which Victor Turner calls "*communitas*" (1969, 96-7). In the process it also rejuvenates and legitimizes a society's belief in itself and the central norms that govern institutionalized interpersonal relationships.

In this connection some authorities have noted the strong resemblance that exists between ancient ritual and human *play* in that the normal distinction between empirical reality and the imaginative realm of fantasy is dissolved (Huizinga, 1950, p.9). The result of this mystical merger is the creation of a new world, one that gives participants the freedom to dramatize their feelings and desires (often in the guise of masked characters and costumes) and to interact with the supernatural, sacred beings which control their current destiny, even as they guided their ancestors in the past. Due to its very nature and purpose, such ritualized communal behavior, as is demonstrated in the Chewa *nyau* (mask) secret society, tends to be of a highly affective and emotive character. It is the total participatory experience which counts, not necessarily some specifiable end result. Thus if such ritual is not corrupted through rote, depersonalized performance, it can render the vital activity of religious communication more meaningful in terms of relevance (i.e., to the particular situation being addressed), significance (i.e., the actual content and purpose of the message), and potency (i.e., the impact and appeal of the message with regard to both senders and receivers--its psychological and performative effect).

Due to the importance and intricacy of the many different types of ritual communication, certain mediatorial specialists are often required in order to ensure the appropriate formal technique during transmission and the correct interpretation of the resultant response. This would apply especially to the proper performance of sacrifice, which is a fundamental component (some would even say the root) of any established religion. Ancient Israel, for example, had its priests and prophets, the former concentrating on the sacrificial cult, and the latter generally serving as a human transmitter and commentator for messages directly from Yahweh. The closest, albeit imperfect, analogues in Central African religion are the medicine man (*sing'anga* 'owner of magic' in Chewa) and the medium (*wolowedwa* 'the entered one' in Chewa). Both roles are similar in that they seek to establish contact with the elemental forces of the universe (cp. the hierarchy of "status" above). The medicine man or diviner-doctor attempts to control the impersonal forces derived from nature as well as personal powers of human origin by means of his magical procedure (including sacrifice) and esoteric knowledge, while the medium desires to be controlled (or possessed) by ancestral agents in order to serve as a vehicle for any special communication coming from these beings to man. In the case of the former, the function of sending messages is stressed; the latter, by way of contrast, emphasizes the role of reception in this deeply personal socioreligious process.

For all practical purposes, then, to give a somewhat different example, the two components of a particular ritual involving the sacrifice of a goat and an associated prayer may be analyzed in basically the same way. In each case, or more exactly, in each communicative event, for two are here combined, there is a source (a person or group of people) who wishes to convey a message to a particular receptor (God or the ancestral spirits) in a given situation, for instance, to ward off a plague which has struck the community. The form of the message is obviously different and so may be the content, i.e., the animal serving as an actual physical (life-bearing) token of the people's desire to appease the receptor(s) on account of some real or supposed wrongdoing is quite distinct from the less concrete verbal expression of that intention. But in this case the general propitiatory function of both religious acts is essentially the same, except that the sacrifice would incorporate an extra measure of inducement. Similarly, the emotions expressed in both the prayer and also the offering of the goat (i.e., as part of the message content) may correspond to a large degree, e.g., grief, dismay, lack of hope, fear for the future, though in this respect the prayer would probably involve greater intensity by conveying these sentiments more openly. The model thus allows for and even encourages the specification of a different mixture of feelings and attitudes in an altered religious setting, e.g., by way of contrast, a harvest offering: joy, gratitude, hope, confidence for the future.

As was mentioned above, the form of the message normally consists of a sequence of signs which are related to one another in a specific way, i.e., as designated by the code, or entire system of signs, from which the form is selected. Other popular codes, or symbol systems, which operate, often simultaneously, in religious discourse in addition to language are: body movements (as in dancing), music (both sung and expressed by instruments), "medicinal" combinations (to bring about this or that therapeutic effect), custom complexes (such as those observed at a funeral), clothing (e.g., to imitate the particular spirit[s] that one is possessed with). Each symbolic sign in its context and in combination with other signs conveys a particular significance or meaning to the receptor(s): cognitive content, attitudes (e.g., favorable or unfavorable), values (e.g., high or low), emotions (e.g., uplifting or depressing), and motivations (e.g., strong or weak), provided that people are familiar with the code that is being used.

The point is that all of these distinct aspects of a given ritual, on several levels of communication within a particular sociocultural setting, need to be analyzed in conjunction with one another in order for one to derive a more accurate understanding of the significance of the whole. The traditional Chewa diviner (*wamaula* 'person of the oracle'), for example, is a practitioner who is particularly adept at manipulating several symbolic media at once (e.g., clothing/dress, ritual apparatus, gestures, words) both in order to impress, and indeed also to mystify, his client(s) as well as to increase the supposed effectiveness of his investigative procedures. It is important to keep in mind that a holistic analytical approach needs to be applied even when one is dealing with a written theological document, such as the Bible. It is not only the words recorded in the Scriptures that communicate, but also the associated actions must be taken into account, especially if there is the possibility that these may bear some social or religious significance within the setting of the receptor culture. Among the Chewa, for example, Christ's act of spitting on the eyes of the blind man he was about to heal would be considered a grave insult (Mk 8:23). The

Tonga, on the other hand, often welcome an honored guest (including a newborn baby) by this gesture.

It is important to take note of the fact that performative ritual action may either succeed or fail in its intended communicative effect--the confrontation between Elijah and the prophets of Baal being a vivid example of both possibilities (1 Kg 18). In this instance the sharp contrast in the actual form of the rites conducted by the respective parties served as an essential though implicit part of the message. To be sure, the 450 prophets directed their self-centered pleas for sacrifice-immolating fire to the idol Baal, while Elijah's intercessory prayer on behalf of the faithless people of Israel invoked the name of Yahweh, their faithful covenant God (vs. 26 and 37). But just as significant in this dramatic contest was the contrast in ritual procedure: Elijah flooded his offering with water to demonstrate beyond a doubt that no magical tricks were involved with his success (though there are those in Central Africa who might view this as an instance of some form of powerful imitative magic--of "like (water) attracting like (rain)"!). Elijah's action was also intended to ensure that all glory would be given to the God of Israel whom he served (v. 36).

On the other hand, the fervent but futile pagan exercises employed by the devotees of Baal—frantic cultic dance (v. 26) along with repeated ecstatic raving to rouse their dormant god to action (v. 29), and above all, a drastic self-inflicted blood-letting procedure to symbolize an actual sacrifice (v. 28)—all this only served to heighten the ignominy of their failure and the impotence of the deity whom they were so boisterously appealing to.

At times, special interpreters of the symbolic code are necessary, as in the case of a message from an ancestral spirit which has been transmitted through a medium. In such situations foreigners, those who come from a different cultural background, often encounter some serious difficulties in comprehension. In the first place they may not even recognize the code that is being used, since it proceeds from a completely different frame of reference. Alternatively— and this is an even greater problem—they may construe what is going on (i.e., the forms of a message) in terms of their own sign-systems, which may vary considerably from the African perspective in both content and function; for example, the giving of names in a Bantu as opposed to a European context. For the former, naming has a definite socioreligious, often mystical and representational, significance, as was the case in early Old Testament times. For a Westerner, on the other hand, names frequently serve no other purpose than to distinguish one person from another. Hence there are times when a Westerner in Africa might treat personal names much too flippantly and in ignorance thereby cause serious offense.

The importance of dreams, too, is not often fully appreciated by a Western oriented investigator. For him they may merely represent the random wanderings of the subconscious or the symptoms of some psychological disorder, and may thus be disregarded. For most people of Central Africa, on the other hand, like the Jews of the Old Testament, the activity of dreaming is an especially important system of symbolic communication. In an African setting the ancestral spirits are believed to transmit vital messages to an individual's inner being or soul. Many hold that, in addition, dreaming can involve a person's soul in specific extracorporeal activity, travel in particular, which is as real as if he were actually awake. It is imperative, therefore, that a dream be quickly and correctly interpreted in order for one to make sense of life's present experiences and also to predict future events. A reliable translator of dream-messages is naturally highly regarded, and the dreamer himself is never despised, as Joseph was by his jealous brothers (Gn 37).

However, even within the same culture and community, certain important religious signs may be misunderstood and/or misapplied. The significance of a death by lightning, for example, may be variously interpreted as being the result of a sovereign, inscrutable act of God; anger on the part of a slighted ancestral (guardian) spirit; the breaking of a solemn oath; or, most frequently, due to the malevolent design of a witch/sorcerer. Furthermore, the import and effect of certain symbol sequences may turn out to be different from the one actually intended by the source, e.g., the apathetic sacrifices of an apostate Israel provoked the Lord to anger instead of propitiating him (cp. Ho 8:11-14). Similarly, when a rain sacrifice is performed and someone among the worshipers is ritually impure (e.g., through an act of sexual intercourse the night before), then no positive response will be forthcoming. In this instance the purpose of the message is distorted by sociological noise, that is, by a breech in security designed to preserve the sacred character of these public rites. In such cases an implicit communication model is used either intuitively or deliberately by divination to determine what caused the failure, that is, precisely where in the process of transmission the breakdown occurred, i.e., due to some fault with the source, receptor, channel, circumstances, or form of the message.

As has already been suggested, religious signs may be verbal or nonverbal in nature. People are generally familiar with the verbal type. Whether or not they have learned to read and write, they all know about the meanings, feelings, and intentions that are associated with the words (and combinations of words) of their language. But they do not always realize the importance of nonverbal communication, that is, how people convey messages by what they do, either deliberately or unintentionally. As they say in English, "Actions speak louder than words," and any type of religious performance, whether public or private, usually involves a great deal of nonlinguistic message transmission. This is true not only in the case of symbolism which is supportive of the verbal element, but also where we find functionally significant behavior which operates to a considerable degree independently of spoken (or written) texts—as when a morsel of food or a mouthful of beer is expelled before eating or drinking, in silent testimony to the communal presence and social position of the ancestors. It is necessary, therefore, to pay careful attention to this frequently neglected aspect of communication during the analysis of any activity suspected of having religious implications, whether in a local cultural environment or, indeed, as described on the pages of Scripture.

This preceding caution applies in particular to ritual action of a seemingly impersonal character, such as that connected with magic. Take sorcery, for example: whether the latter is based upon the principle of association (i.e., contagious magic, e.g., the mystical treatment of some discarded body waste of an intended victim) or that of analogy (i.e., sympathetic magic, e.g., use of a fabricated image of the victim), the activity concerned, namely, the message, often appears to transmit the desired effects automatically, *ex opere operato* by its very performance. However, most respondents point out the fact that not only mechanical procedures, but also the conscious will of the source must invariably be involved. A personal mediator is always necessary at some stage of the communication process, even if in mind only. Religion is thoroughly man-centered in terms of both operation and intended benefit.

Similarly the "medicine" (*mfumba* in Chewa) that a traditional doctor or magician supplies to a client to increase his harvest may be viewed as the message whereby he seeks to control supernatural power for his own advantage. This set of signs consists of a recipe which incorporates both the necessary ingredients for preparing the concoction as well as all of the pointedly specific directions for use that need to be carried out in rigorous precision in order to guarantee, as it were, the successful application of the resultant protective, corrective, curative, or destructive charm, potion, talisman, or spell. But the vital human element of traditional religious practice should not be overlooked here either: without faith on the part of the participants both initiating and sustaining the magical operation, one simply cannot achieve the desired outcome (cp. Mt 9:22,29; 13:58).

To summarize: religion in a Central African context involves a diverse and continual communication process whereby people seek to transcend their limited selves and their limiting socioeconomic circumstances in order to interact in thought, word, and deed with a host of unseen personal and impersonal powers that permeate their world. Such communication assumes many different forms and is motivated by a great variety of purposes (these basic functions will be surveyed at the end of the chapter). Symbolic messages move in both directions between source and receptor as a wide range of religious contacts are established, maintained, broken off, and renewed in a never-ending cycle that consumes much of a person's physical activity and psychological attention. This all-embracing system of traditional philosophy and praxis is in explicit or implicit operation during virtually all of an individual's important life experiences (life as being [state], and life as lived [action]). It begins at the time of his (or her) conception and birth, when others (e.g., parents, elders) transmit crucial messages to the supernatural on his behalf. The process continues throughout the stressful period of youth and family-making, which are always accompanied by various initiation ceremonies that introduce him to the elaborate secrets of these vital communication procedures. Things reach a climax, then, in those critical hours both before and after death, when a person's closest relatives carry out the last great rite of passage as they make final preparations for him to join the invisible but ever-present company of the living dead.

To be sure, the various procedures for signalling religious meaning via verbal and nonverbal signs is considerably more complicated than has just been described. But the preceding introduction is sufficient to suggest the importance of a communication model in helping the investigator to come to grips with what is really taking place during the practice of religion in Africa and elsewhere—in particular, as the basis for an essential sociocultural exercise to analyze both the formal and the functional similarities and differences with comparable objects, roles, events, settings, and situations as presented in the Scriptures.

A Dramatic Model

We might further explore the implications of the communication model in relation to the topic of traditional religion in Central Africa by viewing the latter in terms of a narrative drama. A narrative in the literary sense is a sequence of events that proceeds from some basic problem (e.g., need, lack, task, obstacle, etc.) in the lives of the chief participants through a climactic situation, when the conflict is confronted head-on, to a state of final resolution, i.e., either the conflict is resolved (e.g., need supplied, lack liquidated, task accomplished, or obstacle overcome) or it is not. Six universal role relationships may be discerned in narrative according to the actantial model proposed by the French Structuralist A.J. Greimas (see Patte, 1976, pp.42-43; Calloud, 1976, pp. 29-32). These are specified in their usual formulation as follows:

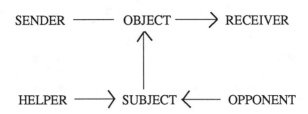

The SENDER is the overall originator of the narrative's sequence of events in that he desires to fulfil some lack or supply a crucial need in the life of the RECEIVER. The SENDER is generally a remote figure who, if he is present at all, usually appears only at the beginning and/or ending of the story. The OBJECT is an essential item which is to be conveyed or communicated to the RECEIVER or receptor group. The SUBJECT is the one who endeavors to see to it that the OBJECT is successfully transmitted to the RECEIVER(s). Normally this role is played by the hero (or heroine) of the plot. Conflict is introduced into the account by the OPPONENT, that is, whoever (the villain) or whatever (in the case of an inanimate obstacle) stands in the way of the SUBJECT or actively attempts to prevent him from carrying out his task. The personal OPPONENT thus maliciously seeks to keep the RECEIVER in a state of need and deprivation. The HELPER, like the OPPONENT, may be human or nonhuman (and in the latter instance, animate or inanimate). He/she/it either works to assist, or is employed by, the SUBJECT in his efforts to complete his mission. It is possible in this scheme for the same personage in the narrative to play more than one functional role, e.g., the HELPER and the SENDER may be the same individual. There are, of course, a variety of ways in which these actants may be realized and interrelated with each other in a given story. The underlying theory and analytical procedures of Greimas are considerably more complex than just described, but the preceding is sufficient for our purposes.

How, then, does this abstract scheme apply to the study of African traditional religion? After a thorough sociological examination and analysis of a large number of actual case studies, one comes to the conclusion that the great majority of religious situations, i.e., social contexts where traditional religion, at least in Central Africa, is practiced, also involve a basic interpersonal conflict of some kind—either overt or implicit, real or supposed—over some vital lack/need. The devotee, who never acts in isolation but always as part of a larger kinship group, naturally seeks a resolution that would eliminate the source of conflict which troubles, or worse, threatens his very existence or that of the entire community. In this sense, then, we might describe such an individual or corporate effort in narrative terms. More than that, one could view life in general as being a cosmic religious drama involving positive and negative forces in dynamic opposition and being played out on the stage of human destiny.

How would the six generic roles be filled in this vast scenario? The following appears to satisfy most of the possibilities:

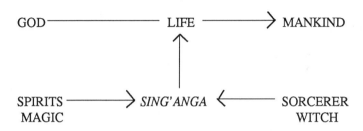

Thus God is universally acknowledged in Central Africa as being the great Sender of every good and perfect gift to the Receivers whom he also created, that is, all humanity. His greatest gift, that Object which is most needful from an anthropocentric perspective, is the force of "life" itself (*moyo* in Chewa, *muuya* in Tonga). As already observed, this a wide-ranging concept which is not only physical in nature (i.e., the animating principle of a living body, endowing it with "life" [also *moyo* in Chewa, but *buumi* in Tonga]), but one which also has many other important dimensions: material (i.e., freedom from want), physiological (i.e., health), psychological (i.e., mental stability), social (i.e., fertility), and spiritual (i.e., it is transformed into the essence of an ancestral spirit at death). Throughout one's earthly existence, however, powerful agents of evil (Opponents) in the person of witches and sorcerers continually seek to either trap or destroy one's life force, or soul, so that they can harness its essential energy for their own nefarious ends. People thus turn to the Subject of this drama, the *sing'anga*, or diviner-doctor/medicine man, for protection so that the gift of life is not cut off from either them or their offspring, through whom their own lives are perpetuated and their future thus guaranteed. The *sing'anga*, in turn, depends upon various helpers, both animate (i.e., the ancestral spirits) or inanimate (i.e., magic, whether white [defensive] or black [offensive/destructive]), to supply him with the power to carry out his vital task.

In a slight modification of Greimas' scheme, we note that as far as the Central African situation is concerned, it is necessary to posit an additional set of Helpers for the Opponents as well. The unique development here is that this category turns out to be the same in essence as the one designated for the Helper. In other words, sorcerers and witches may also utilize either alien spirits or aggressive magic in order to snatch away a person's soul or to frustrate the efforts of a medicine man to protect it. The primary antagonists, then, in the drama of human life may be represented as follows:

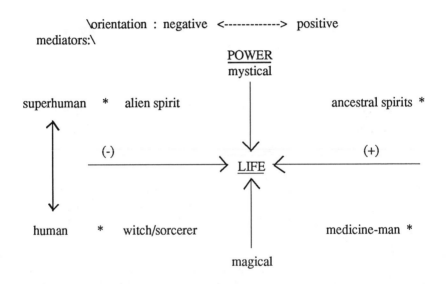

The Power Brokers of Central African Religion

Or, looking at this volatile state of affairs in a somewhat different way, we might say that life confronts the average individual with an unending battle which proceeds in cyclical fashion from conflict to resolution and back again. Social strife, resulting from otherwise unexplainable deprivations and disasters, whether prolonged or sudden in nature, may be attributed by informed intuition or divination to the activity of hostile forces arising from within the ingroup itself (relatives) or from an external source, i.e., the outgroup (nonrelatives). Such disharmony, the product of latent tensions and/or antisocial behavior, is believed to manifest itself in turn through two basic types of affliction: spirit possession, which is often associated with some physical ailment, or the attacks of witches (related) and wizards (unrelated).

Once the diagnosis has been made through the efforts of a diviner and/or medium, another psychoreligious specialist (who may be the same person) is then called in to deal with the matter. This is the *sing'anga*—the medicine man/diviner-doctor, or as he is sometimes misleading and pejoratively termed, the "witchdoctor"—who is consulted in order to obtain either healing or protection, depending on the situation. In the event of spirit-caused illness, the afflicting being is either cast out, if it happens to be a foreign spirit, or if an ancestor is involved, it is allowed to express itself (e.g., through therapeutic dancing) and placated (e.g., by means of an offering or the observance of designated ritual taboos). Where witchcraft/sorcery is diagnosed, on the other hand, countermagic is employed to deal with the spell and its injurous effects. In either case some type of resolution is brought about with varying degrees of success in restoring social harmony and the balance of opposing forces within the community at large. This resolution may be either superficial and temporary or more substantial and long-lasting, but inevitably conflicts are again generated and the cycle of aggression repeats itself on many different levels of seriousness and scope within a given social group. This state of affairs may be diagrammed as follows:

	diagnosis	treatment
spiritual:	spirit possession	exorcism/appeasement
magical:	sorcery/witchcraft	counter-magic
mystical:	taboo-affliction	acts of expiation

CONFLICT <- - - - - - - - - - - - - - - - - - - -> RESOLUTION

The Socio-Religious Drama of Life/Death

A combined "dramatic-communicative" depiction of the heart of the traditional Central African religious process is shown as follows:

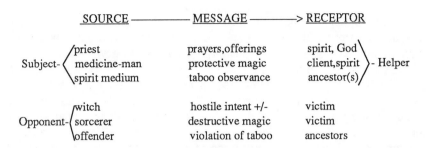

If the symbolic and/or ritual communication has been successful, a concrete result will be forthcoming. Thus the locus of POWER, whether a personal being or a humanly mediated impersonal force, conveys what is desired by the SOURCE (e.g., [+] rain, healing, knowledge, protection // [-] injury, disease, loss—physical or psychological), either to benefit those whom the latter is representing (clients, constituents) or to harm those whom the latter is attacking (victims). In the case of a taboo violation, of course, the process is rather different, since presumably the person involved did not deliberately commit an offense in order to be punished. The receptors, then, are implicit, namely, the ancestral guardians of traditional customs and the preservers of the time-hallowed status quo.

It is interesting to observe in the preceding schema the prominent mediatorial role that is played by the traditional religious specialist. This refers to the *sing'anga* 'diviner-doctor' in particular, but to a lesser extent also to the spirit medium (*wamizimu* 'the one of spirits' in Chewa), who functions as a prophetic voice, the traditional priest (*wansembe* 'person of sacrifices' in Chewa), and in an antithetical sense even to the sorcerer (*wanyanga* 'person of the horn' in Chewa). There is in actual practice only a very fine line that separates the personality and profession of the latter from the positive role generally attributed to the medicine man. In any case, as the Subject of the dramatic action, the ritual leader controls the power of life or death on behalf of ordinary mortals, for he (or she) is supposedly able to preserve an individual's well-being in several ways: by revealing the cause of particular misfortunes and the source of danger; by providing both medicinal as well as protective potions and amulets; by attacking and neutralizing the power of enemies; by offering inspired advice on how to avoid problems in the future; and in a somewhat more questionable practice, by selling individual specifically concocted charms to augment his possessions, both physical and mental (including produce from the harvest, success in business, ability in various skills and crafts, etc.).

So it is that the witchdoctor, the individual (or profession) whom Christianity has attacked as being the epitome and primary agent of Satan in

African society, turns out to be the hero of the religious drama of everyday existence. It is he who defends people from danger and delivers them in the day of trouble. It is no wonder, then, that this socially strategic and ever-adaptable vocation continues to thrive in spite of the tremendous growth of the Christian church in this century and the greatly altered cultural milieu in which it is practiced.

For many people the two religious systems are able to coexist happily in their minds, each with its own sphere of influence and area of specialized activity. A fuzzy dichotomy thus emerges: Christianity takes care of preparing one for a better life beyond the grave, while traditional religion assumes primary responsibility for the here and now—for life as it is lived from day to day in a world that is filled with powers that can be manipulated by a person's enemies to control, gain possession of, or to extinguish his life force and hence the essence of one's being. Such a separation would be most likely to arise within the longer established, mainline, dogmatically-oriented denominations, where all too often there seems to be an overemphasis upon correct instruction at the expense of a genuine personal application of Christian teaching to meet the challenges of daily life in a dynamic sociocultural environment.

For a rapidly increasing number of other adherents, however, especially those of the charismatic persuasion, whether traditional African or of modern Western origin, overt and covert syncretism appears to be the order of the day as indigenous beliefs are simply absorbed into the church with little change in substance, but clothed in a new form, that is, a superficially taught and understood evangelical terminology (or jargon). In such circumstances, God the Father easily assumes the place of the remote, mythic Creator Deity; Jesus Christ becomes in essence the second Lawgiver, analogous to Moses; and the Holy Spirit holds center stage as the Distributor of diverse gifts of power, which enable certain individuals, namely those who have been magically born again, to deal with the hostile attacks of evil spirits, witches, and sorcerers, plus all types of other threatening situations in life.

As was indicated on an earlier diagram, these indigenous beliefs and values constitute the animating nucleus of the world-view of a majority of the population, whether they happen to be Christianized or not. Such thinking cannot be dealt with by merely denying its presence or downplaying its relevance. The avoidance or repudiation as well as the confrontational, power-encounter approach only forces the traditional system underground, where it continues to flourish and operate freely whenever a crisis develops that cannot be handled by a Western-biased rationalistic theological method. Situations vary, of course, and the evangelist needs to have a variety of tested strategies available for application in a given set of circumstances. However, in the manner of the epistle to the Hebrews, it seems best to make a concerted but sympathetic and culturally-relevant effort to gradually effect a paradigm-shift whereby the basic presuppositions of the traditional world-view are modified. This will result in a progressive displacement of that resistant conceptual core to the periphery of people's faith, whence it will eventually disappear due to the influence of sound, contextualized biblical instruction as well as progressive spiritual growth and maturity under the Spirit's guidance.

Following the writer's example in Hebrews, then, effective teaching will focus on the total superiority of Christ the Lord, indeed, the very Son of God (status), over the traditions and practices of the past. As the great divinely appointed MEDIATOR (1 Ti 2:5), Christ integrates all of the familiar dramatic religious roles perfectly: he intercedes with the SENDER, the heavenly Father, to communicate LIFE to his people in all its fullness both now in this world and forever in the next (a theme strongly emphasized also in the gospel of John). Christ also supplies the necessary POWER by sending the HELPER, the Holy Spirit, to guide and instruct his people in the Word of God to enable them to withstand the attacks of their chief OPPONENT, Satan, and any other human antichrist (cp. Jn 14:16,26; 15:26; 16:7; 1 Jn 2:18). Jesus is himself the SUBJECT—the Prophet (God's "Medium," the eternal Word, Hb 1:1-2), Priest (and the "Sacrifice" as well, Hb 7:27), King (or "Chief," Rv 17:14), Healer (the divine "Medicine Man," Ac 10:38), Judge (Jn 5:22), Warrior (Rv 19:11-21), and many more—the One who makes it possible for all people to be victorious in their daily struggle with the various physical and spiritual, magical and mystical forces of this world, thereby fulfilling God's purpose and achieving the glorious end for which they were created (Ro 8:37-39).

But Christ is much more than just a power figure. He also became true Man, the perfect *Munthu* (Pp 2:7-8, Hb 2:14), in complete solidarity with all humanity, to live the life we fail to achieve, to die the death we deserve. He became a curse on the cross, completely "taboo," in our stead (Ga 3:13), so that we might be redeemed from spiritual, religious, and cultural slavery (Ga 4:1-11) and reunited into the extended family, or clan, of God the Father by faith in him (Ga 3:26). Being led by the Spirit of this great Ancestor of ours (Ro 8:14-17, Hb 2:14-18), we are enabled to resist temptation and do the things which demonstrate our relationship to Christ—as his "brother, sister, or mother" (Mk 3:35). Through our oneness with him, everything that is his becomes ours (2 Ti 2:12), including those needs in particular that happen to be most relevant to the society concerned—in Central Africa: life (Jn 10:10) and power (Ac 1:8). We might illustrate this culturally sensitive theological position in terms of our earlier diagram of the paradigm of power and solidarity as follows:

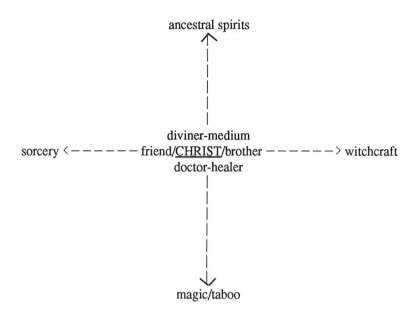

This picture is perhaps an oversimplification, but at least it suggests a conceptual goal that contemporary evangelists might aim to achieve in their communication efforts. Once a person becomes convinced that Christ, the Man in the middle, is in addition also the complete and all-powerful Lord of his life, both in this world and the next, then there will be no need for him to return to the partial and imperfect religious beliefs and practices of antiquity. Such a progressive, step-by-step (as opposed to an "either-or"), people-specific (rather than some universal) and culturally-sensitive (instead of ethnocentric) program of indoctrination combines sound biblical training with a more realistic and relevant approach with respect to the indigenous religious system on the one hand and an indigenized Christianity on the other. It is a receptor-oriented method which honestly and openly seeks to understand his traditional mind-set, even as it tactfully exposes the many failings of an anthropomorphically-based faith by comparing it to the preeminence of Christ, the all-sufficient Savior (Col. 1:15-20, 2:13-15).

The Functions of Religion in Society

To conclude this chapter and to prepare for the next, which presents a more detailed examination of a Central African world-view as this relates to the expression of the people's religious beliefs, we summarize below some of the primary functions of the religious system as a whole within the context of a traditional community. The representation of these functions reflects our application of the three models discussed above, namely, those based on power relations (i.e., status and solidarity), the process of communication (i.e., intentions and effects in particular), and the drama of interpersonal interaction (i.e., participant roles in dynamic interplay). It should be noted that the results of this functional analysis will differ in its details from that undertaken with regard to people of a different sociocultural background—that of a technologically-oriented Western society, for instance. It all depends on the importance that religion has and the level of intensity that it generates among the population at large toward shaping their fundamental thought patterns and in influencing the affairs of their everyday experience.

We have been stressing the notion that in many, if not all, parts of Africa the practice of traditional religion, taken in its comprehensive sense, encompasses the sum total of a society's cultural institutions. This is generally true whether or not the majority of people living in a given area happen to be active adherents—or even members, nominal and otherwise—of other religious organizations, notably Christian or Muslim. Correspondingly, then, their belief system, which is manifested by the continual operation of a diverse and elaborate symbolic communication process, effects a variety of functions within the community as a whole, over and above those which are more obviously ethical or spiritual in nature. Thus every aspect of social organization and activity that religion touches, as it were, may be seen to give expression to some related purpose, one that is naturally connected also with each of the others. The following diagram illustrates the central functional role that religion has with respect to the other major social institutions of Central Africa: kinship, politics, economics, education, medicine, and indeed, the natural environment itself. The so-called religious function, then, is not uniform; it is decidedly manifold:

ecological

therapeutic   sociological

RELIGIOUS

educational   political

economic

Sociocultural Functions

African religion thus affects, even as it is in turn influenced by, all of culture. Take the element of political control, for example: on the local, regional, or national level religion functions either to promote the established structures of power, e.g., the royal lineage and the rule of chiefs, or it acts to control such institutions by operating as an alternative or even competing system of authority. The *nyau* men's secret society among the matrilineal Chewa would be an example of the latter, for from its roots as a dramatic mime depicting mythical nature spirits--or nature in general as opposed to the culture of human habitation--it was gradually taken over by men/husbands living as oppressed foreigners at their wives' villages (i.e., matrilocal residence) to compensate for their lack of local sociopolitical status (Kalilombe, 1980, p. 46). Later this semireligious association broadened its sphere of activity to represent the interests of the common man (the Banda macroclan) over against the established kinship-based royal organization of authority (the Phiri macroclan). Both aspects of this type of political function may coexist, of course, to counterbalance one another within the same community, as apparently was the case in the ancient Chewa situation (ibid., p. 51; also cp. Schoffeleers, 1979, 150ff.)

Other prominent functions and subfunctions of religion among the Chewa people as suggested on the diagram above may be briefly described as follows: *sociological*, to direct and control the key communal rituals of transition in the cycle of life (e.g., at birth, maturation, marriage, childbearing, death, assumption of royal office) and living (e.g., planting, first-fruits, harvest); *judicial*, to discover, judge, and "cleanse" (punish/rehabilitate) social offenders and deviants, such as witches; *therapeutic*, to provide a means of healing for those who have either been afflicted by spirits or attacked by sorcerers; *ecological*, to help ensure the success of man's interaction with the natural environment, particularly with respect to the various means of food production (e.g., hunting, fishing, planting, herding, gathering); *genealogical*, to reinforce the legitimate lines of descent (past, present, and future) via the concept of life force as transmitted from the ancestors through the matrilineage and on to one's descendants.

The preceding has been but a partial description of just some of the many anthropocentric functions that the beliefs and practices of religion carry out in a traditional Central African society. Naturally, these are very closely related to one another, since they all to a greater or lesser extent affect the common concerns of man's existence on a day-to-day basis. Thus it would not be an exaggeration to claim that virtually every act of human communication in an African context involves, to a certain degree at least, some form of religious motivation or influence, whether overtly expressed or simply assumed as being part of the customary way in which things are done.

One might consolidate the preceding surface functions of religion, i.e., as stated in terms of specific social institutions and practices, and express them at a more abstract level of organization. One way to do this would be to apply the general definition of religion as a process of communication and posit the various functions that have normally been associated with the transmission of messages, e.g., expressive, affective, informative, relational, esthetic, and so forth (cp. Nida and de Waard, 1987, ch.2; Wendland, 1985, ch.2). The expressive function, for example, would include suboperations such as revealing man's need, whether individually or communally, in order to manifest his inner feelings and fears about his relationship with the supernatural or the sacred "numinous" (Otto, 1950), both verbally (e.g., prayers) and nonverbally (e.g., thank/fellow-ship offerings). Among other things, the informative function would cover a variety of activities pertaining to the universal human effort to organize, categorize, define, and interpret the cosmos by means of symbols and symbolic behavior. One of the principal affective subfunctions would involve man's attempts to influence or persuade personal divinities, and ultimately the Deity himself, to favor the community with blessings, such as fertility, or to ward off calamities like famine and pestilence.

It may be more helpful, however, in our presentation of a functional framework for traditional religion to remain somewhere between the extremes of generality and specificity. To that end we might posit the following seven basic motives of religious thought which initiate the practice of ritual action and all types of symbolic behavior in a nonurbanized, subsistence-based (tribal) society of Central Africa. The first six are primarily utilitarian and partially overlapping in nature. That is to say, they have a common homocentric perspective and relate in particular to the main social institutions which constitute and govern man's world. The seventh function with its theological focus is somewhat different, in that it reveals natural man's implicit desire, whether spiritually or materially motivated, to establish and maintain a favorable relationship with his Creator, Provider, and ultimate Judge. All seven functions are alike, however, in that, ideally at least, they enable people to deal with or to transcend three principal deficiencies of human experience: *uncertainty*, man's inability to predict and control the future/fate; *frailty*, his failure to manage and direct the fundamental powers of the cosmos; and *scarcity*, his incapacity to satisfy or supply all of the basic needs of everyday existence (O'Dea, 1983, 5).

1. Explanation

Religion is necessary to provide an explanation for the universe, its invisible aspects in particular, and man's place in this integrated whole—nature as well as supernature. Religion gives man an origin, an identity, and a meaning to history by revealing not only who he is and where he has come from, but also where he is going in terms of his ultimate destiny, that is, what happens after death. In the meantime, it enables him to relate meaningfully to the current reality, to provide answers for the way things are in life and how the world operates—as inexplicable as this may seem at times. These basic presuppositions about human existence help him to make sense of the cosmos and his daily experiences as part of an all-embracing framework of substance, being, nature, and essence. This applies especially to those unforeseen and usually adverse events such as accidents, sickness, and death, for which he could otherwise posit no tangible reason in terms of his present world-view.

2. Validation

This function is closely related to the first, in that once man has an explanation for the way things are (were and will be), he can in turn use this to justify the means which his society has evolved over the ages to organize itself—its thinking as well as its behavior. The basic social institutions of government, kinship, education, medicine, and economics operate the way in which they do because of religious sanction; this is how God and his representatives, the ancestors, want things to be arranged and carried out. Traditional religion reaffirms and thus sacralizes the basic value system of society together with its associated set of goals and norms of conduct. In this way it also serves as the foundation for community ethics and moral standards and legitimizes the fundamental roles, functions, facilities, and system of rewards and punishments that are characteristic of the group. This holistic and hallowed perspective thus gives people the confidence and the authority to deal with the various questions and crises which they encounter in life, both as individuals and as a community.

3. Purgation

In partial contrast to the preceding function, indigenous African religion provides a means for dealing with man's inevitable attempts to break the established social norms and to rebel against the prevailing domination by the group. It thus acts like a safety valve to facilitate a release of interpersonal tensions, or to express excess individualism. It also provides an outlet for a displacement of the repressed aggressions that periodically arise in typically small, closed, communalistic, largely nonliterate and pretechnological societies (though these are fast disappearing nowadays). It does this by recognizing various practices of the antinorm, taboo violations and sorcery/witchcraft in particular, and by institutionalizing a corresponding number of methods for correcting such occurrences and for overcoming guilt/shame and alienation, e.g., rites of reconciliation, cleansing procedures, application of protective medicines, propitiatory offerings, and so forth. Similarly, religious ideology furnishes man with a conceptual adaptive mechanism for reducing the degree of contradiction and conflict that may arise during periods of pronounced sociocultural change and increased population mobility (Kraft, 1974, 299). It thus preserves the equilibrium of society by allowing for a certain limited amount of reinterpretation or alteration of the underlying belief and value system to accommodate the disappointing failures in expectation and adverse experiences that inevitably occur in life.

4. Regulation

As an institution of authority, religion performs an important social role by contributing to the maintenance of law, order, and discipline in the community. It upholds the time-tested beliefs and customs of the past in order to preserve the general well-being of contemporary society by regulating public behavior and by hence averting punitive measures on the part of the overseeing ancestors, or even the deity. Religious traditions thus define what is acceptable or unacceptable behavior with respect to one's fellow man, the natural environment, and also the world of supernatural beings. Religious specialists such as the diviner-doctor and prophet then prescribe various forms of chastisement to be inflicted against those who either fail or refuse to conform to the established values and norms; for example, fines of compensation, deeds of penance, social ostracism, and in extreme cases through actual corporal, and occasionally also capital, punishment. In addition an interlocking set of taboos is in force, particularly in the area of social-sexual pollution. The latter facet of the overall corrective system operates more immediately and impersonally to chasten violators of the purity code by means of some physical or psychological affliction.

5. Integration

As the hub of African culture, religion functions to harmonize and homogenize the popular perception of reality (i.e., world-view). It also serves to integrate the different institutions of society and to act as a reference point according to which they all may be directed, evaluated, and adjusted, if necessary, for the common good. This is what Mary Douglas calls the "framing function" of religious ritual (1966, 63). The firmly held beliefs of tradition provide everyone with a unified outlook on the world and human experience. Corporate religious practices, in turn, act as a communal rallying point in times of crisis (e.g., drought), conflict (e.g., witchcraft accusations), and celebration (e.g., harvest), as well as in the special periods of transition during the course of life (i.e., growth and maturation). It thus promotes interpersonal solidarity and fosters a sense of unity which enables a closely-knit social group to withstand the various pressures, both from within and without, that are continually working for its debilitation and disintegration. The concept of "community" of course includes the future generation as well as the company of the departed, the ancestral host, with whom a positive, but not too familiar, relationship needs to be maintained.

6. Preservation

In a sense, this is the sum of functions one to five, for by operating to explain, validate, stabilize, regulate, and organize society, religion acts also to preserve the world-view upon which a group's social institutions and way of life are founded. Its regular or emergency rituals provide security and support both in periods of stress as well as at times of celebration. Its orientation towards the past and the ways of the fathers makes religion a very conservative and hence also a strong stabilizing force in society, one that resists both external and internal pressures for change. By bridging the gap between the objective world of experience and the culturally agreed upon perception and interpretation of that reality (Kraft, 1974, 298), the pervasive symbols of religious belief give adherents the assurance that there is meaning and purpose to life—a comprehensive plan that is based, not upon inferior human qualities and abilities, but upon surrounding distinct but accessible supernatural forces and powers (Nida, 1971, 244). All that is necessary, then, to keep society on an even keel is to faithfully observe the time-hallowed traditions which have been ordained and practiced with good success by those who have gone on before.

7. Theological Reflection

Indigenous Central African religion is more than a homocentric system of belief and a pragmatic social institution having solely a utilitarian function in the community. Like any natural, humanly-devised framework for mediating between man and the supernatural, or between the sacred and the profane within a particular sociocultural setting and physical environment, it also manifests a higher, theological purpose by offering people a means for communicating with the ultimate Being and supreme Force of the cosmos. Central African religion both explicitly and implicitly acknowledges the fact that "God" (*Mulungu, Leza,* etc.) is the Creator and Sustainer of all things, and that all the "powers and principalities" of the universe are ultimately subservient to his sovereign authority, purpose, and rule. Similarly, there is a deeply felt awareness of the greatness and absolute otherness of the Deity—his distinctness from man—primarily in a physical and psychological sense, but to a certain extent also morally and spiritually as well. God is not, and never could be, called or classified as *munthu,* "person/human being/man"!

The concept of divine "holiness," viewed in terms of a fundamental separation, is therefore not foreign to traditional religious thought. Although "sin" is viewed largely in social terms, i.e., as being an offence against humanity rather than the Deity, the idea that the latter has established an ethical standard to which man must conform is definitely included. Such views of the divine "numinous," to use Rudolf Otto's term, are enshrined in the many primal myths of origin that have been recorded throughout Central Africa. Thus God is also recognized as the supreme Judge, who may at times mete out punishments directly (instead of through his representatives, the ancestral spirits) in cases of extreme (e.g., incest) or widespread violation of his principles regarding right order in the world (e.g., apathy in personal/corporate worship). On the other hand, he is also appealed to as a last resort in situations of dire need, when there seems no hope of continued life, with respect to an individual (e.g., disease), the clan (e.g., barrenness), or the community as a whole (e.g., a plague). It is for these and other reasons that most sacrifices and offerings, both large and small, may be viewed as ultimately having a theological function as man's consecrated attempts not only to propitiate, appease, or become reconciled with the Deity, but also to thank, praise, and express admiration for his majesty and magnificence. Such diverse, divinely-directed thoughts and activities are a clear reflection of what theologians have termed the "natural knowledge of God" (Ac 17:22-31; Ro 1:18-32).

Conclusion: A Brief Dysfunctional Perspective

A positive functional approach such as that adopted above does not mean to imply that traditional religion in its various sociocultural manifestations over the years is now or ever was able to solve all of man's problems, whether personal or those of the community at large. Indeed, as Nida observes, there is a definite danger in "defending any and all forms of indigenous belief" (1960, 99). By incorporating tenets such as those relating to divination, taboo, magic, and witchcraft, for example, a natural religious system, whether in Africa or anywhere else, in many cases even promotes attitudes and actions that foster severe discord, dissension, and division within the group. As someone has observed, "Witchcraft feeds upon itself." In other words, the discovery and elimination or cleansing of the witches from a community through explicit ordeals and eradication procedures frequently serves only to sow the seed of latent hostility (envy, the desire for revenge, etc.) which will eventually spring up and bear similar fruit sometime in the future. Or, as O'Dea has expressed it, ". . . both the magical and religious rite anticipate and arouse the anxieties they allay" (1983, 10).

It is for this reason, too, that there are really no natural accidents, according to popular opinion. Rather, there is ultimately a human cause to every possible misfortune in life, whether self- or other-inflicted (e.g., the violation of a taboo as opposed to being felled by a sudden illness). Such a perspective on man's daily experience obviously produces a climate that is most conducive to the generation and maintenance of personal feelings of jealously when others prosper, and a desire for revenge and retribution when the self (or a close relative) happens to suffer. So it is that the three models of power, communication, and dramatic interplay can and must also be employed to investigate the several negative or disintegrative relationships that invariably occur with respect to the three interrelated factors of religion, society, and the wider cultural context.

To put it in local theological terms, "sin," which is passively a serious moral failure resulting in public "shame" (*uchimo* in Chewa), or actively a deliberate destruction of some clearly established ethical principle (*cinyonyoono* in Tonga), is that infectious and pervasive noise which hinders both the functions and the effects of the general religious communication process also in traditional societies. Thus the explanations prove to be wrong, validation is inadequate, stabilization falters and is shaken, compensatory purgation fails, regulating discipline breaks down, social integration is undone, and theological reflection becomes distorted or completely blurred. Or to be more concrete: the misuse, or progressive disuse, of religious beliefs and practices may transform the latter into an overly rigid, conservative force that encourages an uncritical intellectual dependency among the general population, impedes positive social changes, stifles the sense of individual responsibility and initiative, inhibits the development of scientific inquiry and knowledge, and promotes narrow, isolationist, extremist, even fanatical, views with regard to one's own society and usually all outsiders as well. A lot more can and probably should be said about these dysfunctional aspects of religion or, in Geertz's terms, the "cost" as distinct from the "gain" of religious organization and operation in society (1973, 143), but that would require an extensive separate study within the context of a specific cultural group or subgroup.

To such disruptions and incongruities on the internal level of socioreligious experience must be added those of an external nature, in particular the ever-growing influence of science, technology, education, extensive cross-cultural contact, and all that such modern motivations for change entail. Traditional African religion is resistant, but certainly not impervious, to the effects of such ubiquitous forces, which will have a decided impact, on not only the forms of religious expression, but ultimately also upon the underlying belief system itself. For this reason detailed research into this multifaceted subject needs to be continuous, yet at the same time broad and flexible enough to deal with its ever changing manifestations as well as its serious implications for society at large, and for the Christian community in particular.

In closing, we might cite just one graphic instance of the convergence of internal and external factors in the dysfunctional operation of traditional religion in a contemporary setting. The example illustrates the way in which the explanatory and regulatory roles of customary religious belief can act as a barrier that hinders progress and development in the economic sector of a modern African state. It was recently reported on the BBC (Africa Service, the "Focus on Africa" program of August 23, 1989) that peasant farmers in the southern region of Malawi are strongly resisting government efforts to promote more ecologically sound agricultural techniques. The case in point concerned the application of contour-ridge plowing in the extensive fields of maize, which is the country's staple food crop. This practice is believed to anger the legendary semi-divine ancestral spirit of Mbona, who was renowned in the area as the greatest ever "rain-caller" (*woitanitsa-mvula*). As a result, Mbona, who according to tradition turned into a great mystical serpent at death, has in recent years been striking the region with heavy, destructive rainstorms which greatly reduce crop yields.

The radio report ended there, but it might have concluded with the following religious explanation: the contour-ridges appear from the sky as huge snakes covering the ground. The gross multiplication of such imperfect images constitutes a grave insult to Mbona, for in this part of Africa neither God nor the ancestors are ever reduced to the form of human idols. He therefore demonstrates his offended majesty in an appropriate manner, that is, with a punishment that fits the crime. He transforms what in his lifetime was the most outstanding of charismatic gifts (i.e., to counter a lack of rain) into a rod of chastisement (i.e., by providing an excess of rain) which is levelled against an apparently ungrateful and impious people.

The dysfunctional effects of certain prominent beliefs and practices are not restricted of course to indigenous African religion, for they may be observed in connection with many Christian groups as well. When the integrative function, for example, is pushed too far and too literally in relation to selected biblical texts, it can result in a decided, even militant, antigovernment stance in the case of some African independent churches (e.g., refusing to pay taxes, salute the flag, send children to school, vote in elections, hold public office, and so forth). The same motivation may also provoke intense rivalry, which often borders on outright hostility, in the case of certain larger mainline denominations (e.g., between Roman Catholics and certain evangelical Protestant churches in some parts of Central Africa).

We see then that the seven functions as presented above are convenient abstractions and idealizations, described as performing harmoniously in a pristine, utopian society, which of course does not exist anywhere on earth! And yet the effort to specify and define them in such terms is not without purpose, for the critical evaluation of these systems and their cross-cultural comparison cannot be carried out without first having established at least some putative standard or norm to serve as a basis for analysis. From this vantage point, then, the various abberations, imbalances, fluctuations, alterations, and additional developments may be more systematically explored in relation to the other major institutions which constitute the fluid core of any human social organism. In the next chapter, this functionally-oriented, model-guided approach will be applied more specifically to a consideration of the overall belief system that underlies the overt practices of traditional Central African religion.

Chapter 3

THE FOUNDATION OF RELIGIOUS BELIEF:
KEY ASPECTS OF THE CHEWA AND TONGA WORLD-VIEW

World-View as a Filter in the Communication Process

According to the simple communication model presented in the preceding chapter, a receptor or receptor-group receives a given message, whether verbal or nonverbal, which has been transmitted via a particular sensory channel by the source. The receptor decodes the signs of the message according to the rules of the cultural code concerned and then reacts in a manner that is most relevant or appropriate to the occasion (from his perspective), either immediately or some time thereafter, in thought, word, and/or deed. It is important to recognize that this communication process never takes place in a circumstantial vacuum or in social isolation. On the contrary, it always occurs within a particular setting—a surrounding context which no doubt stimulated the message in the first place and which never fails to influence its composition and interpretation.

As was noted, the *context* of communication (as distinct from the textual context) is itself a complex concept. It may be broken down into a number of distinct but interrelated sociolinguistic facets, impersonal and personal (cp. Nida, 1986; Wendland, 1985, ch.3). The *impersonal* context includes such things as the time, place, and dramatic circumstances of the communication event. It makes a big difference sometimes whether a message is transmitted and received in the morning, when the receptor is fresh and prepared to meet the day, or at night, when he is tired and ready to retire. A person is naturally going to respond differently to a message that is conveyed in church on Sunday morning as opposed to in a bar on Saturday night. A Christian worship service held out of doors under the open sky in a rural African village conveys a different atmosphere than a similar service conducted in a large urban cathedral, especially when a severe thunderstorm is threatening to break loose. Similarly, certain behavior communicates differently under diverse external conditions. For example, one does not participate in a football match or throw a party on a day of national mourning, for such action would be regarded as being grossly inappropriate, and in many African countries, even a criminal offense. The coarse, unrestrained type of language and behavior between the sexes that frequently occurs during the burial time of a Central African funeral would not be tolerated at all under any other circumstances.

The *personal* context has two principal dimensions: external and internal, both of which greatly affect the act of communication. The *external*, or interpersonal, aspect concerns the participants who are involved in the event: how are they related to one another (e.g., father to son, niece to paternal uncle [= "father"], a husband to his mother-in-law, etc.); what are their respective statuses and mutual roles (e.g., higher to lower, social equals, master to servant, ruler to subject, pastor to parishioner, etc.); and what is the situational setting under which they are interacting (e.g., wedding, funeral, an interview for a job, an initiation ceremony, etc.). It is clear that this aspect of context can become rather involved. It is crucial, however, that the total sociological environment be carefully analyzed in any study of the effects of culture on communication, for ignoring any one of these factors can lead to errors of interpretation, especially in matters as complex as those pertaining to religious beliefs and practice in Africa.

Take the deceptively simple matter of whether one is to address the Deity with an honorific or a familiar form of language. The traditional Tonga worshipper speaks to God as to a close friend or personal acquaintance. The Chewa, on the other hand, are accustomed to include some formal marks of dignity and social distance in their discourse with God, as in a prayer or liturgical rite. This corresponds to the respective conventions which these two peoples observe when conversing with their traditional leaders, such as a local headman or chief. These long-standing verbal customs may be modified, however, due to the more recent influence of Christian teaching and a perspective that tends to prefer a more respectful linguistic approach towards the Father, Son, and Holy Spirit.

The *internal* aspect of the personal setting manifests a stable and an unstable component (relatively speaking). The *unstable* element pertains primarily to one's personal moods, sentiments, affections, and feelings, which tend to be rather changeable and transient, depending upon the individual concerned and circumstances that he or she happen to be in (the latter factor linking up with the impersonal setting). Nevertheless, such psychological features contribute to a certain degree at least to the total context in which a given communicative event occurs, and hence they influence both the act of message reception and often that of transmission as well. A person who is angry, frustrated, in love, or grief-stricken, for example, will naturally not respond to an admonition from his pastor in the same way that he would if his mind were not affected by such emotions. These internal feelings normally vary also according to personal characteristics such as age and sex, and so do the socially acceptable forms of their public manifestation. Among many groups both in Africa and elsewhere, women and younger individuals tend to display their affections more overtly than men and older people.

But one must be aware of possible cultural differences in the area of emotive expression, during acts of religious communication for example. Upon hearing that "David danced before the Lord with all his might" (2 Sm 6:14), a Tonga audience would immediately identify with the situation, for that is exactly what their traditional religious leader does when approaching the ancestral spirits at a local *malende* rain shrine. Western Christians, on the other hand, would be much more inclined to react like Michal did to a great leader's outburst of religious enthusiasm—with shame and perhaps even a considerable measure of disgust at what they might regard as socially inappropriate behavior. The typical Tonga person, however, would undoubtedly question David's sharply contrasting actions in connection with the illness of the first son that Bathsheba bore him: while the baby was still sick, David "fasted and wept" on the ground (2 Sm 12:22) as "he pleaded with God for the child" (v.16), certainly conduct unbecoming a Tonga man in similar circumstances, though not for a Jew. But then after the child had died, David got up, washed, changed his clothes, worshipped God, and ate (v.20), quite the opposite of what would be expected of a *Mutonga* at the funeral of his son. However, we note that even David's personal servants were surprised by their master's latter conduct.

A person's *stable* internal, or mental, setting has to do with the more deep-seated and enduring aspects of his outlook on life—his world-view, in other words. This general perspective on existence, as was noted earlier, is composed of several elements, notably one's underlying beliefs, values, attitudes, motivations, and goals, all of which combine to establish his norms or standards of thought and behavior. This conceptual framework in turn acts like a filter to block out from any message that is communicated to the individual (or group) all information which may somehow contradict or call into question its underlying premises and assumptions, or even less rigidly held desires, impressions, and opinions. Alternatively, this psychological screen may function to modify the content and tone of any instance of communication to harmonize with one's predetermined perspective on the subject being discussed. In either case, the meaning of the message which was transmitted by the source is not the same as that which his receptors actually apprehend. Because of the culturally specific world-view which guides and directs their thinking, people tend to see, hear, and understand just what they want—or better, what they have been conditioned—to see, hear, and understand. If the message corresponds with the way they think and feel, especially with respect to their basic set of values, and if they perceive it to be relevant to their particular needs, they will respond accordingly, either internally (i.e., with regard to their thoughts, emotions, goals, etc.) or externally (i.e., by what they say and do).

To give a typical example from Central Africa: in November of 1976 the Sunday Times of Zambia reported the remarkable story of a 72 year old woman from Choma (in the Southern Province) who refused to die. This particular individual was alleged to have "died and risen" three times within a period of four months. According to the report:

> She first "died" one night last August. A coffin was bought and a grave dug. But when they started nailing the coffin, a voice complained from inside: "You are hurting me." The dumb-founded mourners opened the coffin and found her very much alive and kicking. She has since then died and risen on two other occasions, so the "Times" was told.

Speaking from a medical point of view, local Western-trained doctors were skeptical, noting that not infrequently a very sick person's body will slow down to the point where it seems from all visible signs that he or she is dead. If no competent medical examination is conducted, and if the survivors are a little too anxious to bury their relative, then, so the doctors contended, it is not surprising that mistakes like this occur. A rational, scientific explanation, however, has little or no effect upon those who already have a way of explaining what had happened—a way established by tradition and no doubt confirmed many times according to the viewpoint of the observers. Thus, in the opinion of those who were on the scene of the "resurrection," such an occurrence is not really mysterious at all (just as it was not for the medical doctors): "The woman who has denied death three times must have taken a kind of love potion called *shabwa*, which prevents her from dying as long as she can see men or hear male voices."

Here we have another clear instance of where the very same event communicates a completely different message—or, we might say, calls forth a radically dissimilar conclusion and emotive reaction—depending upon the underlying perspective from which it is viewed and interpreted. Furthermore, the opposing viewpoints effectively filter one another out in the minds of their respective adherents.

The following is a summary diagram of the various aspects of *context* which interact during any given communication event to modify and structure the processes of perception, interpretation, and response on the part of the participants involved:

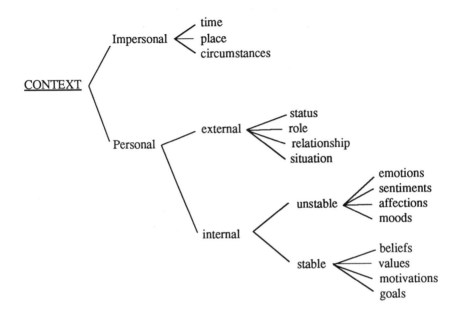

Degrees of Contextual Immediacy

The various elements which comprise the *context* of any act of communication are different in their relative degree of apparentness to the outside observer, particularly if he or she comes from a different cultural background. The *impersonal* features may be recognized by just about anyone on the scene, that is, the *time*, *place*, and *circumstances* of the event or situation in question. The *external* aspects of the *personal* context—the interpersonal relations (e.g., respective statuses and roles) of those concerned as well as the social setting—are not so easy for the cultural outsider to discern, but after some careful observation and study, these, too, might be specified quite precisely.

The *internal*, or psychological, context is a different matter, however. Now the analyst must be able to penetrate the minds of the participants, and here is where some major problems are encountered, for this probing process can only be carried out indirectly, that is, by inference from a people's language and other types of overt behavior. There is not as much difficulty here with the *unstable* features, since these are close to the surface, so to speak, of both individual and corporate expression, e.g., in various religious rites and ceremonies. Nevertheless, despite the fact that one's desires, emotions, attitudes, and concerns will often be revealed in the matter and manner of what he or she says and does, this is by no means always the case. A cover-up, disguise, or alteration of one's true opinion and feeling is frequently resorted to, especially in difficult social situations (e.g., wartime, witchcraft trials, or other interpersonal conflict) for varying reasons (e.g., to save face, avoid blame, gain some advantage). The classic example of emotive dissimulation is of course Judas' greeting of Christ in the Garden of Gethsemane (Mt 26:47), and arising from a completely different motivation, we have the Lord's seemingly uninterested response to the report of Lazarus' illness (Jn 11:3-4; cp. 33-36).

The *stable* factors, on the other hand, that is, those which pertain to the mental constitution of the individual, are not always very apparent even to members of the same cultural group. These are matters which are often simply taken for granted; one does not normally have occasion to discuss or debate them. This is the most difficult, and from the point of view of communication strategy, the most crucial, context to penetrate, for it involves the deep-seated beliefs, presuppositions, and values which derive from the theory of reality and philosophy of life that a person assimilates by being the member of a particular society. And the essential aspects of the religious component of this overall world-view are probably the hardest part of the code to crack because it is so often hidden by several layers of formalism covering all facets of everyday life, as manifested, for example, in preexilic upper-class Israel (cp. Am 5:18-27) or NT Pharisaism. It took the divine perception of the Son of God to expose the prejudice, hypocrisy, and perversity of the latter's self-righteous ethical system (Mt 23), yet he had no greater success in convincing his hardened hearers of the error of their ways than did the Lord's herdsman-prophet with his thundering oracles of denunciation.

Not only is a given world-view difficult to analyze because so much of it is implicit (even those who adhere to it usually cannot describe and explain it readily, if at all), but it is probably the single most important, potentially limiting factor in any communication process. If the source and the receptors share for all practical purposes the same belief system and outlook on life, then, all other variables being the same, it is relatively easy for them to communicate with one another by word or action. In fact, on many occasions one person will even be able to anticipate what a fellow participant in some event is going to say or do. This does not mean that they will always agree, or that there will never be any misunderstanding between them, but one of the most serious barriers to interpersonal interaction will simply not be present.

Unfortunately the converse is also true. As the degree of disparity in world-view between source and receptor widens, so the likelihood of some breakdown in communication or cooperation between them also increases. This seems to be especially critical where matters of a religious nature are concerned, due to the fundamental role that it plays in all human thought and behavior. Examples are Pilate's misunderstanding of Christ and his "kingdom" (Jn 18:33-38), and the controversy that arose between Jews and Gentiles in the early Christian church over the issue of circumcision (Ac 15). And when such a culturally-based incongruity occurs, given the fact that the true nature of another people's world-view is so inaccessible to the alien observer, he will frequently experience some formidable problems in determining just exactly what has gone wrong and why. For the residents of Lystra, there could be no doubt that Paul and Barnabas were really the gods Zeus and Hermes in disguise. The two apostles, who had just healed a lame man, fit the image evoked by an ancient legend and hence fulfilled the people's religious expectations perfectly. It was no wonder then that they wished to sacrifice to these gods in a great public ceremony. Paul and Barnabas could hardly prevent such rites from taking place, let alone persuade the people to change their minds. It was only after some jealous Jews from a neighboring town convinced the Lystrans that the two were frauds that the crowd finally responded, interestingly enough with an attempt to inflict the prescribed Old Testament punishment for defamation of the deity—death by stoning (Ac 14:1-20).

In this chapter we will focus upon the principal elements of a Central African world-view in an effort, first of all, to specify its underlying sociocultural macrothemes, and secondly, to show how these premises influence some of the more apparent aspects of religious behavior (cp. Nida, 1962; Wonderly and Nida, 1963; Welton, 1971). Our survey will take the form of a description, analysis, and illustration of some of the key tenets of this tightly integrated system of beliefs and values which, as we have noted, functions as the central core—or to put it in more dynamic terms, the source of the well or spring (*citsime* in Chewa)—of Bantu traditional culture in this region of the continent.

Seven Principles of a Central African Philosophy of Life

The seven principles to be described and exemplified below represent just one way of analyzing, organizing, and evaluating the masses of data which are available to work with. The main point of this investigation is to delineate some of the basic features of the belief system and the conceptual framework within which these operate. There may well be differences of opinion as regards the following treatment of this material, which concerns, we remember, not a static and lifeless object which can be dissected with precision in a laboratory and examined under a microscope. Rather, we are dealing with a dynamic phenomenon, one that is composed of a multitude of different facets in many specific local settings and all in a continual state of interaction and change, like that of a living organism, within the ongoing development of the culture as a whole. Thus it is felt that differences of formulation and detail need not detract from the main ideas being presented or the inductive methodology whereby they were arrived at.

It is proposed that the linguistic distinction between so-called deep and surface structures is applicable and useful also in describing the essentials of a people's world-view, its primary religious features in particular (Nida, 1972, 15-16). *Deep* refers to the underlying conceptual framework which organizes and directs all thought, perception, feeling, and ultimately also the overt activities and products (i.e., on the *surface* of life) that characterize a particular cultural group or subgroup. Surface experience and behavior, in turn, such as a group's social institutions and their associated conventions, influence the belief and value system in many subtle ways, especially in times of considerable pressure for adaptation and/or change (Filbeck, 1985, 86).

We will proceed, therefore, by considering a set of seven fundamental premises or presuppositions about reality, each of which appears to account for a significant portion of the Central African world-view complex. The individual principles will then be delineated in terms of their manifestation within Bantu society, especially in areas which are of special religious relevance. The focus will be upon those essential values and affections to which a particular belief gives rise, and an attempt will be made to provide concrete illustrations of how the principle concerned is realized in actual behavior. This procedure is crucial, for it demonstrates how the visible forms of a given cultural group may be analyzed with regard to their function, both as symbols which convey meanings, or messages, to all members of the community, and also as indices which reflect some fundamental feature of a people's world-view.

These seven principles should be viewed as broad, overlapping *predilections* rather than hard and fast rules or distinct conceptual categories. Furthermore, while the concepts are interrelated, they do not seem to be equal in their level of generality. Some, in short, appear to be more fundamental to the Central African world-view than others. We will begin, then, with the notion that is regarded as being basic to all of the rest, one that pertains to the average person's underlying outlook on life, namely, a *synthetic* perspective. Thereafter we will discuss two principles which are also crucial to one's understanding of the system as a whole, that is, *dynamism* and *experientialism*. This leads to a consideration of four additional ideas which, while still essential to the underlying world-view, seem to be somewhat subordinate in nature: *gradation, communalism, humanism* and *circumscription*. It will not be possible in the following discussion to exemplify these principles in detail. Rather, an overview is presented which can subsequently serve as a starting point for further, more intensive research on the subject or various aspects of it.

It is also necessary to point out that the different cultural themes presented here are not unique to the Central African scene. In fact, every society will probably exhibit behavior which reflects each of the seven principles to a greater or lesser extent. This would be especially true in a large pluralistic nation such as the United States, which is composed of many distinct subsocieties and cultures. Thus a particular characterization is really a matter of gradients, degrees, or special emphases rather than being an either-or situation with respect to any constituent. One would therefore expect to find these features represented by a series of continua in which each would involve a range of possible values or strengths that fluctuate between one extreme and the other, for example, between a synthetic and an analytical approach, a humanistic and a theistic ethos, or between a communalistic and an individualistic lifestyle. It is possible, too, that one might even find certain variations in prominence from one social institution to the next (i.e., government, education, economics, kinship, art, medicine, and religion) within a given community, though such a complex diversity in outlook does not as yet appear to be widespread in Central Africa. In any case, it is the complete profile which is important, that is, the particular combination of features in their respective strengths and weaknesses as they happen to apply within a given society at a particular point in time. It is hoped that the following also provides a possible comparative framework from which one might begin such an investigation across different cultural boundaries.

1. The Principle of Synthesis

This essential concept, one which pertains to a predominant frame of mind rather than to an exclusive orientation, seems to underlie all of the rest. In other words, an extensive investigation of ancient as well as modern texts, both verbal and nonverbal, reveals this to be perhaps the most prominent feature of the Central African world-view (not only theirs, of course), namely, a distinct preference for a *synthetic* approach toward life. That is to say, there is a widespread tendency to "put things together," no matter how seemingly dissimilar on the surface, in order to attain or ascribe a certain wholeness or unity to whatever is being examined, described, evaluated, or otherwise considered. This perspective leads one to look for what is similar in human experience—the *common components* of life, to use a lexical metaphor—and to link up all of these elements in a communally oriented system where everyone has his/her/its own purpose and place within the whole. There is thus an emphasis upon searching for the relatedness of things, to include rather than to exclude, to ensure that no one or thing is left out, for the entire universe, including its Creator, must function as a unit, with all of the individual parts operating in smooth and harmonious interaction.

There is a host of instances that may be cited to illustrate this central concept, many of which will appear in our discussion of the six derivative principles below. But we might mention here some of the more obvious manifestations. Take the elaborate African kinship system, for example. Within the clan, everyone is either a "mother," "father," "sister," or "brother." Much more precise designations of a person's relationship can be given if needed, but in general conversation the more inclusive designation is employed whenever possible. These familial terms can even be extended to encompass larger group relations, right on up to the tribe as a whole. Such a holistic perspective makes it quite natural to express, with a depth of feeling that approaches that of the original, an idea like "brothers" and "sisters" in the Lord (e.g., Mt 12:50; Ja 2:15). The reference here is to people who believe the same and fellowship together, so naturally they must be related! However, we should also take note of the fact that the correspondence in meaning is not exact; the relationship being referred to in the Scriptures transcends all familial, kinship, ethnic, and national boundaries.

Since a group with a predominantly synthetic outlook on life does not like to leave anyone out or unrelated, they normally devise ways to accommodate the foreigners or strangers with whom they happen to come into contact. Thus the system of clan totems, which is quite common throughout Central Africa (e.g., leopard, elephant, crocodile, hippo, and so on), is extended to include, or at least to recognize, also those corresponding members who belong to different ethnic groups. There are also specific categories reserved for complete aliens—for people speaking foreign languages and observing different customs, but obviously still human, e.g., *mzungu* "white man"—perhaps derived from the Swahili word denoting something strange, wondrous, extraordinary. As it turns out, even the European colonialist would have discovered (had he bothered to look into it) that he was already "related" to the indigenous people whose land he was invading and whom he regarded as being somehow inferior to himself.

The commonly cited practice of tribalism, whereby an individual, usually one in authority, shows favoritism to a person of his own ethnic group as opposed to someone else, does not really contradict this principle. It simply demonstrates that there are degrees of synthetic bonding, and the greater measure of loyalty or assistance that is incumbent upon those with closer social ties must naturally manifest itself in cases where a choice has to be made. This has nothing at all to do with the disparaging attitudes of superiority that are associated with racism.

It is interesting to observe that the noun class and concordial copy system which is such a prominent feature of all Bantu languages reinforces this idea of inclusiveness: every object in the environment, new as well as old, has its designated place within the classification, and hence the syntactic relations of every nominal within a connected piece of discourse are clearly marked. Furthermore, there is a tendency for selected groups of entities, such as trees, rivers, human beings, wild beasts, birds, and animals which function as characters in the oral literature to be put into a common noun class. Accurate semantic distinctions need to be made, of course, and to that end a certain measure of analytical processing is also involved—one cannot have synthesis without at least some form of prior analysis. But the primary emphasis seems to be upon the former, on grouping together items which have a distinct familial resemblance, whether overt or attributed, so that a sense of wholeness and unity is either created or confirmed.

Relations and relatives, both human and otherwise, thus pervade the preferred synthetic logic of African thought. It is felt to be a distinctive feature of man's nature in particular; as the Chewa put it: *tili tawiri ntianthu, kali kokha nkanyama*, "When we're together we are 'people' [i.e., human], a person by himself is like an animal." This will be noticed time and again in any thorough consideration of their religion, too, which is integrally connected in some way or another with all of the other dimensions of culture. Thus religion was not regarded as being essentially distinct from the other major sociocultural institutions, such as the kinship system, political establishment, traditional education, or economic methods. Rather, it was seen to thoroughly permeate them all. Similarly, there was no such thing as separate, antagonistic sects or cults within the overall religious framework of a single, homogeneous ethnic group. The internal competition would come later--even before the advent of Western Christian denominationalism--when such indigenous groups merged with one another, either through force of arms or by mutual accommodation. A good example of this is revealed in the history of the Banda and Phiri clans of the Proto-Chewa and Maravi peoples respectively, each of which maintained, with modification, its central institutions of worship (i.e., territorial rain shrines versus a centralized royal cult), as the groups amalgamated over the years in the country now known as Malawi (cp. Schoffeleers, 1978, 148ff).

This harmonizing, incorporative tendency holds true also for the various specific manifestations of religion. Take the practice of magic, for example: whether the imitative or the contagious variety is being applied, the same basic principle is involved, namely, that a part can be employed to represent the whole, the former being mystically linked to the latter either by similarity or by some other relevant association. Magic, as we observed, is itself connected with each of the other major aspects of power dynamics operative in Central African religion—with sorcery, witchcraft, spiritism, and healing.

All active (as opposed to dormant or dead) symbolism in fact gives evidence of the operation of a profound conceptual synthesis. The analogy which forms the basis (vehicle) for a symbol in the Central African sociocultural context is normally found in nature, which includes the human body and all of its orifices and appendages. The meaning or significance of the symbol (its tenor) relates to critical events or states in the cycle of human existence—points of crisis or transition (e.g., initiation), situations where a separation must be made (e.g., taboo restriction), and times when a certain force must be harnessed, either for individual purposes or for the common good (e.g., use of medicine). The process cannot be reduced to a matter of simple cause-and-effect, nor can it be explained in purely rational terms—to that extent it is thus illogical or mystical. The symbol bridges, as it were, two distinct aspects or dimensions of reality through the mediating efforts of some human agent, whether an average individual or some socioreligious specialist (e.g., medicine man [+], sorcerer [-]), who deliberately or unconsciously activates an additional extrasensory source of power or influence which lies either within or without himself. The synthetic element of such symbolism can go so far as to effect a virtual identification between the vehicle and its tenor, as happens for example when a witch attacks a victim by means of his or her secret, personal name, or when people link the vital presence of an ancestor with the blood of a living relative (as they say in Chichewa, "brotherhood [or sisterhood] is blood," *ubale ndi magazi*).

It may be helpful by way of comparison to point out in somewhat more detail what a synthetic viewpoint contrasts with, namely, an analytical approach. It is the latter principle which guides a great deal of Western thinking. The analyst focuses upon what is unique, individual, and distinct in the world about him (i.e., the diagnostic components of life). He likes to break down what he observes and experiences rationally into neat categories of opposition with their fixed laws of organization, and to demonstrate how one thing is different from another in terms of measurable criteria. Such an empirical approach is, of course, fundamental to the so-called scientific method which governs the Westerner's manner of systematically conceptualizing, captivating, and controlling the environment in which he lives.

Frequently, however, this process of analytic differentiation goes no further than two, and what results is a crass dualism, that is, a division of reality into contrasting pairs of polarized absolutes: fact vs. fiction, visible vs. invisible, civilized vs. primitive, personal vs. impersonal, public vs. private, body vs. soul, matter vs. spirit, truth vs. error, moral vs. immoral, success vs. failure, clean vs. dirty, work vs. play, and so forth. This reductionistic perspective naturally tends to lead the analyst into what may be termed "either-or" type of thinking: if something does not fit into one category, then it must belong to the opposite one; for or against. In such thinking there is no room for "now-and-then," "in-between," or "both-and" possibilities which are allowed for and appreciated by the synthesist.

The difference between the analytical and synthetic modes of thought has some important consequences as far as one's approach to religion is concerned. For the traditionally-oriented African, as we have stressed, religion permeates, promotes, and propels all of life. It is difficult, if not impossible, to fix a dividing line between where religion leaves off and some other sociocultural institution begins. The Westerner, on the other hand, has that particular boundary quite clearly demarcated in his life, and unfortunately, all too often in his thinking as well. For him there is a definite difference between what is sacred and secular in his world, and the border between the two is often reinforced by legal sanction and a variety of laws which are designed to designate either exclusion or inclusion (e.g., the use of religious decorations in public places at Christmas time or the allowance/prohibition of prayers in public schools).

For the sake of good order (and 1 Co 14:40 is sometimes cited in this connection), the analyst likes to have this distinction very clearly marked with respect to both time and space. Thus religion is normally (officially, formally, properly, etc.) practiced on a particular day, the "Sabbath," and at a specific place, within a church building. Any time or place other than this does not really count as much—nor does it have to, once the minimum requirements for worship have been met. So while religion as an activity somehow divorced from everyday life began to diminish in importance and relevance within an increasingly materialistic and secular society, so also did the time allocated to such practice decrease, till at last it has been restricted by many to but a single hour on what used to be known as "the Lord's Day." Interestingly enough, there did not follow a corresponding reduction in the place, or space, of worship. On the contrary, an inordinate amount of material, labor, expense, and adornment is lavished upon religious edifices, perhaps as a way of compensating for the little time that is actually spent there.

In customary Central African practice, on the other hand, a religious "event" such as an initiation ritual or a rain-calling ceremony could last several days and would incorporate everything that was done over that period of time, wherever such activity happened to be carried out within the entire village setting, e.g., prior acts of divination to ascertain the cause of the dilemma (drought), ritual self-preparation, fellowship meals together, singing, dancing, prayers at the shrine, the sacrificial act itself, and various other types of communal interaction. It is tragic to see an imported Western sacred-secular dichotomy exerting ever greater influence upon the thinking of many African Christians nowadays. Thus people go to church--a building which is clearly identified as representing a particular denomination or sect--regularly once a week out of habit just to be a part of the somewhat novel or prestigious rites taking place there. But they tend to leave the basic problems of their lives (those pertaining to health, spiritism, magic, sorcery, and witchcraft in particular) back home where they can be dealt with in the familiar traditional way.

An analytical, as opposed to a synthetic, viewpoint not only concerns one's religious practice, but it also profoundly affects one's perspective on the composition of the universe and indeed life itself. The traditional African, for example, does not formally distinguish between the natural and the supernatural, nor does he evaluate in positive and negative terms the material as opposed to the spiritual, exalting the latter at the expense of the former. Indeed, key religious notions do not revolve around a central antagonistic dualism of good versus evil, whether the latter be conceived of in impersonal or personal terms, e.g., the New Testament antithesis of God/angels versus Satan/demons (Ep 6:11-12). Evil spirits as well as witches/sorcerers are all part of a single amoral conception of the cosmos. Furthermore, the natural and the supernatural comprise but one integrated system of mutually interacting forces in the universe, as was pointed out earlier, and it does violence to the structure as a whole to try and distinguish the various elements as belonging either to one or the other sphere with respect to essence and/or function. Thus what the American would regard as being supernatural may be perfectly natural for the African, though some sort of special concentration of life force or spiritual power may well be perceived as operating in a manner which is personally either advantageous or detrimental.

For example, a newspaper article such as that cited earlier, which reports the fact that someone had "risen" from the dead, is unusual or extraordinary only insofar as such an event does not happen every day. But the occurrence itself is quite natural in the sense that it can be explained in terms of a special manifestation of mystical power, either with or without the application of selected magical substances. Similarly, the appearance of the spirit of a departed relative to someone in a dream/vision would not be thought of as being strange at all, though it may well be a deeply unsettling experience for the individual concerned. It is simply part of the nature of the cosmos (i.e., having no firmly fixed barrier between the physical and the spiritual realms) as it was established in the beginning, when God was actually living down here on earth in fellowship with man—and as things have continued essentially unaltered ever since.

Someone with an analytically-oriented world-view, however, would be inclined to regard such happenings as being supernatural, since they appear to be contrary to proven scientific laws which govern the operation of the universe; or he might consider the possibility of his senses being deceived (e.g., due to drugs or drink); or he may be led to the conclusion that he was beginning to lose his mind because "these things just don't happen!" Many people having this viewpoint would even go so far as to completely deny the possibility of the supernatural having any relevance to human existence at all. Every such occurrence of the extraordinary, therefore, like the miracles recorded in the Bible, must be demythologized in order to remove every trace of supernatural belief and to render them reasonable (i.e., understandable and demonstrable) to someone with a naturalistic and rationalistic mind-set.

Since a differentiation between the sacred and the secular is important for the Westerner, their separateness is continually observed in his day-to-day affairs. Everything (objects, events, places, times, etc.) which constitutes his experience in life is categorized (usually subconsciously) as being either religious or nonreligious in nature. Of course there will always be some overlapping in actual practice, such as when a prayer is said before some secular function, but even then the distinction will normally be maintained, e.g., a clergyman will specifically be called upon to say the prayer. Similarly, the difference between what is supernatural and natural in the world is one that is rather obvious to most people (at least according to their thinking it is), and this perspective governs how they evaluate and react to certain uncommon events, happenings, and situations which they may encounter.

For example, are there such things as haunted houses, demon-possession, witchcraft, monstrous creatures, spirits, gremlins, or good-luck charms? If so, then such phenomena must be supernatural, since they defy a rational, scientific explanation. But if not, then some logical reason in terms of verifiable cause and effect is either presently available or it is to be expected (after the necessary empirical investigation has been carried out). The two pairs of parameters that we have been discussing intersect, giving the person with an analytical perspective four categories according to which he may classify his experience:

	religious	secular
natural	e.g., worship service	e.g., football match
supernatural	e.g., God	e.g., ghost

The reason for the preceding description is to contrast it with the Central African's synthetic outlook on life. As far as his world is concerned, while various precise linguistic distinctions are made where socioculturally relevant, there are no metaphysical divisions, no conceptually closed compartments like those indicated above. The religious merges with the secular and the natural with the supernatural to form a holistic perspective and approach towards all of the experiences of life. Even such a seemingly secular event as a football match may be permeated by what we are calling religious behavior, for example, in the magical charms that players acquire in order to increase their skill, and in the protective medicine that is applied in the goal mouth to prevent the home team's opponents from scoring! Such conviction finds poetic expression in the Bemba proverb: *kwimba kati kusansha na Lesa*,"to dig up a little root is to mix with God." In other words, no charm works without the blessing of the Deity; he ultimately controls all human activity. Furthermore, God is a vital, if not an immediately perceptible, participant in even the most ordinary of man's endeavors.

It would appear at first glance that the elaborate system of taboos observed by societies such as the Chewa and Tonga represent at least one clear exception to the dominance of synthetic thinking in the Central African world-view. To be sure, the clearest possible differentiation (hence "analysis") is made between what is regarded as ritually "pure" as distinct from "polluted" objects, persons, events, and states. The same thing applies to whatever is weak and defenseless ("cold," e.g., a baby, sick person, menstruating woman) as opposed to the strong and possibly dangerous ("hot," e.g., a person who has recently had or is capable of having sexual relations). Thus an individual, or indeed the community as a whole, must maintain the strictest separation from anyone or anything that is even potentially polluting or unclean, such as a corpse. Similarly, the greatest care must be taken so as not to endanger someone, a female initiate for example, who might be exposed to "hot blood," i.e., an antagonistic or overpowering life force, which frequently occurs through illicit or premature sexual contact.

But such strictures must be viewed and interpreted within the framework of the larger social setting. These extensive categories of distinction are undeniably the product of analytical thought. And yet they invariably function as part of a much wider synthetic and symbolic mode of organization. The latter always relates in turn to either the divinely ordained structure of the cosmos or society as a whole (e.g., male/female roles and their division of labor) or to the various internal and external pressures which continually threaten it (e.g., male dominance within a matrilineal group). For the Westerner, "dirt" (anything that is physically, socially, ritually, or spiritually polluting) needs to be excluded or eliminated—swept out, so to speak, from his mind and life. The notion of pollution is present, but as Mary Douglas points out, only in a partial, unsystematic sort of way and relegated to the more peripheral concerns of esthetics, hygiene, or etiquette (1966, 40,72).

For the traditional Central African, on the other hand, defiling "dirt" is an integral part of the overall cosmological and ontological system which constitutes his theory of reality or world-view. Its presence performs a vital explanatory function by accounting for certain of the major misfortunes of life, i.e., as a result of some violation of the taboos concerning pollution. Paradoxically, such dirt can also be utilized in a positive way to inoculate others from the adverse effects which it is believed to occasion, for example, to smear semen on a baby to protect it from those who are sexually "hot." The diverse purity laws that govern his life also serve to impose order on human experience, and hence they are applied whenever the accepted form and arrangement of nature is threatened or violated. The basic institutions of society are thus validated, and human interaction is regulated in terms of what has been traditionally accepted as beneficial for the group. The occasional anomalies in the normal order of things (e.g., "unnatural" creatures such as the bat, mole, ostrich, or barbel fish) can also be dealt with in a satisfactory sort of way—in a manner which harmonizes with the world-view of the culture concerned (e.g., through dietary prohibitions).

In a most perceptive analysis (ibid., ch. 3), Douglas shows how the numerous dietary and other laws regarding "abominations" recorded in Leviticus are not arbitrary avoidance restrictions resulting from an archaic unscientific method of biological classification. On the contrary, they form part of a comprehensive sign system which had the significant theological (and sociological) purpose of celebrating as well as reinforcing the holistic notion of unity, purity, and completeness with respect to both Yahweh and his chosen people. Thus the oft repeated refrain "be ye holy" meant a great deal more than simply "keep yourselves apart from" which a Western interpretation might favor. It had to do with the whole concept of a well-organized universe which needed to be kept ordered and undefiled as a continual reminder of the analogous perfection of its Creator.

The divergence in perception resulting from a preference for one or the other of these two ideological standpoints, synthetic versus analytic, is so wide, at least in the religious sphere, that it often cannot be fully understood or appreciated by proponents of the opposing position. This applies in particular to the rationalistic, scientifically- oriented Westerner—a category that includes those Africans who have adopted a foreign way of thinking and lifestyle, whether completely or selectively. And since the latter group usually initiates, controls, or at least greatly influences, the dissemination of information in Central Africa, both religious and secular—through literature, training institutions (at home as well as abroad), advisory positions of administration, and so on—it is not surprising to find that frequently some breakdown in communication has taken place. The original message, such as a lengthy dogmatic treatise on the divine trinity, predestination, or the two natures of Christ, so precisely formulated in logical, systematic fashion by the Western-oriented source, gets altered, completely changed, or blocked entirely during the process of decoding, due to the effective operation of the filtering system of the local receptor's world-view. And the sad thing is that often the occurrence of such a failure in transmission is not even recognized by either side, the authoritative source in particular. He simply carries on, convinced that he is conveying something most meaningful, when in fact the message is being distorted or jammed during its reception.

To give several practical examples: Christian medical workers, like their secular counterparts, often find that they are unable to treat certain illnesses adequately if they do not adopt a holistic approach, especially when they ignore any possible religious dimensions of the problem. As a result of superficial interviewing techniques, they may not realize that a certain patient believes he is sick because he has been bewitched. And knowing how Westerners normally react to such claims, the patient would naturally be reluctant to volunteer such information on his own. In the same way, health workers cannot effectively propose and initiate changes in the traditional way of life without taking into consideration the total cultural context, the religious implications in particular. In promoting a program of planned parenthood, for example, the sponsor must realize that by asking people to limit the number of their children, they are actually tampering with the parents' own cycle of life and future existence, which is believed to be reinforced by the quantity, not necessarily the physical quality, of their offspring.

In the theological realm, the average American missionary will, according to his world-view and training, have a tendency to emphasize the primarily spiritual nature of his ministry, especially in his presentation and application of the message of Scripture. This stress is frequently so strong in his approach that he completely ignores the physical needs of his African parishioners. He feels that has been called to save his people for the world to come, and thus he must not allow himself to get thrown off course by the corrupting affairs of the present generation and age, least of all by "primitive pagan beliefs." The African, on the other hand, does not see a difference between the physical and the spiritual worlds or "kingdoms." In fact, as far as he is concerned, a religion that has no concrete relevance for this life here on earth—as traditionally perceived and interpreted—is itself irrelevant. This viewpoint is reinforced by the fact that normally the word used to translate "save" in his language has reference almost exclusively to the here-and-now and a rescue from immediate danger (Adeyemo, 1979, 93-95).

Secondly, the missionary tends to limit his concept of what is "spiritual" (and supernatural), or "sacred" (as opposed to "profane") to what he has learned in his dogmatics textbook, dismissing as mere local superstition the very heart and core of the African religious mind-set, namely, the power-complex of spiritism, magic, witchcraft/wizardry, and taboo. He is therefore amazed that "his people" can apparently adhere to such obviously (to him) opposing beliefs as Christian sanctification and traditional sorcery. He does not realize that from a holistic point of view such alleged logical contradictions do not exist, for in the overarching inclusive and integrating universe of indigenous thought there is a time, a place, and a purpose for everything under the sun (cp. Wonderly and Nida, 1963, 24). Further implications of such fundamental differences in perspective will be noted in the following discussion of six more key principles of the Central African faith-life system—all of which derive either directly or indirectly from a predominantly synthetic and religious frame of reference.

2. The Principle of Dynamism

We have pointed out that the concept of dynamism, or life force, dominates the religious thought of Central Africa. This involves, in effect, a total personalization of the cosmos (Douglas, 1966, 88). Every living being possesses such a force (otherwise it would not be alive), and selected inanimate objects of the environment may also function as the locus of this force by serving as the residence or habitat of certain spiritual beings. One encounters some difficulty in attempting to describe the precise nature and operation of the particular power principle being discussed here, because in the languages of Malawi and Zambia, at least, it is not designated lexically by a single term, as is the case of *bwanga* 'magical power, remedy, charm' found in many of the languages of Zaire (Tempels, 1959, 46-49). What we find rather is that each language has several words that cover different aspects of the total area of meaning under consideration, while various terms that are lexically similar to *bwanga* tend to be somewhat more restricted in reference.

In Bemba, a major language spoken close to Zaire in the north of Zambia, we perhaps come the closest with the term *bwanga*, which has taken on a negative connotation, since it refers to this magical power primarily as it is applied in witchcraft and sorcery (e.g., *kupando bwanga* 'to concoct/practice/utilize magical powers/substances'). However, the word also designates the power/charm which is used to counteract or ward off the influence of witchcraft. The Chewa *ung'anga* is a related abstract term that covers in a general way the total practice of the "medicine man/doctor/herbalist" (*sing'anga*). The latter is a ritual specialist who has the ability to discern, defuse, and deploy these mysterious forces of the environment. Similarly, the Tonga term for "traditional healer/protector" is *mung'anga*, while the various magical substances which he provides to clients are often referred to quite generally as *bwanga*. The latter may be regarded as being either good or bad, depending upon its purpose and one's personal perspective.

In any case, for one to be able to account for the various related phenomena which are associated with Central African religious belief and practice, one must make the following assumptions about the operation of the principle of dynamism in the world. Like the primary concept itself, these tend to be abstract observations and conclusions which are based upon a number of more concrete expressions of what people understand about the subject and how they explain their experience and behavior in relation to it. Thus a program of continual testing and assessment is especially necessary in this area of belief in order to check the validity of one's understanding and description of the traditional point of view and to correct this where it proves to be misleading or in error.

The personal power that an individual possesses, which for lack of a better term we shall henceforth designate as his/her soul, is neither a perceptible internal substance nor tangible energy (such as Christ apparently was conscious of, cp. Lk 8:46). It is rather an inherent vitality which is received from God, the Supreme Being, through the mediation of one or more of his (or her) ancestors. More specifically, the latter is normally the spiritual being with whom he/she is closely associated by means of a common, inherited name in what we might loosely describe as a patron-client relationship. Such soul power [*moyo* (Chewa), *muuya* (Tonga)] is distinct from, yet integrally connected with, the manifestation of life, i.e., the state of being alive in a physical, material sense. The former, the "life principle" or "life force," appears to motivate, or we might say activate, the "life" within a person, which in turn reveals itself in such characteristic physiological functions as breathing, blinking eyes, or a beating heart. Accordingly, as one's soul increases in vigor, being augmented either by natural (physical growth) or supernatural (magical) means (looking at it from a Western perspective now), so also one's quality of life improves, increasing in health and strength. Furthermore, one's standing in terms of social status and influence within the community grows as well.

However, it is possible for one's enemies—witches or sorcerers—to gain control of one's soul to serve evil purposes, primarily, to sustain and promote their own life force and/or physical well-being. As such social parasites mystically eat, as it were, the soul power out of an individual, he or she gradually becomes weaker and weaker until at last the soul is no longer able to support life and the person dies. At other times, so the belief goes, a witch can enslave one's soul and compel it to do his/her bidding, thus transforming the person into some type of zombie-like creature—physically still alive, but spiritually (with regard to soul power) quite dead! When a person finally dies physically—whatever the cause, for death is never completely "natural"—it seems (though commentators are not fully agreed on this point) that the "soul" is the particular component of his/her total being which transforms into an eternal "spirit" (*mzimu* in Chewa, *muzimo* in Tonga). That is why, people say, one's "shadow" (*cithunzithunzi* in Chewa, *cimvule* in Tonga) disappears at death; the shadow is but a physical, or more precisely, a symbolical, manifestation of one's inner, spiritual essence.

The force of life originated with the Creator-Deity, and to God it will once again eventually return, unless this intended cycle is somehow interrupted by some agent of evil, as suggested above. Indeed, the person that people fear most in daily life is "the one who can destroy both body and soul" (Mt 10:28). But this great Enemy could never be God; it would have to be a witch. And such personal destruction is not thought to happen in some remote place called "hell"; it rather occurs every day right here on earth!

Now if one's soul power can increase or decrease in potency, and if it can come under the adverse control or influence of others, then it follows that the issue of protection will become very crucial for the average individual. He must be able to defend himself against attack, and to take the process a logical step further, he must also actively seek to augment his own life force, whether qualitatively, quantitatively, or both, in order to enhance his personal well-being and welfare in the community. This vital task is accomplished by means of medicines, that is, concoctions derived from animate and inanimate (including human) sources which are somehow able to tap the energy inherent in their respective ingredients and utilize these for various purposes. Normally a person must obtain such magical potions from a specialist in the field, namely, one who possesses a spiritual (i.e., spirit-guided) insight into the manipulation of specific powers through the preparation and application of potent natural substances. Furthermore, the qualitative state of one's nature or being is partially determined by the vitality of one's guardian spirit, for if the latter is weak, it will not be able to effectively ward off the forces of evil which are directed against that individual.

In addition to such power boosters, a person can also enhance the soundness of his soul's condition through "extension of association" (Nida, 1962, 148), that is, by cultivating solidarity in the form of a good number of dependency relations in life as well as in death. This may be accomplished through individuals who are linked to him by obligation (e.g., as inferior to superior in status), friendship, ritual (e.g., common initiation), marriage, or more strongly, by blood, including one's progeny. The various customs involving the practice of giving a mature person honor and respecting his (or her) authority naturally contributes to the maintenance of his soul power, something which goes considerably beyond what from a Western perspective might be termed one's "self-image." This was undoubtedly one of the primary reasons for polygamy in the past: it provided more offspring to care for one, both during this life and, more importantly, in the after-life, by sacrifices, libations, rituals, and ceremonies for remembering the departed. This type of marriage institution thus had a definite religious intent in addition to its more obvious socioeconomic and political functions.

The principle of dynamism, which is very much a synthetic concept in its holistic, integrative emphasis, is in many respects also basic to most if not all of those mentioned below. It serves to establish the mind-set or conceptual framework within which the other principles operate in close conjunction with one another. Moreover, once such ideas as soul power (human) or life force (especially with reference to nonhuman, animate beings) are correctly understood, it is not so difficult to recognize how the religious system of Central Africa developed into the complex of complementary, coexisting, competing, and sometimes contradictory set of beliefs that it manifests nowadays. The notion of divinely-originated and spiritually-sustained individual forces in continual variation and interaction with one another forms the nucleus, as it were, around which all of the other basic presuppositions revolve, that is, from which the latter derive their validity and credibility as having a definitely religious nature, the debatable notions of magic and witchcraft in particular.

Dynamism, then, is the key that gives traditional religion a vigorous vitality which continues to attract and to influence millions in Central Africa today, Christian and non-Christian alike. Paradoxically, however, this same central belief has also proved to be a debilitating liability to the spiritual progress of many people, since it has condemned them to an endless cycle of existence living at the mercy of inscrutable powers which they can only hope to partially control and ward off through magical methods. It has also led them to pin their hopes on familiar counteragents who employ these same means in order to provide the necessary protection and healing. A strong dependency relationship is thereby created and sustained, one that is firmly fixed upon earthly concerns, human saviors and mystical cures. Moreover there is seemingly no way to break the ever-present personalized cause-effect chain of misfortune in life: provocation (whether real or imagined)–aggression–divination–retribution, for diverse forces in motion cannot help but collide. It is an inevitable part of the human condition, expressed in graphically concrete terms by the Tonga proverb: *matako aali abili taabuli kucumbana*, "two buttocks cannot avoid abrasion."

3. The Principle of Gradation

This principle is closely related to the first two in that any dynamic system of integrated forces will frequently give evidence of a graded, or hierarchical, structure whereby the individual constituent powers are implicitly ranked according to some sort of ascending measure of "potency" (*mphamvu* in Chewa, *nguzu* in Tonga). In the preceding chapter we referred to this as the scale of "status" (*ulemu* in Chewa, *bulemu* in Tonga). The main rungs in this ladder of spiritual power are established primarily on the basis of the esoteric knowledge associated with seniority—that is, according to the natural order of things, which, unless counterbalanced by certain forms of human malicious action, always favors age. The general organization of this hierarchy is shown on the diagram below. It should be noted that this is an etic system, one that has been abstracted from emic manifestation in various types of verbal and nonverbal behavior. Thus, while the overall concept of gradation is clearly demonstrated in the culture, the following classification in all of its analytical detail is not one that would necessarily be recognized and discussed by the people themselves in such terms, except perhaps for the broad categories indicated by capital letters. In this respect once more a synthetic concern for inclusiveness, unity, and harmony prevails.

GOD

SPIRITS

    Clan Spirits (originators, culture heroes)

    Ancestral Spirits (forgotten in name/personality)

    Living Dead (both benevolent and malevolent)

MAN --- chief
           religious specialists (good and bad)
           elders of society
           adults (with family)
           youth (initiated)
           children (with name)
           infants

NATURE

    Animals (also ranked)

    Plants (ranked)

    Inanimate Objects/Places (loci of spirit-forces)

According to this cosmology, God (*Mulungu* in Chewa, *Leza* in Tonga) is undeniably positioned at the top. This is the case not only because he is the supreme power and the initiator of all existing forces in the universe, but also by virtue of his nature (the "complete Other") as well as his longevity: he is the senior "elder" of all living beings (cp. Tonga: *Munamazuba* 'Ancient of Days'). Advancing age is believed to be accompanied by increasing wisdom, in particular, wisdom which concerns the mystical forces of the world and how to captivate and control them.

    The great clan spirits or divinities come next on the ladder. They represent those famous personages of the past who can never be forgotten, due to their outstanding contribution to the welfare of the tribe or clan (which has probably grown tremendously with the passage of time) as leaders, warriors, deliverers, founders, sages, prophets, or healers. Their names are perpetuated among their living kin, for they must be formally mentioned and their persons appealed to in times of prayer during important public rituals (e.g., at a rain-calling ceremony).

Below these great heroes are the ancient ancestral beings who are no longer known and remembered by name, mysterious and often dangerous spirits who inhabit prominent physical locations in the environment: large trees, river banks, lakes, high hills, steep passes, waterfalls, hot springs, deformed boulders, and similar unfrequented spots. Such nature spirits control whatever human activity happens to be carried on in the vicinity, such as hunting, fishing, farming, honey collection, charcoal burning, and mining. They also chastise every magically unprotected or ritually polluted individual who happens to venture too near their abode.

After the nature spirits in immediacy come those ancestors who are still actively remembered by their descendants, the "living dead," as Mbiti has termed this group—or in the language of Hebrews, that "great cloud of witnesses [which] surrounds" mankind (Hb 12:1). Such familial spirits continue to live close to human habitation where they are ever ready to bless man or to punish him, depending on the circumstances. Some of the ancestral spirits are more powerful (i.e., control more life force) than others, degrees being reckoned according to the lifetime status of the persons whom they are derived from. Individual weakness, wickedness, and moral wandering are the occasion for certain of these spirits transforming into the agents of evil, bent on punitive destruction rather than deliverance.

Human society, being more perceptible in terms of actual behavior, naturally reveals the most clearly defined gradation of force-potential, one that depends upon several socially-determined factors, all of which relate to the control of more or less soul power, e.g., age, rank, achievement, magically acquired strength, and primogeniture (rights of the first-born). Lowest on this totem pole of potency are the newborn who have not yet received a name, hence a specific protecting spirit, and are thus not really regarded as being persons at all. In such a social organization, the principle of political equality and individual rights, so prized in Western societies, is neither valued nor sought after. Even modern educational advances do not necessarily give the young an advantage over their elders, for what really counts is not intellectual knowledge, but practical wisdom based on experience: *musinza tuuwidi kubanene*, "soup never spills on older folks" [Tonga].

Furthermore, in the human hierarchy one does not usually see the informality and directness in personal interaction that is often associated with the acceptance of all individuals as social equals. This is particularly true when some important business is being discussed. While one does not encounter in Central Africa the extreme formality found in many Far Eastern cultures, for example the

Japanese, there is a definite status- and distance-preserving procedure that one must observe whenever matters affecting the group are being considered (by the elders, of course), whether within the kinship unit or without, e.g., marriage negotiations and arrangements.

Below the human race, then, we find certain prominent animals, particularly the wild variety, which are known for their additional concentration of life force, e.g., wildebeest, hippo, zebra, lion, elephant. It may be that this was part of the original reason for their choice (along with certain birds, reptiles, insects, and plants) as clan totems in many of the tribes of Central Africa. In any case, they were very closely associated with man in the beginning of history, as ancient myths testify. Specialists in magic are able to utilize these natural resources, i.e., selected animal body parts, in the preparation of medicines either for helpful or harmful purposes—depending upon one's perspective, of course, that is, as a source of the communicative application or as the receptors of its positive or negative force. Frequently these medicines are of an imitative variety, as each seeks to reproduce for the user some stereotyped quality which is believed to be manifested by a particular animal, for example, the strength of the elephant, the fierceness of the lion, or the sexual vigor of the zebra. Other beasts and birds have a more infamous reputation because of certain negative characteristics (as commonly perceived), and these are therefore associated with the malevolent powers of darkness, e.g., as the familars of a witch: the nocturnal owl, the greedy hyena, the deadly mamba snake, and so forth.

Likewise some plants, known for this or that physical feature, are thought to possess similar local forces. Trees, perhaps because of their relative size and diversity, are especially popular in the preparation of magical substances. The term for traditional medicine in many Central African languages is related to the word "tree," e.g., in Tonga and Bemba it is the same for both, i.e., *musamu* and *muti* respectively. Plant parts are thus magically employed either for healing purposes by medicine men, or in exactly the opposite manner by sorcerers to cause a weakening of an opponent's soul power and eventually death, if not counteracted in time. As it is said in Bemba: *muti ukulu tauwa nga kaice*, "a big tree does not fall like a child," i.e., an adult does not die without a reason, and as the end draws near he is expected to reveal his revelatory suspicions regarding those who bewitched him.

And finally, there are certain well-known physical features which, though they are inanimate and consequently lack a vital force of their own, do serve as the means whereby and/or the place at which some spiritual or magical powers are manifested. For example, the ancestral spirits, especially the forgotten ones, are believed to inhabit prominent places in the local environment, e.g., a high rocky hill, a deep-flowing river, an ancient royal burial grove. When the spirits happen to be known by name, as in a chiefly cult, the place may serve as a community shrine (*malende* in Tonga) where people gather on special occasions for worship, e.g., to plead for rain in a time of drought. There are also a variety of earthly materials, such as colored rocks and soil, which do not contain any mystical energy, but which, due to their special symbolic potential, can help to catalyze, transmit, or localize it. These substances too may therefore be exploited by magicians either to augment or to diminish the personal soul power of a human being (in the form of potions, amulets, charms, and so forth).

The loosely structured hierarchical organization of Bantu society, realized primarily in terms of seniority or status, is overtly manifested in a host of customs, both verbal and nonverbal, pertaining to deference and respect. "Shame" results when an individual, an elder or "big person" (*wamkulu* in Chewa) is not accorded the honor he feels he deserves, and this emotion can, in turn, have a serious effect upon the condition of his soul. It can also result in a justifiable curse being called down upon the offender, as Elisha felt compelled to do to those youths who dared to mock his person and position (2 Kg 2:23).

The ladder of status also contributes to the importance of the mediatorial function in social relations: often a person cannot communicate immediately and directly with those who are one or more rungs above him. For that a "mediator" is necessary, someone who is recognized by the community as having the insight and ability to perform this vital function, which frequently has to do with matters pertaining to life and death, whether actual or ritual (i.e., during initiation ceremonies). Such intermediaries are particularly important as leaders in the crucial rites-of-passage which mark critical stages in the human life cycle. The Chewa *namkungwi*, for example, is not only an experienced instructor in traditional wisdom and practice, but she, or he, also performs a vital religious function as she brings her charges, the *anamwali* "initiates," through an extremely dangerous transitional period as they move from childhood to adulthood.

The gradation principle is probably most obviously revealed linguistically through a fairly elaborate system of respect terms which plays such an important part in the conversation of a people like the Chewa. As the social distance between speakers increases, so also the terms of personal reference become more oblique, especially in public contexts of conversation, i.e., from second person familiar to a second person honorific plural to a third plural of majestic designation. This phenomenon has some interesting theological implications with regard to mention of the deity as was noted earlier: is Christ to be addressed either in the Scriptures or in personal prayer using familiar forms as to our elder brother, or should one of the more honorific conventions be employed when speaking to the Lord of all? And how would the various social groups that he encountered during his ministry have conversed with him if they had been speaking Chichewa, e.g., his disciples, Mary his mother, the Pharisees, Roman officials like Pilate, and so on? Obviously the textual and situational contexts also play an important part in dealing with matters such as these (cp. Wendland, 1985, ch.5).

Deferential or honorific speech is normally accompanied by corresponding actions which demonstrate one's social status with regard to another; for example, a young, unmarried woman in the presence of a respected elder would be expected to kneel, clasp her hands together in her lap, look down at the ground, and speak only when invited or spoken to. Similarly, one would not overtly contradict what an elder person is saying or refuse to do what one has been told. Rather, to avoid confrontation and a potentially shame-bearing situation where a genuine difference of opinion is involved, a junior would follow this advice: *kukana mau a akulu ndi kuviika nsalu m'madzi* [Chewa] "to refuse the words of the elders is to dip the cloth into the water [instead of thoroughly scrubbing it]," i.e., rather than to bluntly say no, one would at least pretend to do what was wanted, but in a partial sort of way. In a graded society, then, everyone knows his/her place and how to maintain that position so that the underlying structure of personal forces and relationships remains intact for the good of each and every member. Any accidental or deliberate overturning of this time-sanctioned status quo is likely to upset the balance of powers, an event which is believed to have severe repercussions as far as the overall prosperity and welfare of the community is concerned. The ever-vigilant ancestors would see to that, for their position, too, is at stake.

To be sure, any Western nation also gives evidence of a social hierarchy of sorts, but it is generally one that is based more upon individual achievement and personal acquisition (as in the case of a sports figure, politician, author, entertainer, millionaire, etc.), rather than communal ascription founded on a principle of inherent dynamism according to years of experience, service, and the accumulation of wisdom. And within the Christian Church the ranks are frequently apportioned according to theological expertise (evangelical), ecclesiastical devotion (catholic), charismatic fervor (pentecostal), or political diplomacy (liberal) rather than the Pauline principle of love demonstrated for "the body" (1 Co 12-13).

4. The Principle of Communalism

The concept of hierarchy described above potentially establishes a great number of implicit and explicit distinctions in society, and indeed the cosmos as a whole, on the basis of how much dynamism a particular being either possesses or controls. Such a motivation, if allowed to operate in isolation, would of course fracture a group into many different and competing segments. But there is another prominent force that is active in the organization of Central African society which serves to counteract, or better (from a synthetic perspective), to complement the former by tying all the individual pieces together again. This is the principle of *communalism*, or as we termed it earlier, *solidarity*.

Whenever power is exercised in human culture, there is always the danger of abuse and a consequent division of the group into fragments on the basis of who manages the power and for what ends. The drive to acquire more power, even in the form of self-protection, is thus a strong divisive force in society. The motivation of power-seeking reaches its negative climax in the practice of witchcraft/sorcery, where we find certain individuals actively engaged in promoting their own status (in a mystical sense) at the expense of others. A rather different type of abuse is impiety, that is, the deliberate refusal to recognize and respect the various gradations of power that have been traditionally established, and this includes the authority of the ancestral spirits. Either attitude—the desire to accumulate power or the denial of its relevance to society—whether benign or malignant, must therefore be purged from the community through different methods of behavioral control, e.g., fines and sanctions, witchcraft detection and eradication, exile, ostracization, and so forth. In addition, the tendency toward individualism and factionalism must be counterbalanced by a corresponding drive toward cohesion that draws the various constituent parties together again and helps to maintain the harmony that is so necessary for them to function together effectively as a collective unit.

The concept of community, together with the related notions of mutual participation and sharing, is very strong in all African societies. This point is highlighted in a great many proverbs and sayings, pertaining to both thought and action, e.g., Chewa: *Ichi nchiani nkulinga muli awiri*, "To ask, 'What's this?' only works if you are two;" *Chala chimodzi sichiswa nsabwe*, "One finger cannot smash a louse." We have already noted the importance of the inclusive system of relationships which links all members of the group into some form of association. Every individual, though valued in and of him/herself, is always viewed in relation to the whole of which he/she constitutes a vital part, beginning with the extended family (the fundamental kinship unit), through clan membership, and on up to the tribe as a whole. It is the familial group, including one's ancestors as well as descendants, which gives each person a sense of identity, for everyone has a niche in society and a role to play, no matter how minor this might seem to the outsider. It is very important, therefore, for one to know his proper place in the group and to act accordingly.

The life of a woman living in a traditional society might appear to the Westerner to be especially circumscribed in this regard, though the situation is rapidly changing. Indeed, it would seem that all of the major decisions that she confronts in life are already largely determined by the group: marriage (in many cases even whom she should marry), place of residence, amount of formal education, occupation, even how many children to have (as many as possible). At the cost of her personal freedom in these areas, however, she gains a sense of security and support which cannot easily be shaken. Furthermore, though society tends to be male-dominated, she does not live a life of servitude. On the contrary, women are highly respected, one's mother in particular, and they often wield a great deal of influence in the decision-making process of the typically matrilineally organized extended family unit. As the Tonga proverb goes: *bwami bwaciluli mbwaanda*, "the glory [lit.'chieftainship'] of the roof is the walls [of the house, i.e., the wife/mother in the family]."

For every member of such a closed society, then, all motives born purely out of self-interest must normally give way to a group-oriented perspective. A competitive attitude, the drive to gain success, a concern for personal rights and responsibilities, or one's self-image, are suppressed in favor of a cooperative approach which stresses the need to stimulate and maintain harmony, uniformity, and a conformity to the status quo. Generosity and hospitality ("open-handedness") are virtues held in high regard, whereas all overt manifestations of selfishness, envy, pride, and greed are strongly condemned and often punished, if not by the living, then certainly by the departed members of the community, whose task it is to maintain the traditions which governed their own life on earth.

Mutual sharing, or natural socialism, is a prominent expression of the principle of communalism. All property, for example, is held (not owned, but overseen) for the most part on a corporate basis, that is, by the familial unit and not by an individual. People tend to spend most of their leisure time as well as their working hours engaged in some communal activity, even though the party involved may be small. This is certainly true of most legitimate types of religious practice where group participation is the rule. However, as far as the illegitimate, anti-social varieties are concerned, i.e., sorcery and witchcraft, secrecy is essential, and this is accompanied by an abnormal focus upon one's self. These activities are regarded as being the most despicable sins imaginable, for they directly promote the disruption of social harmony and the poisoning of interpersonal relations at the most basic level, within the bonds of the kinship group as well as the close circle of friends and neighbors. This involves the use of vital force solely for personal ends and for private advantage at the expense of others. Yet even the practice of witchcraft does have its communal aspect in the sense that witches are believed to gather together at night for a diabolical feast when they share the meat of a recent victim.

Since the unity of the whole must be preserved at all costs, an elaborate system of protocol, taboos, purity-preserving regulations, and conversely, strictly observed periods of license, has been developed to prevent friction and tension from building up between closely-related individuals, e.g., between a man and his mother-in-law, a young man and his maternal uncle, a husband and his wives in a polygamous marriage, among cross-cousins, etc. Similarly, we find that many of the restrictions regarding pollution are "enlisted to bind men and women to their alloted roles" in society (Douglas, 1966, 141). Communality is further promoted in all social interaction within the group: both minor and major decisions are made by popular consensus and not by either autocratic degree or by a democratic vote. The ability to seek and effect a compromise where differences of opinion arise, or to bring about a reconciliation where there has been a rift in relationships, is highly regarded. Where a wrong has been committed, the fines or punishments levied are not primarily punitive in nature, but rather they are intended to restore the interpersonal harmony that was damaged by the antisocial action.

Qualities such as veracity and frankness, so appreciated in a Western context, are downgraded in favor of attributes such as friendliness, flexibility, and the capacity to "save face," or prevent shame, among antagonists in a difficult situation. Forthright honesty is therefore much less important than one's ability to avoid hard feelings (mental anguish) in issues where the matter of truth is involved. Habitual or blatant prevarication is of course completely unacceptable behavior, but there are times when the end clearly justifies the means as far as lying is concerned, especially when it is intended to preserve the safety and solidarity of the group. In this light, then, the sin of Sapphira is not seen to be as great as that of Ananias, for she could be viewed as covering up the truth in order to protect her husband (Ac 5:7-8).

In order to facilitate inter- and intragroup action, intermediaries are required at every level of society to help keep personal relations in good repair, especially where delicate negotiations between clans are involved, such as at the time of a marriage, barrenness, divorce, death in the family, and so on. Similarly, man's relations with the spiritual world (both the ancestral spirits as well as others) are guided by religious specialists, that is, by those who can recognize and deal effectively with the various vital forces which are concerned. The departed members of the community, the living dead, in turn, act as agents and mediators between humanity and a God who has for the most part distanced himself from his people's everyday affairs, their mundane needs and problems in particular. The Bemba reinforce this point quite bluntly with the saying: *Lesa talombwa nama, alombwo mweo*, "From God one does not ask for meat, but life." A wide range of sacrifices and offerings, corresponding to the diversity of customs for gift giving in society and the compensation fines levied against the violators of tradition, are employed to maintain congenial relations with the living dead and to repair any ruptures that happen to occur. People can easily identify with Israel's wish that Moses deal with Yahweh on their behalf (Ex 20:18-19); a question remains, however, about how he in his mortal form would be qualified to act in such a grave capacity.

We noted the importance of mediators already under the principle of gradation. Mediation is a thus a crucial relational activity which is absolutely vital to the harmonious functioning of society. This applies both to its vertical, hierarchical aspect, i.e., to acknowledge and preserve the various levels of status (involving values such as politeness, modesty, deference, and respect), and also with regard to its horizontal aspect of degrees of relationship, i.e., to promote the diverse ties of solidarity (involving values such as loyalty, sharing, cooperation, and the avoidance of confrontation). The essential task of the clan mediator, such as the elderly "coordinator" (*nkhoswe*) of the Chewa matrilineage, is to reinforce the various reciprocal and dyadic relations upon which society is based, including those that link the living with their departed ancestors, and to restore such relations through the process of reconciliation where they have been ruptured. On all levels of society, then, in every area of cultural interaction it is necessary to preserve the balance of forces through various customs and rites of veneration, conciliation, cooperation, purification, and propitiation, so that the human community as well as the cosmos as a whole may remain united and in a state of stable equilibrium (cp. Nida, 1962, 147).

5. The Principle of Experientialism

This principle, as it applies to Central Africa (and to ancient Israel), reflects an approach to knowledge that is based primarily upon personal experience backed by an ancient tradition of wisdom, rather than upon what has come to be known as the scientific method, which depends on carefully controlled experimentation derived from logical deduction and hypothesis formation. African empiricism, as distinct from the Western variety, is firmly founded on a synthesizing, subjective perspective that begins with the world around man, and lacks the continual and conscious striving for objectivity which characterizes a rationalistic approach (Douglas, 1966, 78). It is a viewpoint which regards the universe holistically, that is, as a unified, integrated system in which man and nature live in close harmony. The environment is not simply a reservoir of resources, as the

Westerner (the environmentalist excepted) views it, to be coldly dominated, exploited, and controlled for the benefit of man himself. Instead nature, both animate and inanimate, is viewed as a complex living organism, one that possesses its own hierarchy of forces (cp. principles 2 and 3 above) with which man must strive to establish and maintain the appropriate relationships.

Thus the traditional African seeks to participate in or be integrated with his environment, not to manage and manipulate it like a machine. This viewpoint is the same whether the person involved be a hunter, a herdsman, or a farmer. In each case the proper sacrifices will have to be made, as for instance whenever there is the possibility of a break in the harmonious relationships that link man and his surroundings: the hunter before he invades the forest and particularly after he has killed some game; the herdsman when his animals are being troubled by marauding beasts; the farmer when he desires to open a new garden in the virgin bush.

The mechanistically-minded Westerner, like the rich man of Christ's parable (Lk 12:16-21), is impelled by the profit motive and an assembly-line mentality, by the competitive desire to increase his output, ever bigger and better, and hence to raise his economic as well as his social standing in the community. The drive for mass production and greater yields leads to the standardization and specialization of jobs so that the quality achieved may be efficiently duplicated on a large scale. People who no longer are able to produce (the handicapped, the aged, and the infirm) are often reduced in status almost to social outcasts. They become burdens, obstacles to success, and thus are often confined to public institutions designed to remove them from the lives of the potentially productive.

Such thinking (and behavior) is completely foreign to the original Central African, for whom life's primary purpose is not to get ahead of his fellows, but to remain with them through the establishment of friendly interpersonal relationships. This is, of course, also an aspect of the "communalism" discussed above, a perspective which values the aged as much as, if not more than, the very young on account of their wisdom based on past experience in dealing with the problems and perplexities of human existence. One's approach towards work is also much more holistically oriented and related to one's everyday existence. In most rural areas even today a person labors primarily for the family unit, and craftsmen/women producing complete objects (e.g., tools, baskets, pottery, etc.) largely for personal use are still the norm. And in towns, the individual who has achieved some measure of success often serves as a magnet which draws his country cousins who happily share his (their!) wealth while they seek employment for themselves.

Why does the average traditionalist, if left to follow his own inclination, seem to spend so much time visiting, conversing, and socializing with others, even at the expense of some job that he happens to be engaged in? He is not so much concerned about greater output for more profit or about keeping up with his neighbors in life-style; just as long as he has enough for the basic necessities of life, he is content. He lives, rather than "employs," his time (see below) to maintain the various social ties that he has established with his fellowman: *mnzako akapsa ndevu, mzimire* [Chewa] "when your friend's beard catches fire, put it out for him" [implication: one day he'll do the same for you]. After all, if a crisis occurs in his life, he will automatically look to and expect assistance from them. Besides, why should one expend all his efforts in the accumulation of wealth, only to be accused of practicing witchcraft on account of his prosperity (cp. principle 7 below)?!

Time in the traditional Central African scheme of things is not a commodity to be bought and sold as it is in the West. The American's oft-heard excuse, "I have no time," or admonition, "time is money," is quite a mystery to the African. What did God give the person a life for? He ought to use his time, his life, to help satisfy the requests and needs of others, no matter what it costs him as far as personal profit and materialistic gain is concerned. Life is thus experience-oriented rather than time-dominated.

Moreover, the annual calendar is controlled not by hours, days, and months, but by the rhythmic round of nature—the seasons (rains, planting, harvest, dry period, etc.) and the various special events and ceremonies pertaining to the human life-cycle that are associated with them, the so-called rites of passage in particular. Periodic seasonal rituals of renewal are performed to secure the continued vitality and harmony of both man and nature. The boundary between the two is deliberately blurred as the passage from the old/impure/impotent to the new/pure/fertile is celebrated in typically fourfold rites of "mortification, purgation, invigoration, and jubilation" (Gaster, 1961, p. 26). In areas of Central Africa having a strong royal tradition, such as the Bemba do, these annual ceremonies focus on the person of the chief, who stands as an indispensable mediator between his people and the land on the one hand, and between this concrete world of nature and the unseen realm of the divine on the other, i.e., God (*Lesa*) and the illustrious ancestors (*mipashi*). Such ritual practice becomes much more extensive and experience-oriented in the event of a paramount chief's death and the inauguration (or "rebirth") of his successor (cp. Richards, 1939, ch. 17).

The important thing then is not so much exactly when on the clock a particular activity begins or ends, but one's participation in it and the communal benefit which the group derives from their mutual interaction. Thus, one cannot really be "late" for a public function such as a worship service, which, strictly speaking from a traditional viewpoint, ought to begin only after everyone in the group has gathered. Nor can such an experience last "too long," for it ends simply when it is over, when the people have accomplished everything that they came together to do.

An experiential, synthetic concept of time, which is of course promoted by an agriculturally based economy, tends to be cyclical and continuous in nature, rather than being linear (i.e., beginning to ending), discontinuous (i.e., broken up into segments by the clock or calendar), and teleological (i.e., goal-oriented) as the analytical person views it. Thus another more advantageous day will probably come when a particular task may be undertaken. Furthermore, one can easily put off till tomorrow what cannot be done today if the situation arises, especially some human need or circumstance: *tsiku limodzi silioza mbewa*, "one day does not cause a fieldmouse to rot" [Chewa, i.e., one can always prepare, eat, and enjoy it on the morrow]. There is, for all immediate practical purposes, no beginning or ending of time to be concerned about, no pressing schedules to worry about, no real advantage to planning ahead too far into the future. One must only attend to the current active period during which one's life is being lived. For death, the great leveller, may intervene at any moment to initiate one's movement from this world to the next, or better, from the visible to the invisible community. But the past is also a very important consideration in the present: this concerns time which has already been utilized and become a part of concrete tradition and the experience of the ancestors.

This is not to say that the average individual has no notion of the future and no concern for what will happen tomorrow. It is simply that experience has taught him that the lessons of history are more relevant to his daily needs than events which have not yet taken place: *mau a akulu akoma atagonera* [Chewa] "the words of the big-ones become pleasant after they have slept the night." Thus the wisdom of custom and tradition reveals its relevance with the very passing of time. The indistinct and uncertain future, on the other hand, is important only where it promises to be of practical benefit in contributing to one's protection and/or prosperity: *caona mnzako lero, mawa cili paiwe*, "what your friend has seen today will be on you tomorrow" [Chewa; i.e., help him out of his misfortune, and he will reciprocate].

Thus, the dishonest manager of Christ's parable (Lk 16:1-13) does not seem to be all that clever, for it appears as if he decides to cultivate positive interpersonal relationships only when he is about to lose his job. He ought to have been doing this on a regular basis (the ethicality of his action is not at issue) so that the future might take care of itself at any time, should disaster strike and "people [might] welcome [him] into their houses" (v.4).

In contrast, then, to the American who plans ahead for the future and the realization of all his hopes, dreams, and goals, the African prefers to look back to the fulfilled past where he finds the knowledge and instruction about life which enable him to deal with what he encounters in the present. He is also influenced by what has gone on before in a more personal sense by virtue of the continual contact which he maintains with his ancestors, the more recently departed (i.e., living dead) in particular. These ancestral spirits are responsible for his current well-being on earth or, alternatively, if he has violated the customs and mores of society, they are the reason for the misfortune that he will consequently suffer. The African thus has an essentially conservative outlook on life, one that seeks to uphold the tried and true of tradition and of realized experience, one that values and respects the advice of 'those of the ancient rains' (*amvula zakale* [Chewa]), one that promotes maintaining the status quo rather than a continual striving for progress or the "pearl of great price" (Mt 13:45-46). He therefore has difficulty in appreciating the Western penchant for change, innovation, and what is unique or exceptional in the world, including what appears to be an overemphasis upon youth and on remaining young and beautiful.

Another important aspect of an experiential mode of relating to reality is the emphasis upon sound as a vital part of the total human sensorium as opposed to a predominant focus upon the sense of sight. An intellectual, analytical approach to learning tends to stress the visual faculty, which is an individualizing, dissecting sense that concentrates on the external surface of things (Ong, 1967, 258). Thus knowledge, in the Western sense, continues to be evaluated largely in terms of information, that is, how many facts pertaining to a given subject a person is able to store (either in the brain or a computer), retrieve, and put to use, usually in some abstract visualized form that is removed at least several stages from one's everyday experiences in real life. As the performative power of the spoken word to curse, bless, guarantee, heal, adopt, divorce, and so forth is gradually reduced in a predominantly oral-aural society, so also the authority of the traditional speakers—the elders, diviners, priests, and other wise men—is correspondingly diminished in favor of a growing class of young educated elite (cp. the hierarchy of principle 3).

Formerly the educational process in visually-oriented societies was effected primarily, at least as far as the conveying of knowledge is concerned, by means of literacy and the printed word. To be sure, nowadays the video medium, combining the senses of sight and sound together with an electronic mode of communication, appears to be rapidly gaining ground as the principal instrument of such visual message transmission. However, as Ong points out, there is at best only a "secondary orality" promoted here, that is, an orientation to sound which is still heavily based upon and biased towards the use of writing and print (e.g., texts/scripts) and "a rhetoric of the visual word" (e.g., modern display advertising; ibid, 221- 222). Being subject to closure (i.e., a more or less fixed time frame), such televised programs are produced and performed with a great deal of conscious deliberation, technical precision, and a complete lack of interplay with the intended audience (1982, 136-137).

This is quite different from the way in which knowledge is stored, appropriated, and managed in a traditional, preliterate, nontechnological society. Sight is still crucial for one's perception of the world about him, but information about that world is conveyed primarily via the sense of sound in the oral instruction of the elders. Thus sight, whether actual or verbally evoked, is utilized to complement sound, and the education of the young, for example, becomes a pleasant, fun-filled experience (not a drudgery like school), effected by means of folktales, proverbs, riddles, songs, praise poetry, and dramatic historical narratives (myths, legends, etc.) in which either calculated or spontaneous interaction between the speaker and his audience frequently takes place. The learning process was, and still is in these situations, a highly participatory and mutually reinforcing public media event. There is, however, a definite emphasis upon obedience (or more precisely, "listening," e.g., *mvera* [Chewa]) to the precepts of ancient wisdom, and relatively little encouragement given to independent, innovative thinking.

The content of traditional education, then, is not a mere set of facts to be memorized, but case studies, figurative analogies, gnomic reflections, dramatic illustrations, and pieces of common sense and practical advice, intended to stimulate both the intellect and the imagination in the application of these ancient bits of wisdom to the present and one's own personal situation. The inductive method of instruction is clearly preferred, as it was also in the ministry of Christ (Mt 13:34-35). There is thus a conceptual movement from the known to the unknown, specific to the general, concrete to abstract, question to answer, and problem to solution. Many life-oriented examples are used in order to get the audience personally and emotionally involved with the message. They thus learn by doing; that is to say, by imagining and putting themselves into the specific, everyday situations which are called to mind by the teacher-source, they experientially arrive at the conclusion or thematic point that he is leading them to: *ziliko nkulinga utatosa*, "[you can say] 'the mice are there' only after you have checked by poking a stick into the hole" [Chewa].

Thus students progressively grasp the lessons and principles that their instructor is leading them to because he has started where they are, with an explicit recognition of their beliefs, needs, values, goals, fears, and failures. In short, the traditional teacher takes the culture of his receptors seriously and employs this as a conceptual bridge to cross over into some new area of knowledge or experience. Obviously, contemporary Christian communicators, expatriate and national alike, need to follow a more audience-friendly, inductive procedure as they endeavor to proclaim the good news of God's Word in a more meaningful and moving sort of way, for example, when preaching the Sunday sermon or conducting a Bible class.

Since most information storage in an oral-aural culture must take place in human memory (hence the value of elders), the literature of such groups is characterized by a diversity of stylistic devices intended to facilitate the processes of presentation, retention, and recall. Many of these features are no longer appreciated in the sophisticated literary productions of the West, e.g., overt repetition, formulaic expressions, verbal rhythms, parallelism on all levels of structure, standardized themes and vivid character types, a dynamic plot consisting of sharp contrasts treated in terms of exaggerated sets of virtues and vices, as well as an abundance of graphic, down-to-earth imagery.

The vehicle of sound when employed in such a dramatization of the message operates as a synthetic medium in the sense that it tends to personalize the communication process and to promote the unity of the group, i.e., by revealing the "interior" of individuals, that is, their deeply-felt attitudes and emotions (Ong, 1967, ch.3), during what becomes a common esthetic experience. The written word, on the other hand, always divorces the message from the messenger and thus encourages more independent, abstract, and complex systems of thought, for one usually has the opportunity to read and reevaluate a text again (and again) if one does not understand it the first time. This is not to suggest that "The Book" is unimportant, for it is the foundation of all Christian belief and behavior. The point is, however, that a more effective way, both sensorially and logically (i.e., than silent reading/deduction), of conveying the diverse message of the Scriptures to the willing masses of Africa is needed, one which capitalizes on a more familiar, inductive, receptor-oriented communication strategy, e.g., radio/video drama and public performances, like the popular religious mystery-morality-miracle plays of medieval times. (For an introduction to the latter, see Schaff, 1907, pp. 869-75.)

This leads to a final point to note in conjunction with an empirical, participatory approach to knowledge and learning, and that is the importance which it attaches to all forms of nonverbal communication. The Western preference for visual transmission and the medium of print tends to downplay the nonverbal component of messages, except for that which happens to be conveyed by sight. In traditional African societies, on the other hand, a variety of media were utilized for the proclamation and preservation of important messages, both those of an artistic nature as well as those which were primarily utilitarian, e.g., dancing, drumming, singing, clapping, dramatic rituals, and mimes. In particular, the practice of religion employed such a diversity of means in order to convey, in more concrete and vivid terms, vital life-and-death messages, including animal (and sometimes human) sacrifices, both to God and his representatives, the living dead.

Any contemporary religion in Africa, therefore, like Christianity, will have to learn a culturally-specific lesson from the past and diversify its present stress upon verbal, visual, and an intellectually-oriented means of communication (Klem, 1982; Shorter, 1973, ch.4). More participant-centered, fully experiential and dramatic modes of presentation need to be encouraged in order to enhance the effectiveness of the church's evangelistic outreach among people who are accustomed to live their religion and to "talk" to God with their whole selves—body and soul!

6. The Principle of Humanism

Not surprisingly, Central African religious ideology, with its emphasis upon practical knowledge gained both by personal experience and by tradition from the fathers, manifests a strongly man-oriented approach to things. If religion, as we have defined it, is the hub of all cultural life and thought, then man (*munthu*) is the center of religious belief and practice, and theology, as well as what we might call "spiritology," is clearly developed and arranged according to a human perspective. The world revolves around man, and thus regular ritual activity is organized either around the human cycle of existence (i.e., birth, maturation, marriage, procreation, and death), or on those occasions when people find themselves experiencing serious difficulties in life, whether communal (e.g., drought, famine, plague) or individual (e.g., sickness, barrenness, depreciation). This focus is of course typical of many natural religions throughout the world, especially in pretechnological societies.

Thus the Deity, though regarded as being much greater than man, is nevertheless conceived of largely in vivid, contextually-colored anthropomorphic terms with regard to both his nature as well as his attributes (e.g., Tonga: *Luboleka-masuku* 'the One who causes the masuku fruits to rot' [i.e., rain-giver]; *Syakeemba* 'the Great Herdsman'; *Nacoombe* 'Mother of big cow'; *Mutalabala* 'the One who spreads out everywhere'; *Syabusiwa* 'the Owner of grain'; *Luvuna-baumba* 'the One who defends the bereaved'). Though God does possess superhuman qualities and abilities, e.g., with respect to power, wisdom, and presence, he still is believed to exhibit a number of distinctly human foibles and failings such as anger, impatience, forgetfulness, favoritism, or carelessness. He is also ultimately responsible for the misfortunes that man encounters in life: *Mulungu ndi kundzu, unadza cionambo cinacinga nkhalanga mpala,* "God is the One who suddenly strips naked, (thus) you will also see who shaves the guinea fowl's head" [Sena].

Perhaps the greatest divine fault is his somewhat antisocial personality in that he has chosen to live at a great distance, both physically and psychologically, from those whom he did, after all, create in the first place. This is further reflected in the fact that the communication process, which we view as being the heart of the religious system, is initiated for the most part by mankind and formulated according to their physical needs. A concept of divine revelation whereby the will of God is made known to man is thus not very well developed in Central African religious belief, certainly not in verbal form.

In keeping with a man-oriented approach to things, God did, however, as the Great Chief (*Mwami* [Tonga]), make provision for his representatives, namely the ancestral spirits, to fill the gap and act on his behalf in the world. These spirits, too, are noticeably human in their personal attributes, except that they are invisible. In fact, from man's perspective, although they are regarded as being extensions of the human community of beings (and do reflect many of the characteristics of human society in their organization and operation as a corporate body), the spirits are more often than not rather unpredictable and fickle in their personality and hence difficult to deal with. An individual must strive to make sure that he stays on the good side of those in particular who are related to, and thus also responsible for, his welfare and good behavior in life (i.e., by means of sacrifices, prayers, libations, etc.). Otherwise one will most certainly provoke them to anger and invite retribution in the form of sickness or some other affliction.

A humanistic perspective (in the African sense, not the Western variety which is nontheistic, rationalistic, and antisupernatural) is demonstrated most clearly in the religious sphere by most people's interpretation of both their environment as well as their experiences in life. The cosmos is personalized and thought to be responsive to differing forms of symbolic behavior (e.g., ritual incantation, gestures, spells, sacrifices, etc.) which, as we have seen, also vitally depends upon some human agency in both a mental as well as a physical capacity. Similarly the misfortunes that one periodically encounters may in certain instances be viewed as the result of breaking some taboo (*malweza*, in Tonga; *malaulo* in Chewa), especially where the moral code of the community is concerned. In such cases nature itself acts almost like a judge to inflict a prescribed punishment upon the offender(s).

Other accidents, illnesses, and deaths are often viewed as being caused by the machinations of malevolent human agents, including personalized harmful spirits. People have the power, or vital force, to influence others for good or evil, either inherently or as a result of a magical infusion from traditional specialists such as medicine men (cp. Principle 2). Thus, "even powers which are taken to be thoroughly impersonal [i.e., the various forms of magic] are held to be reacting directly to the behavior of individual humans" (Douglas, 1966, 81). Traditional medicine is believed to be discriminating in its action in the sense that it will only affect certain individuals and not others under the right circumstances; for example, to protect one's spouse from an adulterer and to punish the wrongdoer (ibid., 87). A magical potion, amulet, or charm thus operates according to the instructions and will of its owner, as long as the specific directions of use have been correctly carried out.

The humanization, or man-focusing tendency, of traditional African religion appears to have progressed even more rapidly in recent years due to the influence of such diverse factors as education, urbanization, improved medical care, cross-cultural contact, Christian doctrine, Western individualism, and a stronger materialistic attitude generally. For many people today, not only is the Deity remote—in an exaggerated extension of the original indigenous notion, or perhaps even replaced by the Christian God to be worshiped once a week—but also the prestige, relevance, and authority of the ancestors is steadily declining. At times it seems as if they are even completely disregarded, except insofar as they are able to benefit man in some tangible way, e.g., to relieve or give dramatic expression to a specific personal ailment or affliction, or quite differently, through a peripheral nativistic cult involving spirit possession, which augments an individual's status in the community as a result of her/his acquired power of divination and/or healing.

This spiritual void is presently being filled with beliefs that are gradually growing more man-centered in their concerns, specifically with regard to the fear of witchcraft/sorcery. After all, the witch, or sorcerer (the distinction is becoming less significant as the original social/kinship functions of this practice diminish in importance), is a fellow human being. And since this is by far the greatest threat to a person's well-being in life, it is not surprising that both group and individual religious activity should focus upon it. This is especially true because it lies within the province and power of man himself to provide a cure and/or protection from such malevolent creatures, not with the help of God nor even so much the ancestral (guardian) spirits, but through human means, i.e., the insight, instructions, magical potions, and protective charms of the diviner, the medicine man, the witchdoctor, and others. This development towards a more man-centered religion, which includes charismatic cults of possession and an increasing emphasis on magic as a means to attain and maintain prosperity in life, is by no means uniform. Rather, it is progressing at different rates throughout Central Africa, among peoples of diverse ethnic backgrounds and the various emerging socioeconomic classes. In general one could say that this development has had its greatest effect among the (peri-)urban-dwelling, semieducated, lower income groups, but additional research is necessary to establish this.

One thing is certain: the pragmatic, utilitarian nature of traditional religion, which was always a prominent part of the African world-view, is definitely being strengthened. Religion exists, is viable, and is practiced to the degree that it is of physical or material benefit to man. If the indigenous religious system appears to be deficient in this respect, then simply add another to complement it, like Christianity or Islam. Syncretism, whether deliberately practiced (e.g., in African independent churches) or not (e.g., in established mainline denominations), is thus a widespread phenomenon, for in the minds of the people it can only enhance the service of religion to man. Such a perspective is not limited to Africa, of course, but given the compelling local inclination toward synthetic, holistic thought, it does seem to affect more of one's daily life than it would in a Western setting.

In many African countries, the humanistic tendency of traditional religious belief has even been incorporated to varying degrees within the political philosophy of the nation. In Zambia, for instance, this development has actually been termed "humanism" by its originator, President Kenneth D. Kaunda. In the words of one of its spokesmen (Kandeke, 1977, 14, 38):

> Zambian Humanism holds that since Man is the centre of all human activity, then, logically, Man is the SUMMUM BONUM, the chief end of all action, the crowning event to which all things move . . . By putting faith in Man, Humanism induces people to rely on human resources and strength in the process of socio-economic and political development. This factor is the main source of self-reliance so strongly advocated by Zambian Humanism . . .. The task of Zambian Humanism is to see that people, regardless of their social positions, enjoy the fruits of their interdependent labor activities as members of one social being. They all share the nature of belonging to a common humanness. This is the most vital characteristic of Zambian Humanism as a Philosophical ideology for building a Man-centered society.

Thus the emphasis upon man in an African context does not result in an individualistic approach toward life (as noted earlier). No normal person even considers the possibility of becoming an island unto himself: *Munthu ni munthu cifukwa ca banyake*, "a person is a person because of his neighbors (i.e., fellow human beings)" [Tumbuka]. On the contrary, the communalistic pressure of traditional religion (cp. Principle 4 above) is clearly evident in the preceding quotation. The African socialized man is a dyadic personality; he always views himself as part of the community, as the "embedded I." He determines his self-image and evaluates his own station in life with respect to others on both the horizontal as well as the vertical axis of interpersonal power relations (i.e., with regard to both solidarity and status). Such group-oriented influence should also be noted in the fact that, contrary to the tenets of classical humanism as developed in the Middle Ages and beyond, the concept of "god" (as created in the image of man) does have a place in people's lives and is not to be simply discarded or ignored as being irrelevant to human concerns, needs, and goals.

Nevertheless, in any humanistic philosophy, whether the Western materialistic brand or the African spiritualistic variety, Christ's command to "love the Lord your God with all your heart . . ." (Mt 22:37) stands as perhaps the greatest challenge to a genuine personal faith and a consequent motivation in life. Without the Spirit's leading and perfecting (Ep 5:22, Cl 1:8), it would of course be a goal impossible even to attempt.

7. The Principle of Circumscription

A communal, humanistic, experience-oriented outlook on life contributes significantly also to our final basic principle comprising the Central African world-view, namely, "circumscription," or as it has been termed by some social scientists, focusing on its negative manifestation, the concept of "limited good." The members of any subsistence-level economic community, which is usually also a small, closed, tightly-controlled social group, will tend to regard the basic resources of life as being limited in quantity and/or availability: *fodya wako ndiyemwe ali pamphuno*, "it is the tobacco that's in your nose which (finally) belongs to you" [Chewa].

This includes everything which a person has need for or simply desires to have: material possessions, e.g., livestock, crops, housing, clothing; natural resources, e.g., water, arable land, timber, wild game; social bonds, e.g., children, descendants, friends, relatives; physical characteristics, e.g., health, strength, beauty, ability; attributed qualities, e.g., honor, love, courage, power; situational features, e.g., good fortune, peace and security; and most important, the socio-religious key to one's total well-being in life, an adequate supply and control of soul power or vital force. All such resources are considered to be finite at best, and more often than not, in serious short supply. Furthermore, there is nothing that the average person can really do to alter the situation by ordinary means; the supply mechanism lies essentially outside of his personal control or influence.

Now if there is just so much of this world's blessings to go around, then it is easy to conclude that someone who happens to accumulate more than his fellows must apparently be accomplishing this at the expense of others. He can only increase to the extent that somebody else decreases. But in the absence of actual robbery or theft (sins of the highest magnitude in African society), how is such an advantage believed to be effected? This question is basically theological in nature, for if it was God who established the present world order in which man is living, then any alteration from what is the normal pattern (we recall the average person's fundamentally conservative approach towards change) must have religious implications. And so it does, for we are brought back once again to what we have isolated as being the iniquitous heart of the Central African belief system, namely, the operation of witchcraft/sorcery. Any augmentation or diminution either in the quality or quantity of "life," in all of its present as well as potential physical, psychological, social, or spiritual aspects, is directly related to the condition of one's life force.

That is to say, if person X suffers loss with respect to any of areas mentioned above, then, presuming that he has not broken taboo or offended the spirits in any way, the inevitable conclusion is that he is being bewitched, that some enemy has taken control of his soul power for personal gain. Conversely, if person Y begins to enjoy significant increase, then he or she must be practicing witchcraft in order to augment his/her vital force to the detriment of someone else. And it is most probable, if this were a real situation, that the unfortunate fellow would be X. This conclusion would be inescapable if the circumstances were such that there were some hard feelings (a "bad heart") between X and Y. Thus, the divining is all but done; what remains is to restore the status quo by means of protective, reversive, and/or offensive counter-magic, i.e., to destroy the witch(craft). No personal gain or compensation is expected as a result of such an experience (a malpractice suit is decidedly un-African). One wishes only to defend the interests of the clan and to reestablish the social balance between members of the same community.

Any society that is founded on the belief that the opportunities for social and/or economic advancement are predetermined or defined, and hence for all practical purposes not open to adjustment and change, will be characterized by individuals who hold several associated views and values of a restrictive nature. First, there is automatically created an atmosphere where uncertainty, doubt, and suspicion can thrive. A person must remain ever vigilant lest someone else succeed in taking advantage of the soul power and associated charisma that he has been endowed with or the goods which he has been blessed with. Ironically, it is often one's closest relatives that stand first in the line of suspicion when misfortune falls, affines in particular: *ubukamu yombalala*, "(blood) relationship is a spear" [Sukwa]. But this may be because the potential for competition and strife is greatest among the nearest of kin, who tend to live in close proximity to one another.

Then there is the deleterious effect that such a limiting perspective may have upon one's personal initiative: why should I work hard in life only to encourage others to bewitch me (in order to tap my life force) or to become liable myself to charges of witchcraft (since I have distinguished myself from the group)? One's primary goal then becomes to cultivate and to reinforce solidarity with others in the community, not to stand out in any way from them—i.e., to achieve success that would relegate others to one's shadow. The person who is truly progressive, or even ambitious, by nature is almost channelled, as it were, whether physically or psychologically, into the deviant activities of sorcery or the use of magic because that is the predominant expectation which society has burdened such individuals with. The same is true of others who happen not to fit the standard pattern on account of some social deficiency or abnormal behavior, e.g., being an isolationist, iconoclast, spinster, or Scrooge.

Thus far we have concentrated on the potentially negative, antisocial aspects of the principle of circumscription. There are, however, some definite redeeming features which clearly integrate it into the total perspective formed by the other six major components of a Central African world-view. This concept of delimitation serves in a general way to promote a certain spirit of contentment among the various members of the kinship and wider social group. If one's place or status in the community depends more on natural endowment, such as wisdom or strength, and the passing of time (i.e., age), then why should one be overly concerned about personally changing what the Creator has already ordained, which includes the amount of one's possessions and the length of one's lifetime? *Umoyo ni usambazi*, "Life (itself) is riches" say the Tumbuka, and besides, *mali ki soono, a koona ku bulaisa nunya ona*, "money is poison, it can kill its owner (i.e., through indulgence or attacks by sorcerers)" [Lozi]. It may be somewhat easier, therefore, for such an individual—in contrast to a Western social climber—to live within the apparent confines of Christ's injunction in the Sermon on the Mount, first of all not to worry about one's economic standing or physical needs, about the food and clothing which God regularly supplies (Mt 6:25, 27).

Associated with this notion is the security which comes from the knowledge that, since such matters are in divine hands, he will unfailingly provide; one's well-being in life does not depend entirely, or even mainly, upon man's own efforts (vs.32-33). There is also the satisfaction which derives from the assurance that every individual, despite his socioeconomic position, is of value within the group (v. 26), and that all events and happenings, no matter how seemingly chaotic and man-dominated, are nevertheless ordered according to an all-encompassing divine providence. However, the ultimate plan and purpose of God's dealings with man are, as in all natural religions, shrouded in mystery and obscurity. The conceptual limitation in this respect can only be lifted by the light of his Word and, in particular, through the revelation of his Son (Jn 1:1-18).

A realization of the principle of circumscription thus relates in a significant way to most of the others that have been discussed in this chapter. We are obviously dealing with a synthetic, closed, and highly integrated system which is characterized by a dynamic view of the fluid interaction of man, nature, and the supernatural (to employ Western-derived etic categories). It is to be expected that a person will observe his particular station in the graded hierarchy that has been divinely, or at least traditionally, established so as to strengthen the communal bonds which promote the unity and well-being of society as a whole. The humanistic focus in this interpretation of reality stems from personal experience and observation; this is the way things have always been, and this is the way the ancestors, and even the Deity himself, wish things to remain in order to preserve the anthropocentric balance of the cosmos so that "peace" (*mtendere* [Chewa], *luumuno* [Tonga]) and "harmony" (*ciyanjano* [Chewa], *lumvwano* [Tonga]) prevail.

A Concluding Comment on the Seven Principles

The preceding discussion represents just one possible way in which the critical elements of a Central African outlook on life might be organized and described, particularly as it relates to the philosophical and practical aspects of traditional religion. The relevant data could certainly be analyzed and interpreted differently. Other significant distinctions might require additional treatment. We should note, for example, that two important subprinciples are also involved in this nuclear complex of closely interacting religious concepts: *Mediation* on the part of both kinship elders and ritual specialists in particular is necessary in order to maintain the essential balance between competing and coexisting forces, between strength and weakness, bane and blessing, sacred and profane, excess and lack. *Kalulu adatuma njovu* [Chewa] "hare sent the elephant" [i.e., on a personal mission]; that is, when you're in a serious situation, send the best possible representative to act on your behalf. And secondly, we have observed that a pervasive and pragmatic reciprocity of human relationships is promoted on all levels of social and religious organization—i.e., *do ut des* "I give that you may give," or as they put it in Chewa, *kupatsa ndi kuika*, "to give [i.e., to someone else] is to set aside [i.e., an obligation that can be redeemed on another day]." Mutual sharing and the cultivation of crucial dependencies, both between man and man as well as between man and God/the spirits, is essential for keeping interpersonal relationships in good repair and the community functioning for the ultimate good of all concerned.

It is also important to observe that the seven principles and related attitudes not only interact in the everyday practice of religion, but they may also vie with one another to varying degrees in a certain set of social circumstances, particularly in situations of interpersonal tension and conflict. Thus one principle may take precedence over another as people work out or attempt to resolve the difficulties which have arisen. An obvious instance of this is the call for a female clergy that is being heard with increasing insistence and incidence nowadays. Such an appeal, though originating in the West, does strike a responsive chord among those who wish to emphasize the communal nature of the Church. It comes into direct conflict, however, with the precept of gradation and the traditional male-dominated orientation of Bantu culture, even in those which have a matrilineal form of social organization. To date the latter principle has prevailed as being the more necessary to uphold in the majority of Christian denominations, but with some interesting modifications. The vital office of congregational treasurer, for example, is frequently filled by a woman, who serves as the domestic "banker" of traditional societies. Although men (husbands) control the means of production in the economic sector--determining where, when, what, and how much to plant--it is their more thrifty wives who manage the crop storage facilities (e.g., granaries) as well as the wealth of the family in the context of an average rural community.

Another example of what appears to be primary religious tenets in conflict is found in the oft-noted tendency for African independent churches to split, resulting in one or more splinter groups. Now why should this happen, given the fundamental synthetic orientation which we observed as being manifested in so may ways within a traditional, communalistic society? While it is necessary to avoid simplistic explanations for what are usually rather complex and situationally specific phenomena, it is probably correct to view such corporate breaks as instances of the dysfunctional nature of human society in general since the Fall. Things simply do not operate smoothly or as intended no matter how ideal the principles upon which the community has been founded, whether formally (as in political "constitution") or implicitly by way of a set of presuppositions inherited in the traditions passed down from the ancestors.

So in the case of the fracturing of religious bodies, the forces which normally complement one another to keep the group together, i.e., power and solidarity (cp. the preceding chapter), now work in overt or covert opposition to one another and hence result in a fissure within, rather than a consolidation of, the organization concerned. It is an issue of negative dynamics, where rivalry over position and status on the hierarchy of authority overrides the need for unity within the group at large. Although the value of oneness and harmony is recognized and often appealed to in such situations, the power principle almost always prevails, because it is itself based upon an argument for the ultimate benefit of the group—or that portion of it which remains after the split.

In other words, the authority figure (pastor, prophet, healer, or whatever) who wishes either to gain control of or to lead a faction out from an established larger body does so in the belief (or delusion) that he has access to a greater measure of the life force or spiritual charisma (resulting in charismatic gifts) that is so vital for maintaining or augmenting the well-being of all those whom he (or she) represents and is responsible for. All this is in striking contrast, of course to the denominational divisions that occur also in Western Christianity, where the cause for separation, or "defellowshiping," tends to be much more analytical and intellectual in nature. In other words, the offense is more often than not due to some highly specific theological factor, such as a disagreement over the interpretation of a particular proof passage of Scripture or the church's application of it.

World-view and Textual Interpretation: An Example from Job

The Tonga translation team (Zambia) had completed a new rendering of the book of Job and understandably felt quite pleased with themselves, for it was not an easy task. Time and again their linguistic and exegetical ability, as well as their patience, had been taxed to the limit as they struggled to convey the long speeches and the seemingly endless stream of poetic expressions meaningfully in their language. Indeed, there were any number of occasions when the sense of the original Hebrew could not be determined with certainty, and the team simply had to forge ahead with the reading that had the support of most versions and commentators. But at last the job was done—or was it?

During a final check of the translation, the team began to have some serious doubts about what their text actually meant in Chitonga. Oh, they knew well enough what it *said*, but now the question was: what would the average Tonga reader *understand* by it, from his normal cultural perspective, that is. The team soon found that there were some significant clashes in viewpoint, differences in interpretation that arose from fundamental disparities in their belief system and way of life compared with that of Bible times (the latter being represented by the author through the various personages in the debate). The following is a selection of some of the more important of these problems as they were encountered in the third chapter of Job. These examples demonstrate the fact that conceptual interference at a rather basic level can, and often does, occur even when we are dealing with two situational contexts that apparently manifest a relatively high degree of cultural similarity. This exercise also illustrates the overlapping and interaction of the seven principal constituents of a Central African religious perspective (discussed above) as they operate in the process of cross-cultural communication.

As far as the chapter as a whole is concerned, Job's opening speech presents an immediate problem of discourse genre, for while "curses" (*masinganyo*) are certainly known and practiced on occasion, the object of the words of imprecation is always a human being, never an inanimate, and in this instance also an abstract and intangible, referent, i.e., the "day of his birth" (Job 3.1, cp. vs.3,8). In Central Africa, evil is inevitably personalized, and no doubt in a case like Job's the family would be going from one diviner to another in an effort to determine who was responsible for attacking him with so much misfortune. One's birthday is not all that important anyway, for one does not become a person until receiving a name and thereby also an ancestral sponsor and guardian (*muzimo*). An individual might recall the year of his birth, especially if some other important event happened to occur then, but he would not make a special effort to remember the exact day, or even the month. Thus the emphasis upon precise time that runs throughout this chapter (e.g., "days of the year," "number of the months," v.6) sounds somewhat foreign to people who are more experientially than chronologically oriented. It turns out that from a literary point of view Job's words do not seem to be a curse at all, but approximate, in content and tone at least, the intensely personal and expressive sort of bombastic verse known as *ciyaabilo*, which a poet usually composes and performs (in song) either to celebrate or to complain about some special situation in life.

There is, however, another rather serious contextual problem that confronts the Tonga reader in this section. If he or anyone else had experienced the same terrible string of misfortunes that Job did, especially the grave physical affliction which placed him near death (2:7-9), it would not be up to him personally to lament his miserable lot in life. Instead the head of the clan would assume a mediatorial role in order to plead the case of the stricken person, not for the benefit of friends and relatives as it appears here in Job, but before the ancestral spirits in supplication. Illness is not a personal matter in a communal society, but the whole family group is involved, and thus they try to share the burden of the afflicted member. Job, on the other hand, almost sounds as if he is despising his own parents, his mother in particular (cp. vs.9-12), for bringing him into this world of trouble, and this is something that is unheard of in traditional Central African setting. A Mutonga may well have occasion to bemoan the problems he is facing in life (in the form of a *ciyaabilo* song, for example), but any such complaints would be more likely levelled against his personal guardian spirit for not doing a better job on his behalf—never against his mother! As they say, *lukolo lwanyoko talulubwa*, "the breast of your mother is not to be forgotten."

Job begins his lament (v.3) with some pretty strange words from a Tonga point of view. Not only does he speak in abstraction about abolishing the "day" of his birth—which is clearly an impossibility—but he goes on, quite unnaturally now backwards in time, to include the "night" of his conception. If one's birthday is relatively unimportant socially, whether a boy or a girl happens to be born, then the time of one's absolute beginning is even less so. In fact, it is thought to be indeterminable, and therefore no reference is made to the event, not even by one's mother, who certainly would not have guessed the sex of the fetus in any case. But worse than that, it would be highly objectionable--a taboo in fact (*kutondwa*)--for a person to refer, no matter how indirectly or discretely, to sexual relations involving his parents, particularly if he himself were the product of such activity. Furthermore, this part of the verse also deals with the unknown and the unknowable, and anyone who presumes to deal in such matters or who displays a morbid curiosity about them, especially as they concern the "night," must somehow be associated with the powers of darkness, i.e., witchcraft.

This brings up the problem of the poetic imagery which is initiated here and continues prominently throughout the rest of the discourse. A sharp contrast appears to be set up between day and night, between light and darkness (in the development of his mournful theme, Job actually intends to combine these opposites). The great prominence given to this dualistic manner of expression is not at all natural in Tonga oral literature, and neither is the seeming overemphasis on the faculty of sight, at the expense of the other senses, notably sound.

Moreover, the imagery of darkness, particularly when applied to the clouds (v.5), does not necessarily have a negative connotation. From the viewpoint of many peoples in Central Africa, this is usually a good sign, for it is an indication that life-giving rain is near. Thus if the rains fail, a black beast must be sacrificed as part of the ritual conducted at a rain shrine (*malende*), for in the logic of sympathetic magic, likes attract one another, i.e., dark animal and smoke—dark (rain) clouds. In such an ecological context, then, blackness would be a positive symbol, signifying blessing. Total darkness, on the other hand, is a fearful thing, for it facilitates the movement of witches and the performance of all sorts of wicked deeds.

Light, too, generally has a good connotation and may also be employed in figurative usages, not as a metaphor for life (cp. vs.20, 23), but to signify clarity (like a rainless sky), cleanliness, purity, health, or even happiness. However, it is not a good omen when light appears unexpectedly in the night (v.4), for that is a sign of mischievous spirits desiring to play tricks on the unwary. A people's tradition of experience thus combines with their world-view to strongly influence their interpretation of what at first seems to be some rather basic and straightforward forms of poetic expression.

Those who "curse [or: 'cast a spell upon'] the day" (v.8) correspond to the Tonga "sorcerer" (*mulozi*), except that the latter, as noted above, would never waste his time in practicing his black magic upon an abstract, inanimate "day," but would instead direct his attention to human beings who are normally active during that time, namely, the particular parties determined by divination to be guilty or offensive. However, no sorcerer, nor any diviner-medicine man (*ng'anga*) for that matter, would be conceived of having the capacity to control the local equivalent of the mythical "Leviathan," i.e., the malevolent *itosi* serpentine river spirit. This dangerous creature, which is believed to capture men or women in order to live with them under the water, is higher on the cosmic scale of life force, and hence only one's ancestral spirits would have the power to protect one against its attack.

It would be considered most vulgar for someone to talk, whether publically or privately, about "the doors of my mother's womb" (v.10). Such a person would be despised, and perhaps even disciplined, for this lack of respect shown toward the one who brought him into the world. Any individual who persisted in using such demeaning language (cp. also "come forth from the womb" in v.11) would certainly provoke the anger of the ancestors and invite punishment in the form of some accident. Moreover, in a local socioreligious context it would appear as if Job is himself appealing to the practice of witchcraft here—and most strangely against his own mother! Indeed, witches are believed to have the power to "tie up the womb" of some woman whom they are jealous of. Thus, if the appropriate medicine for "untying the womb" is not obtained in time, the poor mother will eventually die in childbirth. Alternatively, in cases of difficult or prolonged labor, the mother is suspected of having committed adultery and must confess whom she sinned with before a normal delivery can occur. In any case, this verse and the next, whether rendered literally or not, has the unfortunate effect of focusing upon the laboring (or bereaved) mother, and not the child, i.e., the sorrowing poet.

As he proceeds through this sad chapter, the Tonga reader would come to the definite conclusion that Job must have been a very old man when he uttered these words, for normally it is only the aged and infirm who would overtly express a longing to die (vs.13,21) since they realize, or assume, that they have become a burden to their family. They would thus prefer to cross death's threshold in order to join the company of the spirits, where renewed powers await them, even if somewhat remotely exercised. The references to "sleeping quietly" and being "at rest" would be understood as applying to Job's own spirit after his death: a quiet or "peaceful" (*waluumuno*) ancestor is not a demanding one. It neither causes sickness for being neglected, nor does it demand (through dreams) too much attention in the form of offerings from its living relatives.

Despite the pervading concept of community in African society, the bodies of ordinary folk would not be buried together "with kings and counselors of the earth" (v.14) in situations where, as is often the case, the latter had been possessed during life with some charismatic spirit, especially one with the power of rain-calling. The graves of such mediums, or saints, are usually established as shrines at which those who happen to inherit their spirits will operate in the future. The graves and associated spirits of other people would profane the place and hence also nullify the rites performed there. Similarly no person would ever think of "rebuilding [at] a ruins" (RSV, cp. GNB), for that would surely invite the wrath of the spirits of the former inhabitants who had lived, died, and been buried there. The graves of most people are dug in the near vicinity of their homes, and their spirits are believed to remain close by.

The traditional and acceptable form of wealth among the Batonga is cattle. Thus any person, whether a "prince" (*muleli* 'ruler') or not, who "filled his house" with inanimate possessions such as money ("gold" and "silver" [v.15]) would become liable to accusations of sorcery. He must have obtained his riches at the expense of others by employing "gremlins" (*tuyobela*), which he would dispatch at night to steal on his behalf. Additional proof for such a charge would be that the individual did not even try to hide his wealth. Burial in the ground is the normal banking procedure for the relatively little cash that people have on hand in rural areas.

Job's reference to "infants that never see the light" (v.16) is pathetically familiar to most receptors in Central Africa, but these words carry with them a number of other associations relating to the life and beliefs of the people. Stillborn infants are buried immediately, usually within the very hut in which the ill-fated delivery took place. This is because the corpse is regarded as "unclean" (or "cold") and therefore dangerous, since it bears a mystical infectious power to harm which can affect others, especially those who are ritually "hot" (i.e., those of child-bearing age who still regularly engage in sexual relations).

Thus no (magically) unprotected person must touch either the body or its grave, and all of the burial arrangements are carried out by old women, who are ritually "cold" and consequently immune to the toxicity of the corpse (this is perhaps a symbolic instance of where opposites repel, with a consequent dissipation of potentially harmful energy).

Likewise Job's observation that in the grave "the wicked cease from troubling" (v.17) would be regarded as a truism also in a Tonga context, but again this would be colored by certain important cultural-religious beliefs. "Wicked" people are invariably witches/sorcerers [balozi], and the only way to get rid of their evil influence is to kill them. That is why persons suspected of such activity (and confirmed either through divination or ordeal) were formerly executed by drowning or burning. Only if the name of a deceased witch were inadvertently given to a descendant would its spirit be able to resume the exercise of its harmful power. Paradoxically, in a Central African setting it is the "righteous" who may cause trouble once they are dead, i.e., as angry or vengeful ancestors out to punish those who deliberately disobey the ancient tribal traditions.

One might object to Job's statement that both "the small and the great" associate together in the state of death (v.19). According to traditional belief, a person's spirit (which is the implication in such passages where the dead are personified) remains by his/her grave in order to watch over the family, to protect its members from attacks of witchcraft, and to punish them for breeches of piety and the established customs. The only meeting of the dead that takes place is when the spirits which have been captured (lit. "pressed out") by a witch are sent out together to go and take possession of another victim. On such an occasion, these spirits may encounter and engage in combat either the spirit-corps of another witch or the protecting ancestral spirits of the family being attacked.

Verse 20 calls to mind the events that take place during a customary "spouse-cleansing" ceremony at the time of a funeral. A "light" is not given to the living, however, whether "in misery" or not. Rather, after an act of ritual sexual intercourse has taken place in the house of the deceased (i.e., between his/her spouse and a close relative), a torch is lit inside in order to attract the spirit of the dead. It is then led by the light of this purifying fire outside the dwelling, where it will remain in peace, not returning to trouble the survivor.

Verse 21 presents a bit of a contradiction from a Tonga perspective: Why would someone want to waste time and energy "searching for . . . a hidden treasure" (NIV, cp. RSV)? Such an endeavor is worth the effort only if one knows where and what one is looking for!

The climax of Job's lament is reached in verse 23, as he intimates for the first time that it is God who is responsible for his wretched condition in words which ironically echo Satan's accusation of 1:10. While his complaint is understandable, it sounds a bit unnatural, if not blasphemous, to fix the blame upon God. According to the traditional religious order of things, God cannot be faulted for personal problems that arise in the human sphere: *cacita Leza tacili cibi*, "what God does is not evil." The error is always due to some failure or wrongdoing on the part of man, and the explanation will be persistently sought in these terms (e.g., a person's *muzimo* is neglecting him; a sorcerer is attacking him—in Job's case, out of envy over his great wealth; he has violated some important taboo, or he is being punished for the sinful behavior of a close relative). Therefore in most situations, unless a community-wide calamity is being experienced or some awful crime has been committed (e.g., premeditated murder), the source of one's affliction must be determined and a remedy discovered with reference to earthly agents, which of course includes the ancestors. This presents the average Tonga receptor with one of the greatest problems of comprehension in the entire book: why does Job continue to berate God for a matter which obviously lies within the province of strictly human affairs?!

Finally, then, what could be "the thing that [Job] fears" so much, the "trouble" which gives him "no rest" (vs.25-26)? For anyone influenced by the dogma of indigenous Tonga religion the answer is quite clear: it can only be *bulozi* 'witchcraft/sorcery.' And the prime suspect would be none other than his unsympathetic wife. Before any traditional court, her very own words would accuse and convict her (2:9)!

The preceding has been a short practical demonstration of the importance of the cultural dimension in Bible translation, particularly the influence of the local world-view upon a receptor's comprehension of the original text (cp. Wendland, 1987, ch.7). This is one of those crucial but covert factors that frequently gets neglected by translators as they are carrying out their work—in the isolation of their offices and under the burden of their many books. Ignorance in this particular area also results from a superficial understanding of and approach to the process of communication, cross-cultural communication in particular. Translators may be fooled into thinking that their task has been accomplished once they have produced a more or less accurate and idiomatic rendering of the original text in their language. But as we have seen—and the examples above were just a sample of what one might meet in Job—this is not the case. The new version might read naturally and be judged intelligible as well as exegetically correct, but on a deeper conceptual level a significant amount of misunderstanding may still occur due to the fact that the perspective of the indigenous philosophy of life (and death) has not been adequately taken into consideration during message transmission.

Much more is involved than the familiar pair of form and content. The entire cultural setting of the communication event—physical, psychological, ideological, social, and moral—enters into the picture (whether the translator is aware of it or not) and often colors the resultant text in ways that were never intended, or even imagined. In Central Africa, at least, religious beliefs and values are fundamental to the very existence of society and of primary significance to the community's outlook on life. They have a great influence on people's behavior as well as their perception, interpretation, and evaluation of all new knowledge and experience. That includes the initial reception and also the continued application of the gospel message of the life and work of Jesus the Christ. One thing is certain: traditional religion in Central Africa cannot simply be ignored or dismissed as "irrelevant." The following Chewa proverb puts the case bluntly: *Dziti mafano, udzafa mano adakayera*, "Say, '[Just] superstition,' and you will die while your teeth are still white!" Any personal commitment to Christ must take such a warning into serious consideration.

Some Concluding Implications for Christian Communicators

The basic orientation of the Central African perspective on reality is "synthesis" (1), the desire or determination to preserve the whole of any aspect of culture in an essential unity, despite the diversity of its components. This outlook is reinforced by an active "experientialism" (5) which establishes the natural human condition and endeavor, both past and present, as the primary criterion for deciding what constitutes knowledge and how to interpret and evaluate what goes on in the universe. Man himself thus serves as the essential measure and central reference point of this "humanistic" system (6). An individual never stands alone, however, but he/she is always conceived of in relation to the "communal" group (4), composed of the living as well as the living dead, of which he/she is a vital member and which in turn gives meaning, purpose, and a certain existential solidarity to his/her life. Though every person has a place to occupy and a role to play in this inclusive community, all are not equal in terms of their social status. Instead there is a "gradation" of authority and potency (3) which is profoundly religious in nature. This is because it is founded on a firm belief in the existence of a great host of vital forces which comprise every living being and control the destiny of all under the ultimate supervision of the Creator-Deity and the practical administration of the ancestors. This "dynamic" complex of interacting principalities and powers (2) does not operate in an individualistic, open-ended, and unrestrained manner. It is rather tightly "circumscribed" by a principle of limitation (7), which ensures that a crucial balance in blessing is effected whereby a stable and harmonious status-quo might be maintained for the benefit of all.

The main enemies of man-in-community, on the other hand, are precisely those who deny or disregard these seven focal aspects of the well-ordered whole: the egotistical, iconoclastic, overly progressive, capitalistic, anti-social, irreverent individualists who have regard for neither God nor man. Since these negative attitudes and attributes are epitomized in the person of the witch, it is only natural that people would consider the primary defender of the local world-view and customary way of life to be the witch-doctor. Thus the savior of all threatened and afflicted individuals in a traditional setting has all too often been labelled as the devil of past missionary polemic. The battle for control of one's soul or life force indeed takes place during this present worldly existence, but the implications and consequences are likewise thought to concern life as it is now lived, and not some indistinct future age when the dead will rise again. What need for a resurrection, so conventional logic goes, if the deceased have been transformed and are already living among us (i.e., as ancestral spirits)?

How is the contemporary Church to respond to this glaring clash in perspectives, which is just one prominent example of the many explicit and implicit disparities that occur when two religions collide? A massive transculturation of the biblical message into local terms is not the answer, for that would only encourage the already- present inclination toward religious syncretism or ideological accommodation. A more or less literal transfer of superficially similar concepts will not do either, for the same reason. A woodenly translated text, whether oral or written, if it is understood at all, will simply be reinterpreted in the light of a familiar indigenous world-view and subsequently applied from that established foundation. It is clear that, as an initial step toward a solution, a careful contrastive comparison of the two distinct symbol systems, source and receptor, must be undertaken in order to specify precisely where the significant similarities, correspondences, and partial overlaps occur: in the area of key-terms first of all, and moving on from there to incorporate all of the major conceptual complexes of Scripture.

Such a comprehensive comparative study of religions in contact, each interpreted first of all on its own terms within its own framework of faith and practice, is thus the essential starting point for anyone, whether insider or outsider, who wishes to transmit the Christian message in a correct but relevant way within an African environment. During this long-term process of research, the investigator will naturally tend to focus upon those critical contrasts that he suspects may exist in one's interpretation of the biblical as compared with the traditional African religious viewpoints. To be sure, there are many obvious similarities which undoubtedly help the communication process along, whether on the level of basic Bible translation, evangelistic outreach and church planting, or the training of an indigenous leadership. Among such conceptual bridges, we might draw attention to ideas pertaining to: the common assumption of the existence of God, the Creator; belief in the occurrence of miracles and the supernatural (which are, as we have noted, from an African point of view quite "natural"); recognition of the importance of the past and the need for respecting the traditions of the elders; emphasis on the concept of unity and fellowship within the context of a group of variously related members; an active awareness of the essential spiritual nature of man; acceptance of the reality of personal agents of evil in the world—to mention just a few.

There are, however, also some significant differences between a biblical and an indigenous conception of religion that need to be kept in mind during the process of cross-cultural communication. Among these barriers to a correct Central African perspective of the Scriptures are the following: the separation of the dead (spirits) from the living during earthly existence; a distinction between the human and the nonhuman, animate, spheres of creation, or nature; the presence of a messianic hope to direct one's thinking towards the future and a heavenly kingdom; the importance of a written scriptures; "wisdom" being essentially divine in origin and in orientation; a personal but nonhuman (i.e., satanic) locus of evil in the world; the relative immediacy of God, through Christ, which allows a believer personal access to the Deity; and a concept of sin which, contrary to local belief, resides preeminently in one's heart (i.e., evil nature) and is, in the first instance, an offense against a holy God rather than a mere manifestation of antisocial behavior directed against one's fellow man.

Such contrasting presuppositions will inevitably influence an uninitiated (i.e., someone who has been exposed to little, if any, Christian instruction) person's understanding of passages where these concepts are focal—for instance, when the Psalmist cries out:

> Create in me a *clean heart*, O God,
> and put a new and right *spirit within me.*
> Cast me not away from *thy presence,*
> and take not *thy Holy Spirit from me.* (Ps 51:10-11, RSV)

Thus, a "clean heart" in customary Chewa thought would mean having a good disposition; a "right spirit" would be a friendly ancestral spirit of possession; no one comes into the "presence" of the Supreme Being and "Owner-of-life" unless s/he is dead and already long forgotten by his/her descendants; and the postulation of a living God who has a (dead, albeit "holy") "Spirit" produces a gross conceptual contradiction.

To bridge such fundamental gaps in perception will require the application of all of the functionally valid models at one's disposal, those emanating from a traditional world-view in particular, coupled with a careful consideration of the sociocultural and especially the religious matrix of both source and receptor groups. The comprehensive aim is to provide the necessary glasses or spectacles, so to speak, in the form of dynamic translations of the Scriptures; penetrating and pertinent accompanying explanatory notes; contextually sensitive commentaries prepared with the local receptors and their preunderstanding in mind; inductive and interactive methods of teaching and application—all intended to promote a clearer vision of the biblical message in its remote original setting as compared with a contemporary African context. Only after the various issues pertaining to conflicting world-views have been clarified, debated, and critically related to a community's dominant social institutions and activities will it be possible for Christian communicators to make a consequential, culturally relevant witness to those for whom the Word of God is intended.

In an African setting, it is indeed important that this "Word" be proclaimed as one which originates from God himself--embodied in his Son--and is conveyed by his divine Spirit. Only that will give it the ultimate authority in terms of power and solidarity to displace the deeply ingrained human models proposed by ancient tradition and to resist the competing secular ideologies that are currently being actively promoted in the sociopolitical sphere the world over. Only Christ, the incarnate Word, working through his written and spoken Word, will be able to motivate the necessary radical shift in a people's basic system of belief and the accompanying total commitment to a new way of life (Hebrews 1:1-4).

Bibliography

(for Chapters 1 to 3)

Adeyemo, Tokunboh. 1979. *Salvation in African Tradition*. Nairobi: Evangel Press.

Banton, M., ed. 1966. *Anthropological Approaches to the Study of Religion*. New York: Praeger.

Barrett, David, ed. 1971. *African Initiatives in Religion*. Nairobi: East African Publishing House.

Calloud, Jean. 1976. *Structural Analysis of Narrative*. Philadelphia: Fortress Press.

Colson, Elizabeth. 1962. *The Plateau Tonga of Northern Rhodesia: Social and Religious Studies*. Manchester: Manchester University Press.

Dickson, Kwesi A. 1984. *Theology in Africa*. Maryknoll, NY: Orbis.

————, and Paul Ellingworth, eds. 1969. *Biblical Revelation and African Beliefs*. London: Lutterworth.

Douglas, Mary. 1966. *Purity and Danger: An Analysis of the Concepts of Pollution and Taboo*. Boston: Ark Paperbacks.

————. 1982. *Natural Symbols: Explorations in Cosmology*. New York: Pantheon Books.

Dundes, Alan. 1984. *Sacred Narrative: Readings in the Theory of Myth*. Berkeley, CA: University of California Press.

Durkheim, Emile. 1954. *The Elementary Forms of the Religious Life*. (Trans. J.W. Swain). Glencoe, IL: The Free Press.

BIBLIOGRAPHY

Eliade, Mircea. 1958. *Patterns in Comparative Religion.* (Trans. Rosemary Sheed). New York: Sheed and Ward.

————. 1958. *Rites and Symbols of Initiation.* New York: Harper and Row.

Evans-Pritchard, E.E. 1937. *Witchcraft, Oracles, and Magic among the Azande.* Oxford: Oxford University Press.

Filbeck, David. 1985. *Social Context and Proclamation.* Pasadena: William Carey Library.

Flatt, Donald C. 1973. "The Cross-Cultural Interpretation of Religion in Africa." *Missiology* 1:3. pp. 325-338.

Forde, Daryll, ed. 1954. *African Worlds: Studies in the Cosmological Ideas and Social Values of African Peoples.* London: Oxford University Press.

Gaster, Theodore. 1961. *Thespis: Ritual, Myth, and Drama in the Ancient Near East.* New York: Doubleday.

Geertz, Clifford. 1966. "Religion as a Cultural System." in M. Banton, ed. (q.v.) pp. 1-46.

————. 1973. *The Interpretation of Cultures.* New York: Basic Books.

Goode, William. J. 1951. *Religion Among the Primitives.* Glencoe, IL: The Free Press.

Hennig, E.W. 1964. "Two Studies of Animism." *Practical Anthropology* 11:1. pp. 47-48.

Hiebert, Paul G. 1982. "The Flaw of the Excluded Middle." *Missiology* 10:1. pp. 35-47.

Huizinga, Johan. 1950. *Homo Ludens: A Study of the Play Element in Culture.* Boston: Beacon Press.

BIBLIOGRAPHY

Idowu, E.Bolaji. 1973. *African Traditional Religion*. Maryknoll: Orbis Books.

Kalilombe, Patrick A. 1980. "An Outline of Chewa Traditional Religion." *Africa Theological Journal* 9:2. pp. 39-51.

Kandeke, Timothy K. 1977. *Fundamentals of Zambian Humanism*. Lusaka: NECZAM.

Klem, Herbert V. 1982. *Oral Communication of the Scripture: Insights from African Oral Art*. Pasadena: William Carey Library.

Kraft, Charles H. 1974. "Ideological Factors in Intercultural Communication." *Missiology* 2:3. pp. 295-312.

Lawson, E.T. 1984. *Religions of Africa*. San Francisco: Harper & Row.

Livingston, James C. 1989. *Anatomy of the Sacred: An Introduction to Religion*. New York: Macmillan.

Louw, Johannes P., ed. 1986. *Sociolinguistics and Communication*. (UBS Monograph Series 1). New York: United Bible Societies.

Lowie, Robert H. 1966. "Religion in Human Life." *Practical Anthropology* 13:1. pp. 34-46.

Maimela, S.S. 1985. "Salvation in African Traditional Religions." *Missionalia* 13:2. pp. 63-77.

Malinowski, Bronislaw. 1948. *Magic, Science and Religion*. Boston: Beacon Press.

Marwick, Max. 1965. *Sorcery in its Social Setting: A Study of the Northern Rhodesian Cewa*. Manchester: Manchester University Press.

Mbiti, John S. 1969. *African Religions and Philosophy*. London: Heinemann.

BIBLIOGRAPHY

―――. 1971. *New Testament Eschatology in an African Background*. London: Oxford University Press.

―――. 1975. *An Introduction to African Religion*. London: Heinemann.

Moore, Robert O. (n.d.) "God and Man in Bantu Religion." *Gaba Reprints*. pp. 149-160.

Mtunda 8. 1982. Blantyre, Malawi: Dzuka Publishing Company.

Mugambi, J. and N. Kirima. 1976. *The African Religious Heritage*. Nairobi: Oxford University Press.

Muzorewa, Gwinyai H. 1985. *The Origin and Development of African Theology*. Maryknoll: Orbis.

Nida, Eugene A. 1986. "Sociolinguistics and Translating." in J.P. Louw, ed. (q.v.) pp. 1-49.

―――. 1972. "Linguistic Models for Religious Behavior." *Practical Anthropology* 19:1. pp. 13-26.

―――. 1971. "New Religions for Old: A Study of Culture Change." *Practical Anthropology* 18:6. pp. 241-253.

―――. 1968. *Religion Across Cultures*. New York: Harper and Row.

―――. 1962. "Akamba Initiation Rites and Culture Themes." *Practical Anthropology* 9:4. pp. 145-155.

―――. 1960. "Religion: Communication with the Supernatural." *Practical Anthropology* 7:3. pp. 97-112.

―――, and de Waard, Jan. 1987. *From One Language to Another*. New York: Thomas Nelson.

————, et.al. 1983. *Style and Discourse*. Cape Town: Bible Society of South Africa.

————, and Wonderly, William. 1963. "Cultural Differences and the Communication of Christian Values." *Practical Anthropology* 10:6. pp. 241- 258.

Nyamiti, Charles. 1977. *African Tradition and the Christian God*. Eldoret, Kenya: Gaba Publications.

O'Dea, Thomas and Janet Aviad. 1983. *The Sociology of Religion*, (second ed.). Englewood Cliffs, NJ: Prentice-Hall.

Ong, Walter J. 1982. *Orality and Literacy: The Technologizing of the Word*. New York: Methuen.

————. 1967. *The Presence of the Word: Some Prolegomena for Cultural and Religious History*. New York: Clarion Books.

Onwu, N. 1985. "The Hermeneutical Model: The Dilemma of the African Theologian." *Africa Theological Journal* 14:3. pp. 145-160.

Otto, Rudolf. 1950. *The Idea of the Holy*, (second ed. trans. by J.W. Harvey). London: Oxford University Press.

Parrinder, Geoffrey. 1969. *Religion in Africa*. Baltimore: Penguin Books.

————. 1954. *African Traditional Religion*. London: Sheldon Press.

Patte, Daniel. 1976. *What Is Structural Exegesis?* Philadelphia: Fortress Press.

Pobee, John S. 1979. *Toward an African Theology*. Abingdon: Nashville.

Ranger T.O. and Isaria Kimambo, eds. 1972. *The Historical Study of African Religion*. London: Heinemann.

BIBLIOGRAPHY

Richards, Audrey I. 1939. *Land, Labor and Diet in Northern Rhodesia*. London: Oxford University Press.

Schaff, Philip. 1907. *History of the Christian Church*. (Vol. 5: "The Middle Ages" [part I]). Grand Rapids, MI: Eerdmans.

Schoffeleers, J.M., ed. 1979. *Guardians of the Land: Essays on Central African Territorial Cults*. Gwelo, Zimbabwe: Mambo Press.

Setiloane, Gabriel M. (n.d.) "Where Are We in African Theology?" *Africa Theological Journal* 8:1. pp. 7-14.

Shorter, Aylward. 1973. *African Culture and the Christian Church*. London: Geoffrey Chapman.

Smith, Edwin W. 1950. *African Ideas of God*. London: Edinburgh House Press.

————, and A.M. Dale. 1968. *The Ila-Speaking Peoples of Northern Rhodesia*. (vols.I&II) New York: University Books.

Taylor, John V. 1963. *The Primal Vision: Christian Presence Amid African Religion*. London: SCM Press.

Tempels, Placide. 1959. *Bantu Philosophy*. Paris: Presence Africaine.

Tillich, Paul. 1966. "The Religious Symbol" In F.W. Dillistone, ed. *Myth and Symbol*. London: SPCK. pp. 15-34.

Turner, Victor W. 1967. *The Forest of Symbols*. Ithaca, NY: Cornell University Press.

————. 1969. *The Ritual Process*. London: Routledge & Kegan Paul.

Utuk, Efiong S. 1986. "An Analysis of John Mbiti's Missiology." *Africa Theological Journal* 15:1. pp. 3-15.

BIBLIOGRAPHY

Van Binsbergen, Wim. and M. Schoffeleers, eds. 1985. *Theoretical Explorations in African Religion*. Boston: KPI.

Van Gennep, Arnold. 1960. *Rites of Passage*. Chicago: University of Chicago Press.

Wach, Joachim. 1944. *Sociology of Religion*. Chicago: University of Chicago Press.

Weber, Max. 1963. *The Sociology of Religion*. Boston: Beacon Press.

Welton, Michael R. 1971. "Themes in African Traditional Belief and Ritual." *Practical Anthropology* 18:1. pp. 1-18.

Wendland, Ernst. 1987. *The Cultural Factor in Bible Translation*. (UBS Monograph Series 2). New York: United Bible Societies.

———. 1985. *Language, Society, and Bible Translation*. Cape Town: The Bible Society of South Africa.

———. 1979. "Stylistic Form and Communicative Function in the Nyanja Radio Narratives of Julius Chongo." Ph.D. dissertation: University of Wisconsin (Madison).

White, C.M.N. 1961. *Elements in Luvale Beliefs and Rituals*. (Rhodes-Livingstone Papers 32). Manchester: Manchester University Press.

Wilson, Bryan. 1982. *Religion in Sociological Perspective*. Oxford: Oxford University Press.

———. 1961. *Sects and Society*. Berkeley, CA: University of California Press.

Yinger, J. Milton. 1957. *Religion, Society and the Individual*. New York: Macmillan.

———. 1970. *The Scientific Study of Religion*. New York: Macmillan.

PART II: Case Studies

Chapter 4

EQUIVALENCE OF RELIGIOUS TERMS ACROSS CULTURES: SOME PROBLEMS IN TRANSLATING THE BIBLE IN THE TURKANA LANGUAGE[1]

Krijn van der Jagt

Introduction

In this chapter we deal with the problem of equivalence of religious terms in translating the Bible into African languages. Translators often have great difficulty with the choice of equivalents for basic religious terms of the biblical text such as "God," "spirit," "Holy Spirit," "sacrifice," or "prayer." The problem is that the translators are bound to use verbal symbols that refer to religious concepts which function in the context of a traditional African religion. When a translator uses specific words in a translation of a biblical text, he assumes that these will refer to the biblical concepts that function in his text, but this cannot be taken for granted. The words have been used in a different religious context and might bring different concepts to the mind of the reader.

Symbols and Concepts

With Geertz we see religion as a system of symbols (1966:4). Everything can become a symbol in a given culture, e.g., an object, a color, a smell, a sound, a word, or an act. For the study of a religious system of a people, three categories of symbols are most relevant: words, objects, and acts.

Symbols are instrumental in motivating the behavior of a people. The meanings of the symbols form concepts of human existence. A researcher has to determine the basic concepts that motivate the lives of the people he is studying. He also has to reveal how these concepts relate to one another and constitute a more or less coherent world view. Geertz makes an important distinction between two types of concepts that are used in the descriptions of cultures and religions. They are experience-near concepts and experience-distant concepts (Geertz, 1983:57). The experience-near concepts are expressed by words of the local language and are mainly used by the people of that language. They are culture specific. It is by means of these concepts that the people express their feelings, observations, and imaginations. Experience-near concepts are in the minds of the people and are often not found in dictionaries. They form the basic conceptual framework of the culture. Experience-distant concepts are expressed with words of world languages and trade languages and are applied across cultures. Experience-near concepts are relatively independent of specific contexts. They are often used in descriptions of religions to serve as a link between a specific experience-near concept and a wider used conceptual framework.[2]

When we attempt to look at the problem of equivalence of religious terms across cultures we have to compare symbols and concepts of two specific religious contexts. In this chapter we compare biblical concepts with experience-near Turkana concepts. Through comparison we explore the continuity and discontinuity that exist between the two types of concepts, and discover the specific problems in translation.

Turkana Culture

The Turkana are a nomadic pastoral people. They keep cattle, sheep, goats, and camels, on which they depend entirely for their daily food. Their main foods are milk, blood, and meat. They move their herds across the stony and sandy plains of northwestern Kenya in search of grazing land and water. Most families migrate in the course of the year within a particular area. In the rainy season there is no need to make frequent moves, but in the dry season people are obliged to change their location many times in order to survive. A married Turkana man who owns a herd that is large enough to support his nuclear family is an independent and autonomous person. He can live wherever he chooses, and is not obliged to stay near his relatives.

Turkana culture is highly dominated by cattle ownership. Cattle breeding is not just an economic activity for the Turkana. The relationship of a Turkana with his animals is not primarily rational; it is foremost irrational, emotional and religious. Herskovitz wrote a well-known article, "The Cattle Complex in East-Africa," in which he demonstrated that all cultures in East Africa share a common cultural matrix which he called "the Cattle Complex." (Herskovitz, 1926). In Herskovitz' terms the Turkana culture is a typical cattle-complex culture. In other words, the central values of the culture are cattle oriented.

We can identify at least six areas within the culture that are molded by cattle-oriented values:

1. Cattle are the prime indicator of wealth in Turkana society. Ownership of cattle is the leading factor in the acquisition of status.
2. All legal procedures require the transfer of cattle. Fines, compensation payments, and bride-price can only be paid in cattle.
3. The main Turkana dance is a cattle dance. In this dance the man represents his dance-ox. A dance-ox is one's favorite animal, the animal one has developed an emotional relationship with from the days of boyhood. While dancing, the men imitate the posture of their oxen. They raise their hands above their heads to indicate the shape of the horns, and they try to move in the same way as their oxen do. At the same time, they praise their beauty and strength in songs they compose themselves. The women and girls represent cows in this dance.
4. All important taboos are related to cattle. On certain occasions people cannot eat meat, preserve milk, or have close contact with the animals; e.g., a woman cannot eat meat or milk animals after child birth.
5. Cattle sacrifice is the central religious act of the Turkana. All important social events require the ritual killing of cattle; e.g., before starting a cattle raid; to reconcile people; to purify adulterers; at birth, initiation, and death.
6. The contents of the stomachs of cattle are considered to be a very powerful substance which is used to cure sick people, to strengthen the life force, and sometimes to kill those who are suspected of acts of witchcraft or sorcery.

In a good number of cases where the transfer or sacrifice of cattle is required, camels, goats, and sheep can be used instead of cattle.

Turkana Symbols and Concepts

The Verbal Symbol Akuj

When Turkana people discuss the vicissitudes of life, they quite often use the word *akuj*. It is not easy to identify *akuj* with one particular being. The word can have different meanings in different contexts. These meanings form important experience-near concepts. In order to be able to determine these concepts, we need to analyze the meaning of the word *akuj* in some detail.

The following are six primary contexts in which the word *akuj* is used:

1. During a mourning ceremony, a number of animals of the herd of the deceased are speared to death by the senior patrilineal member of the extended family. When this person takes up the spear, he speaks the following words: "*Akuj*, I have fed you, I have killed your animals. Don't kill me." The dead man is addressed by the word *akuj*.
2. When one Turkana man was asked what or who *akuj* was, he gave the following answer: "Trees, animals, all kinds of food, that all is *akuj*. When you eat of it, it can give you life. It can also kill you." *Akuj* refers here to a nonpersonal force in nature that can sustain life and also kill.
3. When a Turkana is asked how it can be that witches are so efficient in killing, the following reply is given: "*Akuj* of the soil hears the words of the witch."
4. When somebody is ill one can ask: "What is this illness?" People can answer: "This illness is just *akuj*." *Akuj* refers here to the natural order of things. Illness and old age cause death; this is how things are. Illness and death are also caused by witchcraft and sorcery. When this is the case, one cannot say that the illness is just *akuj*.
5. When people face great difficulties in times of drought, one can hear people say: "This drought is *akuj*. It is totally *akuj*. There is nothing we can do. It is all *akuj*. We cannot overcome *akuj*." Human beings cannot control life. The Turkana experience life as fate. Life with all its hardships is imposed on people by an extraordinary power. This power is called *akuj*.
6. When one asks a Turkana who is *akuj* he will point point to the sky. In that case he refers to a being who is called *Akuj ekasuban*, "*Akuj* the maker." This being is the one who has made all things. He is the owner, the highest authority of all that exists. He is *Akuj ekapolon*, "the senior one." This being is seen as the source of life.

We have now seen that the verbal symbol *akuj* can have different meanings in different contexts.[3] These meanings form a complex Turkana experience-near concept. Within this concept we can differentiate three overlapping subconcepts.

1. *The concept of the supernatural as power controlling life.* Beyond the ordinary world of human beings there is another world whose beings yield influence over the living in such a way that life and death are ultimately in their hands. The powers of the other world are uncountably numerous. They are, however, often perceived as one power: *akuj*.

2. *The concept of source-being.*[4] The Turkana believes in a source-being who is the maker of all life. This concept should not naively be identified with the god concept of the Judeo-Christian world. It is a Turkana experience-near concept.

3. *The concept of the supernatural as a force diffused in nature.* The Turkana believe that life is diffused in nature. This force is in particular located in the earth and in what comes from the earth (e.g., plants). Human beings can apply this force to cure illness, to strengthen life, and to destroy life.

When we translate the Turkana term *akuj* into English, we will use the following glosses: When used in the widest sense of the word, by "the supernatural"; in more specific senses we use "supernatural power," "source-being," and "life-force," in accordance with the context in which the word is used.

The complexity of the concept may be diagrammed as follows:

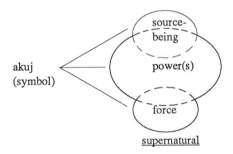

The Verbal Symbol Ekipe

The term *ekipe* is frequently used to refer to the world of the extraordinary. The following six contexts highlight the basic meaning of the term. The sentences are all taken from larger interviews:[5]

1. *Ekipe* kills evildoers.
2. The rainbow is *ekipe.*
3. A whirlwind is *ekipe.*
4. Lightning and thunder are *ekipe.*

5. A child was taken away by *ekipe*.
6. "When your deceased father appears to you in a dream, it is *ekipe*. When you open your eyes, no one is there."

The word *ekipe* (plural form: *ngpian*) is used for all concrete appearances and interventions of the other world among the human beings. The term often refers to a particular kind of beings. These beings are numerous. They are believed to live in water pools, on hills, and in dark places. They are often near to human beings; they see and hear everything. These beings of the other world can appear in a variety of forms:

1. In natural phenomena such as the rainbow, the whirlwind, and fire.
2. In dreams as dead people (*ngikaram*).
3. In objects, in the form of a human being, in the form of shadows (*ngipaara*), in the form of animals, such as hyenas and birds, and in the form of monsters, half human, half animal.

The *ngipian* are often troublesome beings who terrify and upset wherever they manifest themselves. They are not completely malicious, however. Sometimes they are helpful. In general one can say they are ambivalent, on the one hand related to the human beings (ancestors), but also being different from them, like supernatural beings.

The meanings of the verbal symbol *ekipe* form important experience-near concepts within the highly generic concept *akuj*. One of them is the concept of the supernatural as a troublesome and life-threatening power. This concept contrasts with the life-giving force (*akuj*). A second important concept is that of ambivalence.

When we translate the term *ekipe-ngipian* into English, we will use "spirit-spirits."

The Non-Verbal Symbol Ngikujit

The Turkana carry out special study of the contents of the stomachs of the animals of their herds in all their rituals. They call it *ngikujit*. We will present a number of contexts in which this important symbol is used.

1. *Ngikujit* is smeared on a sick person who is ill because the ancestors are annoyed about things.

2. *Ngikujit* is smeared on a person who is ill as a result of witchcraft or sorcery.
3. A child who has been lost for a few days is smeared with *ngikujit* before he or she can enter the homestead. (It is believed that the child has been taken away by spirits.)
4. When someone has broken certain principal laws (*etal*), he or she has to be smeared with *ngikujit*. This is the case with adultery, incest, disrespect for elder people, etc.
5. A woman who returns to the homestead of her father, even for a short visit, before the last ritual of the marriage has been performed, is smeared with *ngikujit*.
6. When somebody has unintentionally made a mistake in the performance of a ritual, it is necessary to kill a sacrificial animal and smear him with the *ngikujit* of that animal.
7. Someone who has killed an enemy in a cattle raid must be smeared with *ngikujit*.
8. The young men at the intiation ritual are smeared with *ngikujit*.
9. The old men smear themselves with the *ngikujit* of the wedding-ox during the marriage ritual.
10. *Ngikujit* is poured out on the ground whenever a sacrificial animal is killed. This act is called: "to feed *akuj*."
11. *Ngikujit* is spread around on the leaves of trees at the rain ritual.
12. During mourning rituals the members of the family of the deceased must smear themselves with the *ngikujit* of the sacrificial animals.

We can summarize the meanings of the symbol *ngikujit* (contents of the stomach) under five different points:

1. *Ngikujit* is curative. It cures sick people (contexts 1 & 2).
2. *Ngikujit* protects against negative reactions of the supernatural world (3,4,5,6,7).
3. *Ngikujit* calms people after conflicts and disharmony (4).
4. *Ngikujit* strengthens people and spirits (8,9,10,11).
5. *Ngikujit* kills people (12).

It is important to relate the meanings of the nonverbal symbol *ngikujit* to the concept of life (*akuj*) and to the concept of spirit (*ekipe*). The Turkana believe that spirits need and desire *ngikujit* to strengthen their modes of life. Spirits also eat human beings. They have to do this in order to remain strong, as people say. The Turkana believe, however, that spirits prefer *ngikujit* to people.

Ngikujit is a life-giving and life-strengthening substance. Animals eat lots of plants which contain medicinal powers. In the stomach of the animal the plants become a powerful mixture. The cows and the goats eat a great variety of plants, some of which have healing powers, others being poisonous. *Ngikujit* can work as medicine or as poison; can heal or it can kill.

Spirits can see the *ngikujit* on the body of one of the victims, and they will eat the *ngikujit* and leave the person alive.

The powerful medicine that is present in the *ngikujit* can make a weak and ill person strong when it enters the body. Spirits can also make a poison, present in the *ngikujit*, enter the body of a person, and that person will die.

The concept of *ngikujit* relates to *akuj* (the supernatural power that pervades nature) and to the spirit world (*ekipe*).

Turkana Religion

The *ngikujit* symbol is the most central nonverbal symbol in Turkana religion. The Turkana people believe that they have to kill animals of their herds to feed the powers of the supernatural world and to strengthen their own lives.

The relationship with cattle has an important religious dimension. Cattle are a source of life for the Turkana, as is seen when we look at the Turkana initiation rite. The initation of the young Turkana men into society takes place during a special sacrificial meal. The Turkana do not practice circumcision. There is no hardship or physical test associated with the initiation. The only thing the candidates have to do is to spear an ox or male goat in front of the initiated men. The contents of the stomach of all the animals are poured out on one spot. The most senior man smears all the candidates with the stomach contents. Then all the meat is roasted and distributed. The candidates receive small bits of all sorts of meat. In addition certain parts of meat that are special, and normally reserved for the most senior men, are given to the candidates. As the sacrificial meal draws to an end, each of the newly initiated is presented with three bones: a bone from the neck, a bone from the back and a bone from the right foreleg. The young men are requested to crush the bones with a sharp-edged stone and suck the marrow which is inside. They appear, however, to be without the power to do so, and they need help from their initiation-father.

The initiation ritual brings about a change in the socioreligious status of the young men. This change is seen as a new birth. The young men have to present themselves as powerless, new-born creatures. The newly initiated crosses the boundary between the impotent world of the noninitiated to the potent world of the initiated. He enters the world of *akuj*. The mediating scheme par excellence between the potent world of *akuj* and the world of the human beings is the sacrificial meal. An animal of the herd, a source of life, is killed, and the meat is shared among the men. The powerful substance *ngikujit* is poured out for the beings of the other world and applied to the bodies of the young men. Turkana initiation mirrors the basic religious structures of the culture. Initiation is the opening up of the channels with the world of the *akuj* through the animals of the herd. The sacrificial meal of the initiated men is the central religious activity of the Turkana. At his initiation a young man "feeds" for the first time the group of initiated men and *akuj* and shares this food with them in a sacrificial meal. In his later life he will do this many times.

Turkana religion is a life-centered religion. The central aim of the religion is not the realization of ethical values, the glory of God, the salvation of the soul, or the escape from the circle of birth and rebirth, but the well-being (life) of the individual and the community. If Turkana religion is interpreted in this light, there is no need to be surprised that there is "a complete lack of ancestor cult" (Gulliver, 1951:229,251). It is indeed true that the ancestor cult is not prominent. The Turkana do not seek and arrange to meet with their ancestors in ritual and dance. The dominant attitude is avoidance and not communication. One does not need to be surprised, either, when one discovers that the source-being is not the object of any form of formal or regular cult, and that the Turkana remain rather indifferent and apathetic towards him (Gulliver, 1951:251).

Thus it is wrong to present Turkana religion as primarily a theistic religion, analogous in structure to Christianity and Islam, as has been done by many earlier writers on Turkana religion. In Turkana thought the essential qualities of the supernatural cannot be confined to a particular being who lives in isolation. The source-being is associated with the life-giving force, all-embracing and all-pervading. The Turkana strongly believe that they can use and profit from the life-force that is in the stomachs of the animals of the herds. The central concept of Turkana religion therefore is not a being but a wider concept. Turkana religion has to be interpreted within the symbolic and conceptual framework of Turkana culture. If this is done consistently, things fall into place.

III. Comparative Discussion of Turkana Symbols and Concepts

1. Akuj and ekipe in relation to universal experience-distant concepts

How do the experience-near concepts *akuj* and *ekipe* relate to experience-distant concepts like God, Supreme Being, High God, spirit, ancestral spirit, demon, and such like? This problem will be addressed in some depth. We will, first of all, review some of the positions taken by researchers of the Turkana culture.

Researchers of the Turkana have identified *akuj* with a good god, and *ekipe* with a bad god or devil. Dundas, one of the first researchers of the Turkana, wrote "They have two gods" (1910:69). He assumed that the Turkana believe in a good god, *akuj*, and a bad god, *ekipe*. Emley had a slightly different opinion: "They have two distinct names for god and evil spirit, namely, *agut* and *agipe*. They are unable to separate them and say that the two constitute one person who lives in the skies" (1927:192).

Gulliver, who studied Turkana culture in detail, is certain that the Turkana believe in one god. He admits that his information is shaky: "Where ideas and beliefs are so vague, even partly contradictory, it is difficult to obtain very full information" (1951:231). Gulliver refers throughout his writings to *akuj* as the high god of the Turkana, and presents Turkana religion basically as a vague cult of a withdrawn high god. As can be concluded from the quotation, above, he did not have a clear picture of Turkana religion. His main observation was that the Turkana people, apart from their apathetic relation with the high god *akuj*, did not pay much attention to the supernatural.

Others, like Best (1978) and Hauge (1986), have followed Gulliver in this. It is interesting to note that, in the theocentric concept of Turkana religion of Gulliver and others, a contradiction is inherent. The religion is concentrated on a *deus otiosus*.

In this essay we do not present Turkana religion as a theocentric religion but as a life-centered religion. The problems that made it difficult for earlier researchers to develop a clear and consistent picture of Turkana religion go back to the semantic complexities of the two key-terms *akuj* and *ekipe*, and the relation of Turkana basic experience-near concepts with universal concepts, like God and demon.

Akuj and the Concept of God

We have seen that the verbal symbol *akuj* can have different meanings. The word can refer to a particular supernatural being that we have termed as source-being. This being is not to be identified with a creator God who has created the world out of nothing. The source-being has its own characteristics. This being is seen as the source of life, which means that life in different forms comes forth, emanates from it, and returns to it. "*Akuj* gives life and eats life," the Turkana say. The Turkana concept of a source-being is a god concept. We have to keep in mind that it is a Turkana experience-near concept. Any naive identification of the

Turkana concept with the biblical god concept or with the philosophical concept of deism leads to distortion. The Turkana god concept is closely related to their concept of life. The source of life is, in fact, not an object of worship. The source-being is not seen as an isolated and independent being at the other side of reality.

It is most useful to compare the Turkana god concept with concepts of god in other cultures so that the distinct features of the Turkana concept can be highlighted.

The Concept of Source-Being and the Biblical Concept of God

There are similarities between the Turkana concept of god and the concept of god we find in the Bible. There are also significant differences.

1. Exclusiveness versus inclusiveness

The Judeo-Christian religion is an outspokenly theistic religion. It has its roots in early forms of the exclusive monotheism of ancient Israel. In Israel's monotheism there is no room for any other power besides the one almighty God. The possibility of an influence of the departed ancestors on the living is denied. Sorcery and witchcraft are put aside as irrelevant and are forbidden, along with all forms of divination or cults for the departed. Religion should be fully concentrated on only the one God.

In daily practice, pagan cults and all sorts of magical practice went on for a long time in ancient Israel, and the prophets of the Old Testament tirelessly warned against unfaithfulness. The God of the Bible is exclusive.

The Turkana concept, however, is not exclusive but inclusive. When the Turkana approach the supernatural world through their rituals, they never address the source-being exclusively. Even if they use the term *akuj* in oral rites, such as "*Akuj*, give us life," the people say that they do not address one particular being, but rather the whole realm of the powers of the other world.

2. Difference in nature versus equality in nature

In the Old Testament it is said that God is spirit (*ruah*), and man is flesh (*basar*). This means that the nature of God, the creator, is totally different from the nature of man. Man is mortal and God is immortal. God created the world and everything that exists out of nothing. So life did not emanate from God; he is not the source of life, but the creator of it. In the Turkana way of thinking, there is no substantial difference between the source and what comes continuously out of it.

3. The ethical versus the nonethical

In the biblical concept of God, there is an important ethical component. The God of Israel has very pronounced ethical ideals. He has created the earth and man with a specific moral purpose in mind: to live with man in a covenant relationship. He loves justice and hates injustice, he protects the rights of the powerless and the foreigner. The Turkana source-being is not associated with ethical ideals. It is often said that *akuj* hears the cry of the one who is wronged. *Akuj* does not exclusively stand for the source-being. With *akuj*, the whole realm of supernatural beings is meant. It is believed that *ekipe* is the one who punishes evil people, but not out of a zeal for ethical ideals. In Turkana society there is no tension between particular ethical ideals and the practice of everyday life, as there was in Ancient Israel.

4. Personal versus nonpersonal

In the biblical concept the personal element is dominant. The God of the Bible enters into a personal relationship with his people. In the Turkana concept this personal element is not developed. The Turkana speak about the source-being in anthropomorphic terms, as the Bible does about the God of Israel. This can be taken as an indication that the personal element is not completely absent. However, the impersonal aspects of the supernatural are prominent in Turkana religion.

Ekipe and the Spirit Concept

The Turkana do not differentiate between good spirits, bad spirits, ancestral spirits, nature spirits, and demons. They just refer to all spirit beings as *ngipian* (plural of *ekipe*). All *ngipian* share the same characteristics. They are all ambivalent beings, sometimes helpful, but quite often troublesome and harmful. The *ngipian* play the role of destroyers of life: they eat people. Since they are numerous and also greedy, they present a permanent threat to the living. The *ngipian* resemble human beings in some points. One of these points is that they also like animals. As living human beings, they can become fond of a particular type of an ox, and in that case people have to kill that animal. Whenever an animal of the herd is ritually killed, the contents of the stomach are poured out on the ground. This is an important act and not just the dumping of a waste-product. The contents of the stomach of the animal contain a powerful substance. The *ngipian* need to eat this regularly in order to remain strong, the Turkana people say.

The ancestral spirits also belong to the group of the *ngipian*. The Turkana do not make the effort to establish good relationships with their ancestral spirits. There is no regular ritual to appease them. Only when things go wrong shortly after the death of someone do people sacrifice near the grave of the deceased and offer him or her meat and other kinds of food. The general attitude towards the deceased is one of indifference. The Turkana do not introduce ancestors in their dances, they do not possess masks, they do not carve images of their ancestors, neither do they maintain shrines for them. Ancestors are *ngipian*. Getting rid of them is more important than relating to them. However, one cen never ignore the existence of *ngipian*, as they always impose themselves on the living.

Ekipe and the Concept of Evil Spirit

We have seen that earlier researchers of the Turkana have identified *ekipe* with the universal concept of the evil spirit or demon. The translators of the New Testament in the Turkana language have taken *ekipe* as an equivalent for Devil (*diabolos, satanas*). The Devil of the New Testament is a supernatural being who seeks to rule the world in opposition to God. This being both tempts and accuses people. He is completely evil, the real enemy of God and man. The New Testament reveals that at the end of history Christ will defeat and destroy this evil spirit. The following table presents an overview of the characteristics of *ekipe* and devil.

Turkana Religion	New Testament World
Ekipe (ngipian)	*diabolos (diaboloi)*
There are many *ngipian*.	There are many *diaboloi*.
The *ngipian* can be grouped in order of seniority.	The *diaboloi* have one leader (*satanos*).

The ancestors are also *ngipian*.

There is no identification of *diaboloi* with spirits of the dead.

Ngipian can enter animals. They can possess people and cause diseases.

Diaboloi can enter animals. They can posses people and causes diseases.

Ngipian can communicate with diviners for the good of the people.

Diaboloi are completely evil.

Ngipian live in deserted places.

Diaboloi live in deserted places.

Ekipe is not the enemy of the source-being.

Satanas is the enemy of God.

In Turkana religion the "spirits" (*ngipian*) are not completely evil. They are highly ambivalent. The personification of one spirit as chief who becomes an adversary of God is typical for the New Testament world. The same is true for the eschatological final battle between God and his armies, and the Devil and his armies.

The distinctions between God (source-being) and spirits are blurred in Turkana religion. In the New Testament we have very sharp distinctions; God and the devil are antagonistic beings.

Translating the Bible into Turkana

The Term for God

Translation of the biblical text demands an in-depth study of the religious concepts of both the source text and the receptor language. The translator has to compare the experience-near concepts of the Bible with the experience-near concepts of his language. It is often helpful to relate both the experience-near concepts of the source language and the ones of the the receptor language to universal experience-distant concepts. The first step in this process is the comparison of the verbal symbols that refer to the relevant concepts in the source text with corresponding glosses in the receptor language. We have seen that the verbal symbol *akuj* may refer to the source-being, but can also refer to other related concepts. The verbal symbol Jahweh has only one referent: the God of Israel. We can visualize the translation process in the following way.

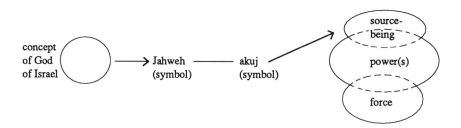

The verbal symbol *akuj* incorporates different senses within its overall area of meaning. If one wants to make sure that the symbol refers to the source-being uniquely, one has to use a qualifier: *akuj ekapolon* (the great akuj). Even when the term *akuj ekapolon* is used, we do not have a symbol that can bring the experience-near concept Jahweh (personal creator, God of Israel, God of the covenant) directly to the mind of the Turkana reader. There is a substantial difference between the Turkana concept of source-being and the concept God of Israel. The terms are therefore mismatched. Translators should be aware of the extent of the mismatching when they translate important religious terms from the biblical text into an African language. In many cases, translators of the Bible have used the verbal symbol that referred to the concept of supreme being or source-being that existed in the African language they worked with, as equivalent for the term that is used to refer to the God of the Bible. By doing so they assumed that the god concept of the Bible was identical or almost identical with the experience-near god concept of their culture.

Not all translators have done this, since they felt that the god concept that existed in the African language differed significantly from the concept of God which we find in the Bible. In quite a few translations of the Bible in African languages, a loanword is used as verbal symbol referring to the concept of God. Such loanwords like Allah (Arabic) or Mungu (Swahili) function as symbols that refer to experience-distant concepts. They are useful to bridge the discontinuity between the African concept and the biblical concept.

Theological Implications

The use of indigenous terms for God in Bible translations has certain missiological and theological implications. There are writers who strongly believe that the traditional African names for God should be used in Bible translations. They base their opinion on a theological evaluation of the traditional African religions. One of these writers is John Mbiti, who believes that the similarities between the concepts of God in Africa, and the biblical God concept are far more important than the differences. For him there is no discontinuity between African traditional religion and the Old Testament. In an article in the *International Review of Missions* (Mbiti, 1970), he states that the African Church does not need the Old Testament as preparation for the Gospel. African traditional religion can replace the Old Testament. The African God is not different from the God of Israel. It is the same God who has revealed himself in different religious forms to different peoples.

Mbiti does not distinguish between concept and being. Concepts of God are experience-near concepts. They exist in the minds of people, they are part of a system of symbols (religion). To say that the same being has revealed himself in different ways to different peoples is a theological statement which cannot be verified empirically. Even when one accepts this statement as truth, it is not automatically so that different peoples have the same conceptual development about the one being who has revealed himself.

Not everyone agrees with Mbiti. The writer Okot p'Bitek accuses Western scholars and their African disciples of dressing up the African gods with the beautiful garments of Greek philosophy and Judeo-Christian theology (1970). It is importent, indeed, to safeguard the concepts of African religions from reinterpretation in terms of foreign concepts. This is in particular relevant for the God concept. Translators should be aware of the discontinuity between the God concept of the Bible and the concepts they find in the African languages. They should not base their choice of equivalents on a naive identification of biblical concepts with African traditional concepts.

The Term for Evil Spirit and Holy Spirit

We have compared the Turkana concept *ekipe* with the New Testament concept "devil" (*diabolos, satanas*). We noticed significant differences. The Turkana do not know about a being that is the enemy of the good god. Turkana religion is not antagonistic. There are binary structures within the overall concept of the supernatural, but these do not form an antagonistic dualism such as we have in the New Testament. The translators of the Turkana Bible use *ekipe/ngipian* for "devil" and "evil spirits." In the New Testament these terms are used exclusively for powers that are completely evil, while the Turkana context *ekipe* and *ngipian* can function outside the evil. *Ngipian* warn the diviner about imminent disasters, *ekipe* kills evil doers, etc. In the context of the Turkana New Testament, *ekipe/ngipian* refer to exclusively evil powers, and this fact made it impossible to use these terms for neutral and positive meanings.

The Greek word *pneuma* is a highly generic word for spirit being. It is used in the New Testament for Holy Spirit (*pneuma hagion*). The Turkana equivalent for *pneuma* would logically be *ekipe*. The translators were forced, however, to look for another term to translate Holy Spirit. The solution they found was the use of the word *etau* (heart). Holy Spirit became *etau akuj*, "heart of God." The meaning of "heart" goes beyond the physical heart, but in the Turkana language the heart is not regarded as being able to act on its own. A further complication is that the Turkana believe that the heart leaves the body after death. As often in the translation of the term "Holy Spirit," the choice is not at all satisfactory.

The Term for Prayer

Whenever a Turkana utters words that are addressed to beings of the otherworld, he uses *akuj* as a term of reference. A man who is in difficulty will say, when he comes out of his sleeping place in the early morning: "*Akuj*, help me." He does not address the source-being *akuj* explicitly, but he turns to the world of the supernatural in an inclusive manner. When you ask him to whom he speaks, he may even say that he has no particular being in mind. At the end of the sacrificial meal of the initiated men, an oral rite is performed (*agata*). One of the most senior men stands in front of the others who are seated in a semi-circle. He acts as "prayer" leader.

He says: "Our children will have life."
The other men reply: "They will have."
He says: "Rain will fall."
The others reply: "It will fall."

When we ask the men to whom they speak their words, they may say: "We just say our words. *Akuj* hears our words." *Akuj* refers here to the whole realm of the supernatural: source-being and spirits.

In the New Testament several terms are used for prayer,[6] but the meaning of the term is to speak to or make requests of God. Prayer is a particular form of personal communication between human beings and God. It is clear from the examples of the Turkana religion that this type of communication is different from the Turkana oral rite (*agata*). The translators of the Turkana New Testament have not used the term *agata* for "prayer," but the term *akilip*, which just means "to ask." A comparison of the two experience-near concepts shows a basic discontinuity. The awareness of this has led the translators to look for a different verbal symbol than *agata*, although it seemed at first sight to be the closest equivalent symbol.

Let us look in more detail into the extent of discontinuity that exists between the Turkana concept of *agata* and the biblical concept of prayer. There are at least three important differences.

1.   The words of the *agata* are not addressed to one particular being exclusively.
2.   The words of the *agata* can only be pronounced by the initiated men. The Turkana people believe that the words of old people are heard by the supernatural powers.
3.   The words of the *agata* always have a positive effect, the Turkana believe. They are believed to have magical power. The *agata* can be both benediction and curse.

Prayer in the Bible is addressed to God exclusively, and all persons, young and old, have the same access to God. The one who prays is completely dependent on God; he or she has no power to implement the wishes or request mentioned in the prayer.

The term *agata* falls in the semantic domain of ritual. The meaning of the term is constituted by the context of Turkana religion, just as the meaning of prayer in the Bible is by the Judeo-Christian religion. The main differences in meaning between *agata* and prayer reflect distinctive aspects of the two types of religions. These aspects have a bearing on the meanings of a good number of terms in the domain of ritual. It is therefore useful to describe these aspects in some more detail.

1.   In ritual the Turkana do not approach one particular being who is far away. They turn to the otherworld, always near in the multitude of spirits. The borderline between the world of man and the otherworld, the world of *akuj*, is transparent and flexible. Also the distinctions within the world of *akuj* are blurred. Source-being and spirits are together. In ritual the Turkana turns to the world of *akuj*, a world of which he himself is part.
2.   The old men have better access to the world of *akuj* than the young people. They are closer to the borderline. The world of *akuj* is structured in

accordance with seniority as Turkana society is. The most senior spirits are most powerful. The source-being is the most senior one of all the beings of the other world. A ritual performed by an old man has more effect than a ritual performed by a young person.

3. Man is part of the world of *akuj* in the sense that he can handle to some extent the powers of life and death diffused in nature. In other words man is not completely dependent on the beings of the other world. There is room for manipulation. In magic, witchcraft, and sorcery, man attempts to influence his life with the help of the forces and powers of the supernatural.

In the Judeo-Christian religion all borderlines are sharp and distinct. This is true for the borderline between God and man, God and spirits, the deceased and the living, the spirits and man. In ritual there is a sharp distinction between religious components and magical components.

In the sphere of religion man manifests his dependence on God; in the sphere of magic man manifests his audacity. In Judeo-Christian religions the two cannot go together. All magical practices are regarded as signs of unbelief and disloyalty to the one God. In the Turkana context magic and religion do not oppose one another, but they complement each other. The three aspects of the Turkana religion--the inclusiveness of the supernatural, the hierarchical structure of the supernatural, and the complementary character of the religious and the magical components--color the meanings of the terms that relate to ritual.

Conclusion

The translator of the Bible in an African language is bound to use religious terms that have been coined in the context of African traditional religions. This poses specific problems. In this chapter we have given examples of this type of problem from the translation of the Bible into the Turkana language. Both the methodology we applied to approach the problems and the practical solutions to the problems may be quite useful to translators of the Bible in the African situation. A translator of a biblical text must carefully analyze and compare the relevant symbols and concepts of the source-text with the analogous symbols and concepts of the receptor language. On the basis of this research, choices of equivalents are to be made.

When we analyzed the problem of the translation of the term for God into Turkana, we discovered that the possibility of ambiguity and mismatch occurred at two levels: at the level of symbol and at the level of concept. By using the general word for the supernatural (*akuj*), the focus would not be exclusively on the source-being but on a wider concept. In order to avoid this ambiguity, it was necessary to add the qualifying word "great" to the generic term *akuj*.

The second problem was related to the concept "source-being." Since there are significant differences between the biblical concept of God and the concept of source-being, one could not opt to use the word *akuj*, but could use the Swahili word *Mungu*. The translators of the Turkana Bible have not done this, but it was one of the options. When in such a case a loanword from the world language or trade language is used, reference is made to an experience-distant concept as an intermediate concept.

In translating the term for Holy Spirit, a different approach is followed. A word that has a particular meaning ("heart") is given an extension of meaning in the translation. The word "heart" must take up the additional sense of "spiritual being." In the translation of the word "prayer," yet another solution is found. The specific Turkana term for oral rite is not used but a generic Turkana word that conveys some components of the biblical concept. These examples from the Turkana context show how complicated the translation of the biblical text is. Translators must have an open and creative mind and base their choices of terms on research of both the biblical text and the culture of the receptor audience in order to assure a faithful transfer of meaning.

Bibliography

Banton, M. ed. *Anthropological Approaches to the Study of Religion*. London: Tavistock Publications, 1966.

Best, G. *Von Rindernomadismus zum Fischfang*. Wiesbade: Steiner Verlag, 1978.

Idowu, E. Bolaji. *African Traditional Religion: A Definition*, SCM Press, 1973.

Dundas, K.R. "Notes on the Tribes Inhabiting the Baringo District." In *Journal of the Royal Anthropological Institute*. 60:49-72, 1910.

Emley, E.D. "The Turkana of Kolosia District." In *Royal Anthropological Institute*, 57:157-201. 1927.

Geertz, C. "Religion as a cultural system." In M. Banton, ed. *Anthropological Approaches to the Study of Religion*. London: Tavistock Publications, 1966.

———. *Local Knowledge. Further Essays in Interpretive Anthropology*. New York: Basic Books, 1983.

Gulliver, *A Preliminary Survey of the Turkana*. Cape Town: University of Cape Town, 1951.

Hauge, H. *Turkana Religion and Folklore*. Stockholm: Studies published by the Institute of Comparative Religion at the University of Stockholm, 1986.

Herskovitz, M.J. "The cattle complex in Eastern Africa." In *American Anthropologist*. 1926.

Van der Jagt, K.A. *De Religie van de Turkana van Kenia*. Ph.D dissertation, University of Utrecht, 1983.

BIBLIOGRAPHY

————. *Symbolic Structures in Turkana Religion.* Assen: Van Gorcum, 1989.

Mbiti, J.M. "Christianity and traditional religions in Africa." In *International Review of Missions.* 1970.

P'Bitek, O. *African Religions in Western Scholarship.* Nairobi: East African Literature Bureau, 1970.

Notes

1. For a description of Turkana religion, see my *De Religie van de Turkana* (1983). The data on Turkana religion that are presented in this chapter are taken from the above-mentioned book.

2. I prefer the use of the more meaningful terms of Geertz to the more widely used emic-etic terminology. The term "emic" corresponds with Geertz's experience-near, and the term "etic" with experience-distant.

3. The word *akuj* can have additional meanings different from the six we have presented. The word is also used as synonym for sky, rain, and illness. It is also used as a qualifying word. It can mean: extraordinarily generous, extraordinarily large, extraordinarily powerful.

4. The term "source-being" has been borrowed from E. Bolaji Idowu. (1973.)

5. See van der Jagt 1989:16-18.

6. The Greek words *euche, proseuche* are normally translated by "prayer." The term *deēis* differs slightly in meaning. It is used for "urgent request," "supplication," sometimes also by "prayer."

Chapter 5

THE TRADITIONAL RELIGIOUS UNIVERSE
OF THE LUO OF KENYA: A PRELIMINARY STUDY

Aloo Osotsi Mojola

1. Introduction

At the outset it is worth noting that for the Luo as for other traditional African cultures religion is not a distinctive area of culture. In fact, in Luo culture the distinction between the sacred and the secular, the spiritual and the material, the natural and supernatural is not easy to make out.

One seeks in vain for terms or concepts in most African languages which refer to these distinctions or convey these conceptions. This is clearly the case at least among the traditional Luo. Such terms as do exist now in this regard are borrowed. E.E. Evans-Pritchard was quite right in his observation that for African religions, the "'sacred' and 'profane' are on the same level of experience, and, far from being cut off from one another, they are so closely intermingled as to be inseparable. They cannot, therefore, either for the individual or for social activities, be put in closed departments which negate each other, one of which is left on entering the other" (1965:65). Religion in this sense is pervasive and all-embracing. There is no sphere of existence that is excluded from its grasp. The presence or absence of rain, the well-being of the community, getting married, naming a child, success or failure, the place and form of one's burial among others, all come into the scope of religion. Nothing is left out.

We must not think, however, of Luo or other African traditional religions as a static reality. Religious reality, as with other realities, is dynamic and responsive to pressures and crises related to a community's survival needs. It is such pressures which act as levers of change in the religious sphere as in others. Religious reality has accordingly changed in response to the survival needs of the various historical moments in the life of the African peoples. Thus the Luo traditional religious reality as now known is not the same as that of fifty or a hundred years ago. That is not to say that the two bear no relationships whatsoever. In fact the present traditional reality is a product of the earlier traditional reality. Both are, however, products of their time and of their antecedent realities.

Hence Luo traditional religion today, while bearing a direct link to the past, has adapted itself of necessity to present realities. It has had to contend with colonial occupation as well as with the onslaught of Christianity and Western culture with its accompanying technological artifacts. In addition it has had to contend with new political realities, the formation of new identities, and interaction with the surrounding Bantu cultures and religions. We could therefore argue for the possibility of syncretism among traditional religions, not least that of the Luo of Kenya. Adherents of present day traditional religions have borrowed a lot from Christianity and/or Islam, in the same way that many practicing Christians or Muslims have retained or embraced many aspects of the traditional religions. A casual study of the new independent or African instituted churches reveals that these Christian churches, which draw heavily from the Old Testament, are also deeply rooted in traditional beliefs and practices. Indeed, there may be cases of independent churches which can no longer be called "Christian" because they have syncretised "Christ" out of their religious system!

2. Two Illustrative Cases

a)   *The S. M. Otieno Case*: Silvano Melea Otieno was a prominent lawyer who died in Nairobi on 20th December, 1986. He was a Luo from Siaya district, where his clanspeople still live. His wife, a Kikuyu by name of Virginia Edith Wambui, wanted to bury Otieno's body at Upper Matasia in Kajiado District where they owned a farm. In a controversial and unprecedented court battle which lasted several months, Otieno's kinspeople contested the right of a wife to bury her husband contrary to the beliefs and practices of her husband's people. The judge, F.C. Shields, who no doubt did not really understand African worldviews, in his judgment had argued that "S. M. Otieno was Luo by tribe, educated in Makerere and India and had a very substantial and varied legal practice in Nairobi. He married the plaintiff, a Kikuyu lady from one of Kenya's leading Kikuyu families, and numbered among his clients people of all tribes and races. He was a metropolitan and a cosmopolitan, and though he undoubtedly honored the traditions of his ancestors, it is hard to envisage such a person as subject to African customary law and in particular to the customs of a rural community" (case of S. M. Otieno 1987:6). He stated that the plaintiff, Otieno's wife, had "accordingly established a highly persuasive *prima facie* case against the defendants to obtain relief by way of injunction against the defendants to restrain them from removing the body of the deceased or taking possession of it or burying it" (ibid).

Otieno's kinspeople immediately disputed this judgment and the matter was moved to a higher court. As the judges of the higher court put it: "The question that lies at the heart of this matter is whether or not the deceased is subject to the Luo customary law" (op cit, p14). The defendants' appeal questioned judge Shields' view that: a) it is only the widow who has a right to her husband's body, completely ignoring the claim made to it by his kinspeople; b) a person's education, marriage, association and professional success are sufficient to take away his "tribal identity," and that such a person is not governed by or subject to the customary laws, traditions or culture of his people; and c) anyone who marries under the Christian marriage act automatically ceases to be governed by or to be subject to his ethnic customs or laws.

An equally important question which this case was posing was the following: in the case of a man and his wife, who is his or her next-of-kin? For judge Shields in the case of S. M. Otieno, it was obviously Otieno's wife. For Otieno's kinspeople it was not so clear. In fact Otieno's wife was not traditionally considered as next-of-kin. A key issue brought out clearly by this case was the spiritual importance of the ancestral land to the Luo community. For the land of one's ancestors provides the link with one's past and communal identity.

In this case the suggestion by Otieno's wife that her husband had expressed a wish to be buried away from his home was rejected by representatives of the clan. They held that wishes or instructions that did not comply with Luo customs could not be honored. They maintained that these customs could not be lightly flouted without serious repercussions to the community. In fact the ancestors, the "living dead," have a stake in the maintenance of these customs. They could haunt the living because of going against the customs of the community. Thus Amos Tago, one of the witnesses, stated that "It does not matter whether you are educated or not, you still have to follow these customs and beliefs to avoid ghosts haunting you or calamities befalling you." Mrs. Magdalena Akumu, Otieno's stepmother, who claimed to be a Christian, admitted that Christians recognize these customs in a symbolic way, for example, with regard to the custom of shaving hair after burial. She said: "Among Christians, only a little hair is shaved, while those who are not Christians shave a lot of their hair" (op cit p. 68). She also admitted belief in spirits and ghosts. Asked whether the ghost of her husband haunted her, she answered: "Since proper burial rites and ceremony were carried out, he will not haunt me. But if as a wife you run away, then he will haunt you."

Another witness, Mr. Johannes Mayamba, who claimed to be a Christian, admitted belief in ghost haunting, which requires a cleansing ceremony to make it disappear. He cited the case of a Mr. Ofafa, who had been haunting his kinspeople (p. 70).

A bishop of an independent church, Bishop Japheth Yahuma, in cross-examination also emphasized the belief in spirits and demons. He held that "If you have done something terribly bad, then demons will come to you" (op cit., p. 73). Such demons, he added, come as a punishment from God to people who break respected customs. Asked whether customs change from time to time, he maintained that "The world is changing, but certain customs which were given to us by God do not change" (op cit., p. 74).

Prof. Odera Oruka of the University of Nairobi, who has done research on Luo beliefs and customs, was called to give evidence in support of Otieno's kinspeople. He described a number of Luo beliefs relating to the setting up of a new home and how to tell that gods and spirits are in favor. He also described customs relating to burial. For example, he reported that if a Luo dies and his body cannot be found or given proper burial, then some object symbolizing their body has to be buried and proper ceremonies must be carried out. He pointed out that fear of spirits and ghosts reinforces those practices. Asked whether as a professor in a national university he still believes that there are spirits, he responded: "I am still looking for a reason why I should not believe in spirits" (op cit., p. 81).

It is interesting that both parties tried to appeal to the Bible to support their case. Wambui's lawyer argued that Luo customs were "primitive" and inconsistent with "civilized values," and "repugnant to justice and morality." He held that Luo rituals " . . . are un-Christian practice. They have been condemned by Christians" (op cit., p. 88). On the other hand the lawyer for Otieno's brother and his clan stated that these customs were beautiful. He argued that "Christianity is not against culture." He used the Bible to show the importance of ancestral land, citing the case of Joseph's bones being taken for burial from Egypt to Canaan. He cited the book of Ruth to show the similarity between levirate marriage customs in the Bible and in Luo tradition. It was further claimed that most of Otieno's clanspeople were Christians but respected Luo customs.

In the final judgment it was decided that Mr. Otieno's body should be buried at his ancestral home in Nyalgunga, Siaya District, after the judges decided that he was subject to Luo customary law, and that the loss was not felt by his wife only, but also by his children, stepmother, his brothers and sisters.

This case illustrates very clearly the continuing influence today of Luo traditional beliefs and customs on the present generation, even on many who claim to be Christian. It highlights the continuing beliefs in spirits, demons and ghosts, and in witchcraft generally. It demonstrates the continuing centrality of the community ethos as opposed to individualism. It underlines the conflict between the city and its values and the rural community and its values.

This case has become a classic. It received wide publicity and coverage in the Western media in such countries as West Germany, France, the United Kingdom, Canada, and the United States. In the *Washington Post* of 25th May, 1987 the report and discussion of the judgment was given nearly one and a half pages. Interestingly, the media in these countries tended to interpret this as illustrating the ugly head of tribalism in Africa, and in this case tribalistic conflict between the Kikuyu and the Luo. They were no doubt misdirected by some Kenyans who interpreted the intensity of feeling about this case as tribally motivated.

In reality, however, the issues raised by this case were more fundamental and include the following: what is the role and place of traditional world outlooks which are generally religious in a modern African state? Are traditional customs and beliefs compatible with a modern concept of law in a modern state? What are the sources and foundations of law and morality in an African state today? A recent publication, *Casebook on Kenya Customary Law*, by a leading authority, Eugene Cotran (1987), has included this important case of *Otieno vs. Ougo and Siranga* as their 88th in the book. Mr. Cotran's controversial lecture given at the University of Nairobi, in which he criticized the Kenya Court of Appeal judgment on the above case, as well as Mr. Otieno Kwach's (the Luo defense lawyer for this case) retort to Mr. Cotran's lecture, have generated much interest in this debate and some of the related issues. (Notice that the *Nairobi Law Monthly*, April, 1988 includes these lectures as well as some other discussions on this problem.)

b)   *The Omieri Case*: The Omieri case raises similar and related questions and focuses our attention on an aspect of the Luo religious universe. This case took place in mid-1987. When I was trying to locate the newspaper story that reported it, I checked the Jan-June 1987 issue of "Media News and Information - Clip Service on Religion" (available from Stic Services, Box 402, Njoro, Kenya) which supposedly collects cuttings from all stories in the local media on religion in Kenya. Interestingly enough this story of Omieri was not considered by the compiler to be of religious interest. It was only included as part of a brief letter to the Editor of the *Nation* newspaper dated June 5, 1987, in which the writer of the said letter was admonishing Luo people to stop worshiping snakes and to worship the true God.

The facts about Omieri are that a fire in some bushes in Nyakach of Nyanza province, Kenya, where a section of the Luo live, badly burnt a big python named Omieri. Subsequently the python Omieri was found by some conservationists and taken to the National Museum in Nairobi for both treatment and protection at the Snake Park of the Nairobi National Museum. The Luo people of Nyakach are said to have been extremely displeased at this and quickly demanded the return of this python. They argued that Omieri's presence in Nyakach is a good omen, and that this reptile is a harbinger of good fortune, contributing to good harvests, rains, and even the general well-being of the community. The member of parliament for Nyakach, Mr. Ojwang K'Ombudo, took this matter up with the government through a lively presentation of the case in the Kenya parliament. In spite of the unwillingness of the conservation authorities, the reptile was eventually returned to Nyakach. This contributed much to the fortunes of K'Ombudo in returning his seat to parliament in the 1988 parliamentary elections.

On January 31, 1989 the death of Omieri was reported in the front pages of the Kenya daily papers. *The Standard* reported on 31st January 1989: "The National Museums of Kenya yesterday announced a brief press statement that the controversial snake, which portends good omen to the people of Nyakach, died in Kisumu during the night of last Saturday 'after a long illness.' The statement said the deed was regrettable."

In *The Standard* of 1st February 1989 (p. 28) it was reported that "Residents of Nyakach, Kisumu District living in Nairobi were in Nairobi mourning after the death of Omieri . . . ," and that a senior elder of Nyakach in Nairobi had stated "The people of Nyakach had learnt with sorrow the untimely death of Omieri . . . Nyakach people are in mourning now following the death of Omieri. We send her husband Nyakach, condolence messages during this time."

The paper reported the local member of parliament, Mr. Ojuang K'Ombudo, as blaming the sudden death of Omieri on the defiance of the wildlife authorities to heed the village elders' call to have her repatriated to her natural home. The MP is said to have appealed for the remains of the snake to be buried in Nyakach as a show of respect to the "dead."

It is interesting to note that the officials of the National Museums of Kenya were of the view that the dead reptile should be kept at one of the museums in Kenya for historical, cultural, or touristic reasons.

The letter cited above which accuses the Luo of worshiping snakes, as well as statements following the recent death of Omieri alleging Luo snake worship, are actually based on a misunderstanding. These charges fail to appreciate the religious cosmology of the Luo, in particular the belief in spirits which possess persons, animals, plants, or inanimate objects for the good or ill of the community or some persons within it. Pythons or any of the other creatures are not worshiped but may be revered or command certain religious attitudes, depending on the spirits possessing them. Omieri the python, then, was not revered and his presence in the community desired because he was a python, but because it was believed that he was possessed by some good ancestral spirit who in concert with other good spirits guaranteed the good of the community, provided that the community in turn acted in accordance with rules and traditions handed to them by the ancestors. Since the Omieri incident other related incidents have come to the attention of the wider Kenya public through the news media!

It is necessary to at least give a description in part to the Luo traditional universe in order to place the Omieri case and some aspects of the S.M. Otieno case in their traditional religious context. Let me note, however, that the two cases illustrate well Professor Mbiti's observation that "Traditional concepts still form the essential background of many African peoples, though obviously this differs from individual to individual and from place to place. I believe, therefore, that even if the educated Africans do not subscribe to all the religious and philosophical practices and ideas . . . [of their peoples], the majority of our people with little or no formal education still hold on to their traditional corpus of beliefs and practices. Anyone familiar with village gossip cannot question this fact; and those who have eyes will also notice evidence of it in the towns and cities" (Mbiti 1969: xi-xii). It could be added that many of those who embrace new religions or different world views usually retain a belief in some of the fundamental presuppositions of their communities, especially those who have grown up or have been brought up in such communities. Ernst Wendland (this volume) is certainly right in his claim that "For many contemporary African Christians, this same dynamic core of traditional beliefs remains very much alive at the center of their thoughts and lives. The 'faith' and practice of their respective denominations may be reflected quite strongly on the outside, especially when the going is good. But when times get tough, there is a great, almost overwhelming, temptation to revert to the religious traditions of the past, to spiritism, magic, wizardry, and witchcraft in particular." This is one of the lessons illustrated in the two cases cited above.

3. A Luo Cosmology - A Brief Sketch

3.1 Some Underlying Principles and Ideas

Ernst Wendland in chapter two of this volume presents some of the fundamental principles underlying black African belief systems or world outlooks. These principles seem to be valid and applicable to the African societies I know, including the Luo society under discussion here. The first principle is the *principle of synthesis*. This principle expresses the strong tendency within African societies for unity, for community, or for inclusion. It emphasizes what is common to a set as opposed to what divides it. It is more interested in wholes than in singles. It is communalistic and holistic rather than individualistic. It is more synthetic rather than analytical.

But even though this attitude may be dominant and widespread, we must avoid the false impression that its opposite attitude is lacking. Those who take this view have been tempted to conclude that Black Africans have a primitive, prelogical, or even childlike mentality which is incapable of rational, logical or analytical thought. Nothing could be further from the truth. A dominant synthetic attitude does not preclude logical or analytical thinking within its terms. This principle explains the prevalent practice and love of togetherness, community and *ujamaa* among the Luo. (*Ujamaa* literally means "familyhood," i.e. "brotherhood/sisterhood" or "kinship," as well as "togethernesss" and "sharing." A political reinterpretation of these concepts underlying the term *ujamaa* is the basis of the Tanzanian form of socialism.) Nevertheless the Luo communities are not collectivistic in the sense of being opposed to expressions of individuality or individual achievements. On the contrary, in Luo society expressions of individuality and individual achievements are strongly encouraged and recognized by the community. In fact the Luo society encourages individuals to sing their own praises and to give themselves praise-names. Luos are fond of heroes and practice to a certain extent hero worship. This is, however, subjected to the interests and needs of the community, which are always primary. The legends surrounding such Luo heroes as Luanda Magere or Gor Mahia clearly illustrate this. (See for example Hauge 1974: 37-44).

Secondly the *principle of dynamism* expresses the hierarchy and interaction of "life-forces" within the Luo universe. This is the principle which determines the operations of the *Juok* or *Jok*. This is a central concept among Nilotic groups closely related to the Kenya Luo, such as Padhola, Alur, Acholi, Lango, Shilluk and Dinka. *Juok* is the life-force or power which sustains or makes possible various levels or types of life. Dr. A.B.C. Ocholla-Ayayo, a well-known Luo anthropologist, explains that there are three basic premises related to the concept of *Juok*, namely:

1. All living creatures as well as nonliving material, material objects, contain some forms of power.
2. Man and animals possess spirits, soul and shadow beside their physical forms.

3. The spiritual attributes of man and animals continue to exist after the decomposition of their physical shapes (1976: 170-171).

Dr. Ocholla-Ayayo adds that "sometimes the Luo identify *Juok* with the wind or the air. It is the elders of the spirits which determine human destiny. Animals, plants and various natural phenomena and objects constitute the environment in which man lives. They provide the means of human existence, and since they also have some power and spirits of their own, certain ritual relationships are found to be established with them" (ibid). Moreover in Luo communities there are various experts, sages and practitioners who have deeper understanding of *Juok* and can acquire more of these powers and manipulate or use them to varying degrees for the good or ill of the community or of individuals in it. Among these are *Ajuoga, Jabilo, Jakor* and *Jajuogi*. The whole area of so-called sorcery, witchcraft and magic is best understood as illustrating the principle of dynamism.

Thirdly, closely related to the above principle is the *principle of gradation*. Thus when Ocholla-Ayayo says that "Man is above animals because he has more supernatural power" (op. cit., p. 171) he no doubt has the gradation principle in mind. The hierarchy of power or vitality among the Luo is similiar to that of many Black African communities and is roughly like that presented by E. Wendland (page 83ff) for Central African peoples. God (*Nyasaye*) is at the top of the chain, followed by spirits, including clan spirits, ancestral spirits and the living dead (both benevolent and malevolent). Thereafter come human beings who are further graded in the same way in a community: the community leader comes first where he is recognized, and he is followed by the various religious specialists, elders, adults (with family), youth (initiated), children (with name) and infants. At the bottom of the ladder is the world of nature--animals, plants and inanimate objects or places. This principle determines degrees of honor and respect accorded to various beings according to their place within the hierarchy and according to their perceived "life-force."

Wendland's fourth principle, *communalism*, which emphasises a common life of sharing and togetherness, really follows from the first principle of synthesis and is no doubt fundamental and pervasive among African communities, including that of the Luo. The fifth *principle of experientialism* is likewise central and pervasive, and hence essential for the understanding of life and culture throughout Africa, not least among the Luo. The emphasis here is experience, participation in common activity, and free expression of emotions according to the occasion and the context. Black African experientialism has nothing in common with modern Western empiricism or positivism. It is not a closed but an open experientialism.

The sixth principle, *humanism*, places the human person in community at the center of the cosmic process. As Wendland puts it: "The world revolves around man, and thus regular ritual activity is organized, for example, either around the human cycle of existence (i.e., birth, maturation, marriage, procreation, and death), or on those occasions when people found themselves experiencing serious difficulties in life, whether social (e.g., drought, famine, plague) or personal (e.g., sickness, barrenness)" (Wendland page 103). The application of this principle is widespread among Africans, the Luos being no exception. Needless to say, African humanism is not similar to Western or modern humanism, which tends to be nonreligious, rationalistic and scientific in the materialistic sense. As has already been noted, it has religious reality at the center, i.e., "notoriously religious," to use a phrase from Mbiti (see Mbiti 1969: 1). This humanism affects the Luo person as most other Africans in their understanding of nature, phenomena or events. For example, the idea of causation tends to be given a humanistic interpretation according to which human relationships and actions provide a framework for understanding diseases, calamities, or suffering in general affecting the community.

The last principle suggested by Wendland is that of *limitation*. He interprets this as a kind of principle limiting the distribution of resources and goals in the community and also limiting and controlling competition and strife in the community, especially among close relatives. Perhaps a better way of characterising this principle would be to see it as a *principle of fairness and egalitarianism* which is to safeguard the interests of individual members in the community as well as ensuring equal access to the community's goods or resources. It is intended to ensure justice in the community. It is closely linked to the first principle of *synthesis* and to that of *communalism*. These taken together provide a framework for understanding many of the ideas underlying, for example, Nyerere's *Ujamaa socialism* in Tanzania.

Now, although the traditional Luo of Kenya are guided by this principle, they do not oppose or obstruct individual growth, wealth or influence as long as these are in the interests of the community. In other words the principle is not to be interpreted as encouraging a status quo. There is no caste system. Hard work, demonstration of personal skills, efforts and initiative are greatly encouraged in Luo society. The above principles can also be seen as illustrative of how the concepts of power and solidarity operate in African communities. Power may be seen to represent the vertical aspect of human relationships in society, while solidarity represents the horizontal aspect. Power is related to authority structures, control and manipulation of spirit forces as well as persons or communities. One's power status determines one's overall place in the social and communal hierarchy. This explains why so much emphasis is placed on power.

Solidarity on the other hand is not unrelated to power. Solidarity gives both the individual and community the identity, unity, and strength they need to face adversity and hostile forces. Solidarity in community makes individual existence possible, safeguarding it while at the same time drawing strength or power from it. Solidarity seems also to have an interest in power for purposes of the survival of the community. Eugene Nida has emphasized the role and significance of these concepts of power and solidarity. He has also correctly pointed out the value of an agnatic approach in dealing with such contrasts as wholeness and uniqueness (or community and individualism, egalitarian and hierarchical), as well as change and conservatism, in considering how these are perceived in African communities.

3.2 God and Spirits in the Luo universe

The Luo of Kenya believe in one supreme creator God, considered the source of everything, whom they refer to as *Nyasaye*. He is variously referred to as *Jachwech* (maker, moulder, creator), *Jakwath* (herder, guardian), *Were* (kind, merciful one), and *Nyakalaga* (omnipresent one). There is no doubt that many of the present Luo ideas of God are influenced or borrowed from their Bantu neighbors. It is even arguable that the name *Nyasaye* is borrowed from the same neighbors who also share in its use, as they do the other name of *Were*. Whisson (1964:3), who makes the same suggestion, may be right. It may be that originally the Luo of Kenya, like their cousins in Uganda and Sudan, shared the term *Juok* or *Jok* for the supreme being. Hauge's (1974:98) claim is partly right when he states that "if the word *Juok* or *Jok* has also been used in the past as a name of the God by the Luo of Kenya, it has lost its original meaning, although some supernatural aspects are still attached to it." Ocholla-Ayayo notes (1976:177) that "The spiritual being, *Juok*, is normally a totality of spirits, souls, shadows and ghosts. *Juok* manifests itself through a living organism, i.e., a totem or through a vision, natural phenomena, or dream." Ocholla-Ayayo also depicts *Juok* as the "infinitely oldest" of the Luo spirits. "He represents the very belief on age as the accumulation of knowledge and wisdom. He is the wisest, the one who has knowledge beyond our knowledge. He is the source of supernatural power and the one with the highest power" (ibid., p. 173).

Ocholla-Ayayo creates some confusion in giving the impression that *Juok* is on a par with *Nyasaye*. He elsewhere calls *Juok* "the supreme spiritual being" (ibid., p. 174), yet he nowhere equates or identifies the two as referring to one God. This is misleading. *Juok* may thus be taken as an alternative name for the supreme being, i.e., *Nyasaye*, which has gone into disuse as Hauge suggests, or as the principle of supernatural power or "vital-force," or simply as a name for spirit or spirits (*Juogi*, pl.) among the Luo of Kenya.

Juok as the supreme spiritual being, or *Nyasaye* as creator is detached and far removed from the everyday life of the Luo. It is evident that people pray to him/her for help and protection. On the whole, however, it is the spirits who dominate people's lives or the human life-world. This derives from the fact that *Nyasaye* is associated more with the sky. He/She may have originally been conceived of as a sky god. In contrast, the spirits have their abode among people and in the surrounding environments. Hauge has aptly observed: "Although it seems that a great many people, especially among the younger generation, have lost their faith in Nyasaye, this does not seem to be the case with the belief in the spirits of the dead. Practically all Luo people, including those who are Christian, appear to believe in the existence of these spirits" (Hauge, op. cit., pp. 111-112). Both the S.M. Otieno case and the Omieri case are examples of this strong belief in spirits.

The Luo believe in various types of spirits (*Juogi*), including natural spirits, animal spirits, clan spirits, ancestral spirits, and the living dead, both benevolent and malevolent. Natural spirits are those spirits associated with natural phenomena, e.g., spirits of animals, snakes, mountains, rivers, lakes and jungles or thunder and lightning, or objects such as boats (*juogi yie*) or rocks.

Clan spirits and ancestral spirits are really in the same category and include spirits of ancestors who are believed to have been leaders of Luo communities, clans, lineages or families. The spirits of great warriors, renowned personalities and heroes are included here.

There are also spirits of ordinary members of the community. For the Luo every person has his own spirits (*Juogi*). The good spirit is referred to as *chuny-maber*, and the bad spirit as *chuny-marach*. However, when a person dies his/her *chuny-marach* is referred to as *Tipo* or *Jachien*. This is a kind of ghost that troubles its relatives. Such a *Jachien* creates trouble either as a form of revenge of demanding his/her rights or restoring fairness or justice. Clan and ancestral spirits can indwell animals or such natural phenomena as trees, hills or rocks. Thus they could appear in the form of a snake such as Omieri, as harbingers of blessings, good harvests, rain, prosperity, or good health in the community.

In general, then, these spirits are believed to be sensitive to happenings in the human community, the good spirits striving always to promote the community good. Yet their actions are not arbitrary. They are caused by good or evil deeds, or by the manipulations of various experts.

Some Western scholars have interpreted this relationship with ancestors (or ancestral spirits) as "ancestor worship." The truth of this view obviously revolves around one's definition or understanding of the term "worship." If this can be called worship, then the Roman Catholic relationship to its saints must also be termed as "worship." In fact, this similarity between the two is so strong that one Luo independent church, the *Legio Maria*, has included Luo ancestors in its repertoire of saints through whom one can seek intercession.

Some have termed the belief in various spirits indwelling natural phenomena (including animals and reptiles) as "animism," that is, they have categorized Luo traditional religion, and all African traditional religions, as "animistic." Again, if this were granted, then the Pentecostal or some charismatic forms of Christianity could also be called "animistic" because they speak of a multitude of spirits (or demons) indwelling people, animals, reptiles or natural phenomena! It is interesting to note that some Pentecostals see the cause of some diseases or ill health, among other calamites, as due to evil spirits. Indeed, it could be argued that the strength and vitality of Pentecostal or charismatic Christianity in Africa derives from its ability to take over this cosmology. (Of course, in this framework the whole pantheon of African spirits is said to be demonic or satanic, and power to overcome or control the evil influences or effects thereof is granted through belief in Jesus and the power of the Holy Spirit!)

3.3 Experts and Powerbrokers of the Luo World

Among the Luo, individuals with knowledge of the hidden or spiritual world affecting individuals and communities, and who are able to control or manipulate the power of this hidden world, usually exercise a lot of power and influence in the community. Power in the Luo universe, then, is inextricably linked to knowledge or expertise in a given field. The degree of power or influence is proportional to its effects or use-values for the community.

The experts and powerbrokers among the traditional Luo fall broadly into two groups which need not be mutually exclusive. One group specializes in the use of what Ocholla-Ayayo calls "magico-medicine" (op. cit., p. 154) and spells. These could be positive and protective, for the good of an individual or the community, or negative and destructive, for the harm or evil of an individual or community. *Bilo* is a positive and protective charm or medicine, while *nawi* is a negative and destructive charm or medicine. These usually have a magical component, as their use is normally believed to involve "the manipulation of 'natural forces' existing in the living creatures and plants" (ibid.). Such creatures as crocodiles, leopards, snakes and certain birds are used for such purposes. Verbal spells called *Sihoho* are also used. The second group specialises in the manipulation of spirits (*Juogi*). Here again the one possessed by good *Juogi* (spirits) uses his powers for positive and protective purposes in the community, while the one possessed by bad or evil *Juogi* is essentially antisocial.

Among those whose power derives directly from the *Juogi* for the good and protection of the community is the *Ajuoga*. He may also use *bilo*, that is, positive magico-medicine. His main functions include healing the sick, divining and advising on important social events including war, and performing sacrifices or oath-taking ceremonies. He also protects the community from the influence of evil spirits or negative magico-medicine.

Jadil specializes mainly in preventing the negative influence of evil spirits on individuals. He may quieten or exorcise evil spirits and thus prevent them from causing harm or suffering or bringing calamity to an individual or community. Ocholla-Ayayo calls *Jadil* "the expert in ghosts' and demons' affairs" (op. cit., p. 164).

Both *Jasihoho* and *Jajuok* are believed to exercise their power in a negative way. The *Jasihoho* harms through the look of evil eyes. *Jasihoho*, usually female, has an evil eye which is believed to harm not only people, especially children, but also domestic animals or food. Her power comes from evil spirits which control her life. *Jajuok* also exercises his/her power in a negative way. He/she is associated more with darkness and is believed to operate mostly at night. *Jajuok* can also harm people by means of magico-medicine. It is believed that the children of these experts or power brokers of the spirit-world usually inherit their parents' powers and access to certain spirits.

Among those experts who are believed to specialize in magico-medicine spells we find *Jabilo*. *Jabilo* is greatly revered and considered as one of the foremost in hidden knowledge. *Jabilo* is believed to have extensive knowledge of plants, herbs and objects which are used for the protection of individuals and the community (*bilo*). Thus *Jabilo* uses *bilo* in a positive and constructive way to counteract evil forces. *Jasiuria* uses magico-medicine to create good relationships among people, whereas a *Jasasia* uses it to create bad relationships. An individual could be both *Jasiuria* and *Jasasia* at the same time.

Janawi and *Jamkingo*, on the other hand, practice evil magico-medicine. Both are greatly feared. *Janawi* uses *bilo* in a negative and destructive way to create harm or calamity on individuals or the community. It is believed that *Janawi* can cancel the effects of his *bilo* if necessary. *Jamkingo* also harms people through *bilo*. He or she may also use *bilo* for good. Both are believed to use verbal spells to transmit evil forces or power to the intended victims.

These then are some of the most important power brokers of the Luo universe. They may be said to exercise much influence, but they are always subject to limits and controls determined by the community. The Luo society is highly democratic, with power not centralized in any individual. Power is acquired through individual achievements, skills or supernatural gifts. At the same time every head of the family is considered a leader in the community. Age also increases one's power in the community. Age is always associated with wisdom and knowledge, and in traditional Luo society wisdom or knowledge is power. Sages are therefore highly regarded and play an important role in determining community affairs, as Professor Odera Oruka of Nairobi University's Department of Philosophy has noted. His research has been reported in *Thoughts of Traditional Kenyan Sages*, with special emphasis on the Luo community. Sages usually give advice, settle disputes and also offer sacrifices and prayers. Usually *jobilo* are considered sages if they are elderly or advanced in age. In fact most community leaders are considered sages or *jobilo* and are often thought to be both.

4. Some Implications of the Foregoing:

Failure to understand the dynamics of the Luo world has led to numerous problems, including a failure in communication by most modern institutions operating there. For example, while dicussing the concept of "ill-health" in African communities, Okot p'Bitek posed some fundamental questions, as follows:

> What is the concept of "ill-health" to the African in the countryside? The medical student ought to try to get an answer to this question. He must learn about witchcraft, about the vengeance ghost, about the cult of the ancestors. The study of African religions ought to be made compulsory at medical schools. What do you do when your patient complains of a splitting headache, and adds that he has been bewitched by his neighbors? How do you handle the case of someone who believes that it is the ghost of her mother who is troubling her? Medical students should turn their attention to the works of the diviners. Our medical schools ought not only to carry out research on the medicines used by the diviners, they must also do serious studies on the African concepts of ill-health; and the study of African religions forms the core of this work (1973, p. 88).

Okot p'Bitek's focus on the medical profession's imperative to understand the dynamics of the African traditional world could be extended to other institutions and professions, not least the Christian church. It is interesting to note that the success of the so-called independent or "African instituted" churches depends upon their adaptation to and their use of concepts, models, languages, principles and traditions of the African world. These churches have affected a continuity between the cultures and beliefs of Black Africa and the new movements. The resulting product or institution has not been viewed as foreign but has been accepted as "a place to feel at home." (See F. B. Welbourn and B. A. Ogot, 1966.) Of course, many of these churches have been accused of syncretism. In making this claim it is often forgotten that the Western Christianity brought to Africa is not pure and undiluted Christianity. A case can be made for it also being syncretistic. Its major approach whereby African cultures, beliefs and traditions were rejected as demonic and totally evil can no longer be defended. In fact, many churches and institutions are slowly learning to free themselves from this misleading idea.

Similarly a complete and uncritical acceptance of African traditional beliefs and practices can only undermine and render irrelevant the ministry of the Christian church and of any other institutions which seek to serve and ameliorate the African condition. As Osadolor Imasogie rightly observes: "In light of our contention that the African world view is charged with spiritual forces, most of which are inimical to man, the most viable starting point for the Christian theologian in Africa is a recognition of that understanding" (Imasogie 1983:79).

This observation leads Imasogie to enunciate the principle that the Christian church in Africa needs to come to "a new appreciation of the efficacy of Christ's power over evil spiritual forces" (op. cit., p. 79). This as well as its "emphasis on the role of the Holy Spirit and the present mediatory efficacy of the living Christ" is the secret of the success of Pentecostalism in Africa (op. cit., p. 81). Equally valid and extremely important is the need for the Christian church in Africa to place "a new emphasis on the omnipresence of God and the consequent sacramental nature of the universe." These guidelines of Imasogie are best understood in the context of an appreciation of the real-life cosmology of an African people such as the Luo of Kenya.

It is clear that a demythologized Christianity along the lines proposed by Bultmann cannot speak to the problems or needs of the majority of African peoples. Neither does a Westernized form of Christianity, incorporating Western world outlooks and values, including certain presuppositions about science and philosophy.

It should be borne in mind that African worldviews are in fact closer to the biblical world view than the contemporary Western secularized one which informs much of modern Western theology.

Notwithstanding this closeness between the biblical world outlook and that of traditional Africa, it must be admitted that there are still major gaps of understanding between the two. In moving from one to the other, there is always the danger of understanding the other and of interpreting symbols, images, objects and entities on the basis of the familiar. One is tempted to transpose or impose the familiar world on to the other as the basis for its understanding. The result is, of course, a distortion or a misunderstanding.

This is sadly what has happened in many African independent churches, or for that matter in many African missionary churches, or in all modern Western theologies. The fundamental problem is whether or not we can grasp the essence of Christianity, undiluted, undistorted, in its pure form. We may receive consolation in the fact that in the final analysis Christianity is not an abstract system but a living reality, a relationship with God himself and the risen Christ himself, a relationship which transforms our individual lives in community and the culture in which we live as well. Such a transformation of individual lives or of our cultures or communities is, contrary to popular opinion, not an overnight thing. It is a process which moves us closer to the heart of God and his Kingdom.

The problem of translating terms from the biblical world into the Luo language is similar. It is not clear that the biblical God is identical to the being who is the reference of *Nyasaye* or *Were*. Notwithstanding, the two have many similarities, and in spite of their differences the Luo term could easily be adopted and seen from the viewpoint of the biblical world-outlook. In other words, it could be Christianized. Alternatively the term *Nyasaye* could be taken in some Luo independent churches as identical to the Christian God, and yet be seen from the viewpoint of the Luo world outlook. This is the inherent translation problem: from which viewpoint shall we translate? How about other spiritual beings such as spirits or demons? Are these beings identical in both worlds? Are the biblical demons or spirits which Jesus cast out, or which got into pigs, the same demons or spirits as the Luo spirits, either spirits of ancestors or other natural phenomena?

How about the benevolent spirits, those opposed to evil in the traditional universe? The Bible does not speak much about them, and yet the persistence of those who have faith in them will lead them to smuggle them into their conceptions of the biblical world outlook when they become Christian! In the Luo Bible (*Muma Maler*), the term *Jachien* is consistently used to translate "demon," "evil spirit," or "ghost" whenever they occur in the Bible. In a few places, especially in Ephesians, for example in 2.2 & 6.12, the word *chuny* is used for the evil spirits or powers. The problem is whether the biblical understanding of evil spirits is identical with the Luo one, or whether this usage tempts the Luo reader to understand the biblical world on the basis of his cultural understanding of spirits, i.e., of *Jachien* or *Chuny*, or of *Juogi*, generally. It is interesting to note, however, that for the Holy Spirit a borrowed word *Roho* is used. *Roho* is normally used in Swahili in the same way, instead of the indigenous Swahili word *moyo*. *Roho* is of Arabic or Semitic origin. It is a cognate of the Hebrew *ruach*. The use of this borrowed term suggests that the translators of both the Swahili and Luo Bibles sensed a problem in using the indigenous Swahili and Luo terms. This, however, has not solved the problem, for the Swahili term is simply understood on the basis of the equivalent Luo term with all its associations! More rethinking is called for in this area.

It should, however, be borne in mind that this is not just a translational problem but an existential one as well. Christian scholars need to grapple with these problems continually. They need to point the way toward what F. Eboussi Boulaga calls "Christianity without Fetishes" (see Boulaga 1984).

Bibliography

Atieno-Odhiambo, E.S. Some Aspects of Religiosity: The Boat Among the Luo of Uyoma." In *Journal of East African Historical Association*, Nairobi, 1973.

———, and D.W. Cohen. *Siaya: The Historical Anthropology of an African Landscape*. Nairobi: Heinemann Educational Books, 1989.

Banton M., ed. *Anthropological Approaches to the Study of Religion*. London: Tavistock Publications, 1966.

Boulaga, F.E. *Christianity Without Fetishes*. New York: Orbis Books, 1984.

Cotran, E. *Casebook on Kenya Customary Law*. Nairobi: Nairobi University Press, 1987.

Evans-Pritchard, E.E. *Theories of Primitive Religion*, London: Oxford University Press, 1965.

Geertz, Clifford. "Religion as a Cultural System." In M. Banton, ed. *Anthropological Approaches to the Study of Religion*. London: Tavistock Publications, 1966.

Hauge, H-E. *Luo Religion and Folklore*. Oslo/Bergen: Scandinavian University Books, 1974.

Imasogie, O. *Guidelines for Christian Theology in Africa*. Accra: Africa Christian Press, 1983.

King, Noel. *African Cosmos: An Introduction to Religion in Africa*. Belmont, CA: Wadsworth Publishing Co. 1986.

Malo, S. *Sigendni Luo Maduogo Chuny*. Nairobi: Eagle Press, 1951.

BIBLIOGRAPHY

Malo, S. & William G. *Luo Customary Law*. Nairobi: Government Printer, 1961.

Mbiti, John S. *African Religions and Philosophy*. Nairobi: Heinemann Educational Books, 1969.

Mboya, Paul. *Luo-Kitgi gi Timbegi*. Kisumu, Kenya: Anyange Press, 1938, 1983.

Mugambi, J & Kirima, N. *The African Religious Heritage*. Nairobi: Oxford University Press, 1976.

The Nairobi Law Monthly, April 1988, "The S. M. Otieno Burial Saga Debate Rages."

News Media and Information - Clip Service on Religion. Stic Services, Box 402, NJORO, Kenya.

Nida, Eugene A. and Jan de Waard. *From one Language to Another*. Atlanta: Thomas Nelson, 1987.

————. *Religion Across Cultures*, New York: Harper and Row, 1968.

Ocholla-Ayayo, A.B.C. *Traditional Ideology and Ethnics among the Southern Luo*, Uppsala: Scandinavian Institute of African Studies, 1976.

Ogot, B.A. *History of the Southern Luo*. London: Heinemann, 1967.

Oguda, L. *So They Say: The Luo Folklore*. Nairobi: East African Publishing House, 1967.

Ogutu, G.E.M. & Scharlemann R.P., ed. *God in Language*. New York: Paragon House Publishers, 1987.

Ojwang', J.B. and J. Mugambi, eds. *The S.M. Otieno Case—Death and Burial in Modern Kenya*. Nairobi: Nairobi University Press, 1989.

173

BIBLIOGRAPHY

Ominde, S.H. *The Luo Girl from Infancy to Marriage*. London: Macmillan, 1952.

Otieno S.M.: Kenya's Unique Burial Saga, Nairobi: A Nation Newspapers Publication, 1987.

P'Bitek, Okot. *Religion of the Central Luo*. Nairobi: East African Literature Bureau, 1971.

————. *Africa's Cultural Revolution*. Nairobi: Macmillan, 1973.

Ray, Benjamin. *African Religions: Symbol, Ritual, and Community*. Englewood Cliffs, NJ: Prentice-Hall, Inc., 1976.

Robertson, Roland, ed. *Sociology of Religion: Selected Readings*, Hammondsworth, Middlessex U.K: Penguin Books, 1969.

Welbourn, F.B. & Ogot, B.A. *A Place to Feel at Home*, Oxford/Nairobi: Oxford University Press, 1966.

Whisson, M. G. *Change and Challenge: A Study of Social and Economic changes among the Kenya Luo*. Nairobi: Christian Council Kenya, 1964.

Zahan, Dominique. *The Religion, Spirituality and Thought of Traditional Africa*. (Translated from the French by Kate Ezra & Lawrence M. Martin). Chicago & London: University of Chicago Press, 1979.

(NB: I acknowledge with thanks valuable critical remarks on an earlier version of this paper by Drs. Eugene Nida and Ernst Wendland.)

Chapter 6

THE RELIGIOUS WORLD OF THE GODIÉ WITH A VIEW TO BIBLE TRANSLATION.[1]

Lynell Marchese Zogbo

This chapter looks at the religious world-view of the Godié, a Kru group living in Southwest Ivory Coast. Though they number no more than 20,000, their way of life and their world-view is similar to that of many thousands of Kru peoples[2] living in Ivory Coast and Liberia.

Who are the Godié?

The Godié live deep in the forest region, approximately 30 miles north of the port of Sassandra. They practice slash and burn agriculture, raising mainly rice, cassava, and various vegetables. Protein in the diet comes from hunting and fishing; cash crops include coffee, cocoa, and palm nuts. The Godié live in rectangular mud houses, covered with woven palm leaves called *papoo*, but they spend most of their day either in the fields, doing various chores outside in the courtyard, or resting and chatting in groups under the trees. The kitchen unit is a short distance from the house and usually contains a small "attic," where dried foods, especially rice, are kept.

Like all Kru peoples, the Godié live within a small clan system, differing from the neighboring Akan-type organization with a king and well-structured hierarchy. Neither are they like their Gur or Mande neighbors to the north and west, with their well-defined social classes. Though they presently have "chiefs," this system is nonindigenous (the word for "chief" is either *kífí*, coming from British "chief," or *séfʋ*, coming from French *chef*). Villagers are governed by elders, who are sometimes designated with special tasks. For example, *dʋdʋkʌnyɔ* (ground-have-person) sees that land is equitably distributed. In general, however, all decisions are arrived at by consensus in lengthy town meetings, and thus it could be said the Godié practice a form of democracy.

Elders participate in a system of village justice, gathering in a circle to hear accusations and the defense, all transmitted by an intermediary *porte-parole*. Crimes such as adultery and theft result in the imposition of fines to be paid in cloth, livestock, and/or money. In the past, serious crimes such as murder could result in a person being banished or sold into slavery. A person suspected of the worst crime, sorcery, was subjected to a horrible ordeal, being forced to drink poison sasswood to determine guilt or innocence. Today the most serious crimes are handled by local government authorities.

The Godié are patrilineal and exogamous, with most of their wives coming from neighboring Kru groups (Dida, Bete, Neyo). Though a dowry system used to exist, the present system is quite informal. Usually a third party (often the bridegroom's friend) accompanies the future husband to make the arrangements. The virginity of the bride is not a prerequisite; indeed, if she has one or two children, it speaks in favor of her fertility. Following the marriage there is a surprising amount of sexual liberty. Adultery is defined, almost Biblically, as taking another man's wife. But in such cases the man is simply reprimanded and fined, while the woman receives little more than a warning.

Tradition and language are passed on by the male members of the community, along with their nonmarried or divorced sisters (the *ylʊ́kwàlʉ̀*), who have considerable influence on village affairs. Wives and mothers are always "strangers" (usually speaking a very closely related language). They return to their own region periodically for rest, and definitively in the case of marital difficulties.[3] In normal circumstances, however, they remain in the village of their husbands, even when they are widowed.

Rites of passage are few and far between. Compared to many other peoples, birth and marriage are rather uneventful. Unlike peoples to the north and west, there is no initiation, and seemingly no secret society.[4] Godié males are not circumcised, and are considered "children" until they are at least thirty. Life is a continuous flow, only interrupted by death. And it is this event that inspires no small amount of ritual, ceremony, social gatherings, and public demonstration.

By nature, the Godié are warm and open. They value generosity and cleanliness, and consider a good name more important than any riches. A "big man" (i.e., one who is to be respected) usually has many children (and possibly many wives), but his greatest asset is his name, obtained through heroic or good actions. Traditionally status comes with age and wisdom, and though contact with the West has brought in secondary values of wealth, job status, and education, in day-to-day village life, age is the most important measure of authority. Even women, who as noted come from the outside, have a very high status by virtue of their age, especially if they qualify as the "first wife."[5] Despite the status of age and name, however, the good of the community is more important than the good of any individual. (See Wendland, this volume, for a broader description of the notion of community in Africa.) The goal of the individual is not to excel personally, but rather to contribute to the welfare of the community and, in particular, to one's immediate or extended family. Indeed, anyone who succeeds too quickly is suspected of sorcery. Even a good luck streak in fishing is not to be publicized. The rule of thumb is to not rock the boat.

While contact with Europeans began as early as the 15th century with the arrival of Portuguese and Dutch ships, Christianity as such has had only a limited impact in the area. There may have been some contact with the itinerant African preacher, the Prophet Harris, who traveled the coast in the early 1900s and prophesied that whites would eventually arrive with God's word. Roman Catholics and Methodists may have had a few converts in the area, but overwhelmingly, traditional religion has dominated for centuries.

With the possible exception of those who have moved to cities and internalized a lifestyle which has much in common with the West, the Godié represent an oral-based culture. The transmission of knowledge is done through their rich literary genres--songs, proverbs, folktales, histories, and procedural discourses ("how-to" narratives). Indeed, while literacy in French is growing, attempts at rendering the Godié (and most Kru peoples, for that matter) literate in their own mother tongue have for the most part been unfruitful. What is striking about the Godié is this: masks are nonexistent, and art work is limited to the carvings on drums and a few drawings on house walls. The treasure of the Godié is the *word*, which entertains, informs, reprimands, and guides in all areas of life.

Religious Beliefs and Practices

There appear to be four important participants in the world of the Godié: *Laagɔ* 'God,' *zlⁱ* 'divinities' or 'spirits,' *kuə* 'spirits of the dead,' and human beings. As is emphasized in all the studies in this volume, there is no dividing line between spiritual and human entities; the combination of all these elements constitutes reality.

1. *Laagɔ*

As in most West African belief systems, Godié religion takes as given the presence of an all-powerful creator God. He is known as *Laagɔ* or *Laagɔ Tɛpɛ*

(*Laagɔ* being the "big name" and *Tɛpɛ* being the "little name"). Though the word *Laagɔ* is homophonous with the word for "sky," [6] there is no sense in which he is considered a sky god. He is clearly a supreme being whom no one has seen. He has created and ordered the world and is higher than any human or spiritual being. Though he is personally distant, his omnipresence and omniscience are unquestioned.

Neighboring Kru languages to the east also refer to God as *Laagɔ*, and with the exception of one language, the name is always homophonous with the word for "sky." In Western Kru, however, God is known as *Nyɛsʋa* (or some variant), which, according to contemporary thinking, derives from *nyɔ sʋa* 'person old' (Jlarue, Sayon, and Tisher, personal communication). Thus these groups identify God with a first being or ancestor. Holas, in a detailed study of the Kru (1980:223 ff.), however, believes the term *nyɛsʋa* and its Kru variant *gwɛ nyɛsʋa* come from *gunyɔ sʋa* 'sorceror old,' and suggests that the identification in the West of *nyɛsʋa* as "Supreme God" is a recent innovation, replacing a former supreme deity. Given the linguistic conservatism of the east and the transparency of the components of *nyɛsʋa*, it is highly likely then, that *laagɔ* is the older of the two terms and probably represents the unknown supreme deity Holas speculates about (p. 225).

Laagɔ is a prominent character in Godié folktales, which either teach how the world as we know it came into being or give certain lessons of moral value to the community. Though these folktales are recognized as being humanly created for amusement and edification, they nevertheless present a certain image of *Laagɔ*'s character. *Laagɔ* of the folktales is all-powerful and a righter of wrong, but also at times a kind of trickster who can himself be duped![7] For example, in one folktale, thanks to the way *Laagɔ* established the seasons, a person who has been wronged is able to carry out his revenge (in this case, trapping the one who "stole" [committed adultery with] his wife). But in another folktale, a human who has a supernatural birth dupes God by stealing his wife! *Laagɔ* intends to kill the man, but when he sees him, he is struck by his handsome face and bright shining smile. "I could have killed you," he says, "but you are so handsome, PRRRR! (ideophone for "bright"), you will be the moon!" While in this tale *Laagɔ* seems somewhat merciful, in yet another he seems downright mean! He tricks Woodpecker into believing that if he knocks down enough trees, he will win the hand of his daughter. Poor Woodpecker! Every time he finishes one bunch of trees, *Laagɔ* gives him more work. To this day Woodpecker is still there trying to complete his task!

While it is doubtful that any Godié takes these tales as gospel truth, the folktales do reveal *Laagɔ* to be master of the universe, the one who gives each animal his nature, the one who puts natural cycles in motion, and the one who assures that moral order is upheld in the world. His way of weaving in and out of every kind of story (be it fiction or fact) underlines how unquestioned his existence is in the traditional Godié mind.

But despite this frequent reference to *Laagɔ*, in everyday dealings people have to do, not with *Laagɔ*, but with a host of other beings which populate their world. Most importantly these include *zlĭ*, spirits which inhabit rivers, trees, ponds, and rocks, and *kuə*, spirits of the departed. *Laagɔ* is inaccessible, impersonal, too great to be approached.[8]

2. *ZlĬ*

ZlĬ, or as they are often translated into French, "genies," are spiritual beings who readily enter into contact with humans. These spirits or divinities are in no way related to the spirits of the ancestors (discussed below), nor are they named or ranked in a hierarchy, as in some West African cultures (Yoruba, for example). They are ambivalent creatures, who can grant happiness, yet at the same time are responsible for any amount of pain and suffering. They must be worshiped (*bubɔ* 'adore'), sometimes at regular intervals (once a month or once a year), and periodicially when some disaster strikes.

There appear to be many different kinds of spirits such as a spirit of the river and spirit of the forest. To ensure, for example, that fish will be plentiful, the spirit of the river must be worshiped. All the villagers, including children, will go to the river's edge. A sacrifice is usually made by slitting the throat of an animal such as a chicken. This action is accompanied by an informal prayer, which might have the following form:

> Divinities of our ancestors,
> Me, our fathers left me here.
> Me, XX (name of the person), me, I'm talking.
> Divinities of the spirits of the dead,
> Where we have come to worship,

The river we have come to worship,
We haven't been able to get any fish.
That's why we have come to worship,
So you (singular) will give us fish.

The woman fix food, everyone eats, and this is followed by singing special songs (ɓuɓulu), and dancing, accompanied by tamtams. Following these ceremonies, if the spirit is pleased, the request will be granted.

If disaster strikes, divinities must also be appealed to (ɓiɓie 'begged') and sacrifices made. For example, if someone disappears after having gone fishing, it is assumed that the spirits have killed him and are holding his body. The relatives of the missing person will go to the people who own that part of the land where the man disappeared. They will take a chicken and ask the spirits to release the body. The chicken is thrown into the river with its feet tied. If it sinks to the bottom, drowning, the zlī have accepted the sacrifice, and the dead person's body will surface and be returned to his people for burial. But if the chicken breaks loose, the sacrifice has been rejected, and the dead man's body will stay with the spirits.

These bush and river spirits also trick people by transforming themselves into animals or human beings. It is commonly believed, for example, that a deformed child is probably a spirit trying to trick people. Thus the newborn will be left in the bush overnight. If the child is still there in the morning, the child is human. If the child is gone, it was a spirit. (People hiding in the bushes to watch what happens report seeing the child turn into a snake, which slithers away.)

Twins are also considered spirits, and so they must be worshiped, whether dead or alive.[9] The worshiping place is usually right in the courtyard where the twins live. They may be represented by two stones (or in the case of triplets, three stones), or there may simply be an altar (poyuə) next to the house. This altar consists of a miniature fence about one foot tall, made of bamboo sticks. The fence forms a little circle, and often there is a small tree growing in the center. In front of the altar are two offering bowls. Eggs, rice (both white and "red" [mixed with palm oil]), along with palm wine, will be offered each month when the moon is full. This worship must be carried out so that the "soul" (zuzu, see below) of the twins will "become strong."

Spirits may confront human beings in a physical form, surfacing up in the water or appearing in the deep forest. Much speculation surrounds the nature of their physical appearance. One description goes like this:

ZɪI are very tall and thin, with hair down to their waist. But instead of flowing down the back, the hair flows over the face. When attempting to see, the *zɪI* sweeps his hair back on each side over his shoulder. The feet of *zɪI* are huge, with the heel extending far back (as long as the foot extends forward). When they point a finger, it lights up and shows the way in the forest.[10]

What is the relationship between *Laagɔ* and *zɪI*? Obviously *Laagɔ* as creator of all things is more powerful than *zɪI*. But there is an incredible fluidity in the Godié world, so much so that at times it is difficult to define any boundaries between one entity and another. *Laagɔ* is the ultimate source of everything, so as one person put it, "If you worship (*bʋbɔ*) a spirit, you are worshiping (*bʋbɔ*) God. When you go to worship the spirits, you use the name of God."[11] But if this fluidity extends upward, from the *zɪI* to God, it also extends downward through humans, into the animal kingdom, and the world of nature. Thus, in a text explaining how one goes about retrieving a body from the river (mentioned above), the speaker appears to mix references, one moment saying it is the river who killed the man, the next, saying it is the spirits. He then goes on to make the following statement:

. . . but if you fall in the river, the thing that is there in the river, it's that which will grab you. It's that we call '*zɪI*.' A crocodile, it's a spirit. A river animal, it's a spirit. At this time, inside the river, things that do battle, they are many. Those that are spirits, it's these you will bow your head to (i.e., beg for the return of the body).

This interpenetration of what we would call the supernatural and the earthly is one of the main characteristics of the Godié worldview. This fluidity between entities is also applicable in the domain of the spirits of the dead.

3. *Kuə*

The word *kuə* or *kudukuə* designates those individuals who have died but who still participate in the Godié world. (The term "living dead" used elsewhere in this volume is thus very appropriate here.) *Kuə* live in *kudukú* ("dead village on"), a kind of neutral resting place for all deceased. The New Testament concept of hell, with its suffering and the separation of the "bad" from the "good," is not applicable. Rather *kudukú* seems similar to Sheol of the ancient Hebrews.

Kuə are greatly feared because of their thirst for vengeance. People are very careful not to provoke their anger. For example, when someone dies and is buried, very personal items such as a pipe, a belt, or a hat will be laid on top of the grave, for fear that the spirit of the dead will come back to attack the person who tries to assume possession of these articles.

Kuə are especially feared if there is reason to believe that they have been wronged before their death. If this is the case, then they must be begged (*ɓiɓie*), much like the divinities or spirits are, so that they will not take out their revenge on the living. A case in point involves a young man who became seriously ill four months after his father died. He was, in fact, near death himself. He was visited by concerned parties who asked him to confess his wrongdoing towards his father (since the causal link between the father's death and the young man's sickness was obvious to all). The son promptly confessed that he had insulted his father shortly before his death. It was now the duty of the oldest member of the family (in this case, the dead man's younger brother) to appeal to the spirit of the dead father for the life of the son. The uncle went to the tomb, spoke to the spirit, acknowledging the guilt of the son, making a sacrifice (typically a white cloth, palm wine, a chicken or a sheep), and "spitting water." This latter action, accompanied by the word *kifia* (meaning unknown), is an integral part of any confession, be it to the *kuə* or to another human being. Following these rituals and a treatment of Western medicine, this young man eventually recovered.

But dealings with *kuə* are much more complicated when sorcery is suspected to be the cause of death. In past times (the practice is presently outlawed) the fingernails and hair of the deceased would be taken and tied in a piece of cloth onto bamboo poles. These poles would be carried on the shoulders of two men. The spirit of the dead would be invited to indicate his killer. Thus he would "take hold" of the men and the poles, pushing them to the place where the killer was hiding. This person would then be tried for sorcery, and the spirit of the dead would be appeased.

This interaction with the spirits of the dead goes on today, but in varying forms. Often the wishes of the *kuə* are made known through dreams. The *kuə* may appear to a family member and request a certain ritual, so that no harm will come to the family. Dreams may also play a role in indicating who is responsible for a death. In one case a girl of twelve fell ill, went into a coma, and died within the space of three days. Her mother reported that before she went into the coma, she had a dream in which a certain man was forcing her to eat meat. This could mean only one thing: it was the man who killed the girl through sorcery. The man denied the story, but approached the dead body, placed a knife in the girl's hand, and licked her forehead, challenging her to come back to kill him if he were the murderer. Months later, when the man came down with an undefined disease that left him almost crippled, the community's mind was made up: the man had indeed killed her, and the girl had taken her revenge. (Years later the man recovered.)

Kuə manifest themselves in other ways as well. Sometimes they come back to be reborn into their own extended family. Every so often a child will be born who is troublesome, crying and fussing continually. If all efforts at comforting the child fail, people may begin to wonder if this isn't a father or mother who has recently passed away. The child will be renamed with the deceased's name. If the child quiets down, it is clear that the deceased has returned in the form of this child.

Kuə also hide out in fields which are usually quite a distance from the village. There they may appear as ghosts, scaring people and keeping them from working. A complicated ceremony ensues whereby a palm branch is placed over the tomb and then taken to the place of appearance. There will be singing and the tapping of tamtams. The person holding the palm branch will be possessed: *ku kù-ɔ kú* (spirit-of-the-dead is-him on) and the person will tremble, *badu ɔ bɛɛ*. When the ceremony is over, the living dead will no longer bother the living!

What is perhaps difficult for the outsider to understand is how the person who has been loved and respected in his or her lifetime can suddenly turn into a vengeful spirit of the dead, seeking to harm even those closest to him in this life. The explanation may lie in the notion that no death is natural; therefore every living dead must be actively seeking to avenge his or her death.

4. Human Beings

We have seen in the preceding discussions that within the spirit world there are no dividing lines separating the physical and the spiritual. As we turn to the fourth participant in the Godié world, the human being, the same is true. Each living human has a nonphysical component, called his *zuzu* (translated as "spirit," "soul," or "shadow"), which is believed to be on his back. When a person dreams, his *zuzu* leaves the body and is said to be "far away." People are not usually conscious of the *zuzu*, since feeling, thoughts, and will are seated in the heart (*plɛ*). Despite this, moral qualities may be attributed to the *zuzu* of a person: *nầa zuzù nyu kpanyι* (your spirit evil/ugly much) or *zuzu nyonyu kʊ̀ ɔ mɥ́* (spirit ugly is him inside), both meaning the person is bad.

Another element is also identified as the spirit or soul of a person, but this *wɥ́gʌ* (possibly a composed word coming from *wlɥ́* 'head') differs from *zuzu* in that it seems to incorporate some notion of fate. According to the elders, people "carry" (*ɓɛɛ*) or "have" (*kʌ̀*) a "soul" (*wɥ́gʌ*) in "heaven" (*Laagɔdu* 'God's village'). This soul determines what work you will have on this earth. The Godié say that each man has his own road (*bɔlɔ*), and if you find your road, you will succeed in life. But if your *wɥ́gʌ* "isn't right with things," you will try and try, but not succeed. Some souls are destined to "know paper," some to go to France. Others are just *bɪ-bɪ-wugʌ* (walk around- walk around-souls), not knowing their place in life. This belief must account, in part, for a certain passive resignation which dominates the Godié world-view. As one speaker noted:

> All my friends, I went to school with them, and now they have work. That's how it is, and I won't be going to work. My *wɥ́gʌ*, it's what accounts for this.

Interestingly, the *wɥ́gʌ* probably had some kind of supernatural power before birth and possibly through the first months of life:

> When you learn to speak, you can no longer *see clearly* [emphasis mine]. You see only the world. But you don't see the *kuduku* (spirits of the dead) any more. You don't see men's *zɪzɪ* (spirits/souls) any more. At that time, *your eyes are broken. . ..* This is us: we, the men of this earth down below who suffer.

It's as if this man regrets losing the supernatural knowledge and power he had *prior* to his own birth.

However, certain human beings (male and female) are endowed with strong supernatural powers, be they good or evil. These people include the *sʌ-nι-nyɔ* (clear-see-person), translated into French as *clairvoyant*, and the *gu-nyɔ* (sickness person), translated as *sorcier* or "sorcerer."[12] Because of their supernatural power, both individuals are feared. Evans-Pritchard (1937:387), among others, noted a similar distinction among the Azande of Southern Sudan. A sorcerer "uses the technique of magic and derives his power from medicines," while the witch (corresponding to the Godié "clairvoyant") "acts without rites and spells and uses hereditary psycho-psychical powers to attain his ends."

The *sa-ni-nyɔ* can do evil or kill a person (especially if attacked) but his primary role is to save a person (*puə* 'save,' 'heal,' 'make whole'). He is an incredible asset to the community because he can discern the cause of sickness or misfortune; he can ward off evil by prescribing certain sacrifices before the evil occurs; he can discern what medicines can make a person well.

The *gunyɔ*, on the other hand, does not save; he only kills. He "takes his *zuzu* to do evil things." *Gunyɔ* is the most feared of all men, and at times he may not even be aware of the evil he is carrying out (as his *zuzu* may carry him away at night to kill and destroy). This is why people are reluctant to deny an accusation of sorcery, because they could have done an act without even being aware of it.

The word *gu-nyɔ* is a compound coming from the word *gu* 'sickness' and *nyɔ* 'person.' Like the word *gwʌsʉ* 'medicine,' the word *gu* is ambiguous. It can refer to a simple sickness such as malaria, or a real curse or sorcerer's spell. Likewise, the word *gwʌsʉ* 'medicine,' can refer to simple medicine, like malaria tablets, or to supernatural medicine which can either save or kill a person. *Gunyɔ* only use their *gwʌsʉ* for evil, however, and in almost every death or misfortune, a sorcerer or a spirit of the dead is suspected of causing the "unnatural event."

Beside these special categories of people is the everyday layman. Unlike Western religions, where religious thoughts and practices are set off for a special day in the week or a certain time in the day, the Godié religious mind-set permeates every waking moment. Someone who is neither a clairvoyant nor a sorcerer may readily enter into contact with the *zĺi* or the *kuə*, as was the case with the uncle who begged for the life of his nephew. A layman can protect his own fields by the placement of magical elements (*ɔ pu ɔ́ di*, he protects his field).

If someone dies and rain is threatening to spoil the funeral, the maternal aunt of the person who died has the ability to chase away the rain by circling the village and throwing ashes in the air. In one case, a woman cursed (*ɓʉti*) the village because the proper customs were not followed when her brother died. The entire town was in an uproar, and people were sent to beg this woman to undo her curse. Examples are unending of how ordinary people interact on a daily basis with the spirit world.

There is obviously a repetitive pattern characterizing these dealings. Divinities, spirits of the dead, and people who have put curses on others, are "begged" (ɓiɓie, African French: *pardonner*) to not carry out vengeance. Likewise the role of *oral confession* is paramount, as seen with the dealings with the kuə. People will confess to incredible crimes to ensure that some greater evil does not befall them. In one case an old woman died of tetanus as a result of receiving an injection with an unsterile needle. When the spirit of the dead revealed that her younger brother had killed her through sorcery, the man readily confessed and became mysteriously ill, being unable to walk on one leg. Though the man was assured that he had not killed his sister (and that a sickness from the ground had), the man did not improve. One day, however, he sacrificed a chicken (on the advice of a fetisher) and began to walk within hours.[13]

Confession also takes place when there is a misunderstanding between two people. Each one will orally present the reasons for the offense. The two will then "spill water" (nyu-nə-sʌ-lɩ 'water-mouth-spill-nominalizer'), each one taking a small amount of water into the mouth and spitting it. This ritual marks their reconciliation.

It has been mentioned that Godié society does not have striking rites of passage, but there is one event that supersedes all others: the Godié funeral. The Godié are a demonstrative and very vocal people. The news of a death, usually passed from mouth to mouth, is received with great emotion. People wail, weep, tear off their outer clothing, and sometimes throw themselves to the ground. They cover themselves with mud and will often fast for one or several days. Death in Godié country hits hard--emotionally (which is inevitable) but also economically. People come from miles around to participate in the funeral, and these must receive food and lodging. And, unless the death is somehow tainted (suicide, death through childbirth, etc), the funeral lasts four weeks in the case of a man, and three weeks in the case of a woman. [14] The extreme importance of the funeral and participation in it cannot be stressed enough. All work in the fields stops. People living in cities leave their jobs and travel long distances to attend. There is no activity in the whole realm of Godié experience that demands as much energy, as much money, and as much self-sacrifice as that given over to death.

5. Syncretism

Even in areas where one would think Christianity has never reached, traces of some Christian contact or influence can be seen. This is true not only among the Godié but in all Kru cultures. In Godié country this contact has resulted, not in the formation of independent Christian churches, as in many other African contexts, but in the subtle adaptation of traditional religion. Indigenous religious movements, surging up and slowly dying out, spread far and wide in the whole Kru domain.

An important case in point for the Godié is the religion called "Lalou," whose influence was extremely strong from the 1950s through the early 1970s. A Godié woman named Marie Lalou, having had some contact with Catholics, came back to her region and experienced a series of revelations in the forest. As is typically the case in such indigenous movements, the person is imbued with power stronger than any other power existing in the region. She could divine and break the power of any other person in her presence. The woman has died, but her movement remains, an incredible mixture of traditional religion with symbols borrowed from Christianity. Adherents meet frequently, responding to the sound of a bell (also used in traditional Godié dance). They wear black on Fridays, the day of Christ's death, and white on Sunday, the day of his resurrection. They circle the town singing, and go to their place of worship. Despite overt symbols--crosses and even a Godié version of a confessional--what remains of the Lalou religion is anything but Christian. One message included an explanation of why trees in the forest periodically fall on people and kill them (say, during a severe storm). The reason is this: evil men killed Christ by nailing him to a tree. Because of the tree's participation in this crime, God is angry with trees. To get back at people for involving them in such a sin, trees kill people when they can! Along with the teaching of such "truths," prayers and practices which have nothing to do with Chrisitianity are carried out. In their worship, adherents pray for protection for themselves and for destructive forces to be released on their enemies. If a supposed evildoer has some calamity come into his life (sickness, loss of possessions or family, or even loss of his own life), if there is not rejoicing, there is at least a very strong reaction of relief and satisfaction. This theme of enemies getting what they deserve permeates the Godié culture, surfacing not only in Lalou, but in proverbs, songs, and especially in an unlimited number of folktales.

Another example coming from just outside the Godié region illustrates again to what extent Christianity is at the service of traditional religion. In Dida country, a certain preacher named Jeannot has made a name for himself, gathering many followers who travel hundreds of miles to consult him. Jeannot's power is not his own. His older brother died unjustly, was buried, and evidently rose from the dead (when they looked in his grave, he was not there). Later the power of this brother came upon Jeannot, enabling him to divine, to determine when people had been the object of sorcery, to cure mental and physical illness, and to put protective spells on people (no one can harm the protected person, and anyone trying to do so will die himself!). All this is done in the name of the older brother. Quite predictably, Kru peoples from all around (Godié, Dida, Bete) are flocking to the area to benefit from the man's gifts.

The syncretist movement by definition takes over the terms and practices indigenous to the region. Thus, to take Lalou as an example, practices find a direct parallel in Godié culture. If Lalou "grabs" or possesses someone (like the divinities or the spirits of the dead), the person must publicly confess to his wrongdoing. The Lalou prophet (like the eldest member of the family) "begs" (ɓiɓie) that the offender will not suffer the consequences of his actions. And, of course, adherents of Lalou feel it is God, Laagɔ, who oversees and condones all their actions.

It is against this backdrop--the physical, the cultural, and the religious life-- that the Bible translator must work.

Translation Problems

The person translating the Bible into Godié meets a biblical world that is not altogether foreign to him. The world-views of the biblical Hebrew and the Godié are somewhat similar. Religion is not *part* of life; it *is* life. It touches on every moment, every event. It is meant to explain all.

Certain cultural notions found in the Old Testament are quite understandable in the Godié context. The notions of community, if not identical, are remarkably similar. Mourning practices have points in common. Sacrificing, be it grain, drink, or animal, and, in the distant past, perhaps even human,[15] is so well known in Godié culture that the Old Testament sacrifices and, to some extent, even the sacrificial death of Christ, have a sounding board certainly not found in any Western minds.[16] Memories of warring times easily provide vocabulary for alliance or convenant and reconciliation, as well as imagery quite close to that found in the Bible.

Another meeting ground is the incredible force of the oral word--in creation, in blessing, in cursing, in promising, in confessing. The concept of the name, as an expression of greatness, as an almost causative agent ("in the name of") finds a near perfect match. Indeed, things like demon possession or messages from the beyond, which we only read about in books like the Bible, find an approximative expression in everyday life among the Godié.

On the other hand, the problems the translator faces are considerable. How can one superimpose a different vision and organization, as it were, of supernatural powers and beings on one that is already a living reality in the Godié mind? What particular problems does a translator face as he goes about translating the New or Old Testament for such a group?

1. The Term for God

As we have seen, there is no other word for "God" except *Laagɔ*, and his personal name *Laagɔ Tɛpɛ*. There are certain aspects of *Laagɔ*'s character which coincide with the Judeo-Christian God: his omnipotence, his ultimate separation from all other beings, his role in creating and sustaining everything in this world, and his role in judgment (i.e., seeing that wrongdoers are punished for what they have done).

On the other hand, it is the character of God in folktales that makes the translator a little uneasy; the God of the Bible is not a trickster, nor a liar, nor can he be duped. Furthermore, *Laagɔ*'s anthropomorphic family (his wife and children) are a far cry from the anthropomorphic figures in the Bible that center around God's love (through images involving marriage and parenting). These misgivings, however, can be put aside, given the fact that these are popular notions, often not taken seriously at all. Folktales are true to the extent that *they teach us moral values*; they do not present truth from a historical point of view.

There are two more important problems, however. The first has to do with the *psychological distance* which exists between *Laagɔ* and his creatures. *Laagɔ* is not the "God of the Godié" in the same way that Yahweh is the God of the Hebrews. He is God of the created world--seen and unseen. Though he is depicted as interacting with humans, it does not seem his main purpose or role to do so. But this distance between *Laagɔ* and man should not keep us from using the name *Laagɔ* for God. The message of the Bible is that God has entered into a relationship with man, first through the convenant and later through Christ. And this message is always new, whether it is first heard by a Godié (who feels God is far away and not willing to interact with man) or by a person from any other culture (who may even have doubts about the existence of God).

The second problem comes as a result of *Laagɔ*'s seeming involvement with beings that are sometimes clearly evil. Thus, is it possible that Godiés believe *Laagɔ condones* the acts of the divinities and spirits of the dead? Is Holas' description of the Grebo situation, where there is a basic supposition of "l'existence d'une seule source divine d'où émanent toutes les autres substances transcendantes" (1980:199, 200), applicable to the Godié case as well? If so, is God so intertwined with these beings (by creating them and allowing them to exist) that his own good nature is questioned? This crucial question needs to be examined more closely. It is perhaps worth noting, however, that even in the Scriptures, the exact relationship between God and Satan is touched upon only briefly, and the eternal question "If God is so good, why is there evil?" is still left unanswered even in the minds of many believers.

Despite these obvious problems, in all cases I know, translators in Kru languages have been unanimous in conserving the term *Laagɔ* in the east and *Nyɛsoa* in the west, with no modification. People know *Laagɔ* is the unique creator God, and no appeal to an outside or foreign name could ever be acceptable, as occurs in some places in East Africa. (See van der Jagt, this volume.) Certainly, adopting *Allah* would be the surest way of alienating all Godié, since they have resisted Islam for centuries. Nor can *Laagɔ*'s name be qualified in any adjectival way. (Indeed in some West African languages, adding a qualifier such as "mighty" to God's name diminishes rather than increases the notion of his greatness and power.[17]) The best solution in this case has been to accept that the traditional notion of God does not coincide exactly with the biblical perspective and usage, but to hope that through the translation itself the real nature of this *Laagɔ*, who is so distant and impersonal, will eventually be known.

Speaking of God as father is quite natural and even culturally-based. Thus, to refer to God as *a tʉ Laagɔ Tɛpɛ* ('our father' *Laagɔ Tɛpɛ*) or *a bʌ Laagɔ* ("our father God," a vocative) is quite natural, while "my father" would be quite shocking, implying an exclusive claim on him on the part of the speaker. The intimate *Bʌbʌ* 'Daddy' or 'Grampa,' is also to be excluded on grounds of inappropriateness. What is virtually impossible to express, it would seem, is the unpossessed notion "*the* Father," a form the use of which is often attributed to Christ in the New Testament. Thus, John 10:15 "just as *the* father knows me, so I know *the* father" can only be translated as: "Just as *our* father *Laagɔ* knows me, so I know him." As noted above, adjectival phrases--already quite rare in everyday speech--are unacceptable as modifiers of *Laagɔ*. Descriptive relative clauses are greatly preferred. Thus, while one would never say **glïglï Laagɔ* (*great great God), one can express the notion with a sentence or relative clause: *ʋ̀ glï kpanyι* 'he (who) is very great.'

There is no problem in expressing "Lord," since several expressions are available. *a kʌmʌnyɔ* (our command-person) is one possibility, but an even better expression is *a kʌnyɔ* (our have/possess-person). This term, meaning "our owner," is used to designate the person who has responsibility to care for a person. In consequence, the person cared for is to respect and obey his *kʌnyɔ*. The term is used in various situations; for example, when a stranger comes to town and is given over to a specific household for care, the *kʌnyɔ* will see to his needs but will also protect and advise him. Likewise if someone needs to send his or her child to another town, he or she will put the child in the care of an overseer (*kʌnyɔ*). Most Kru languages readily use this term to mean "Lord."

As is the case with "Father," *kʌnyɔ* is always possessed, thus usually "our Lord" and not "*the* Lord."

2. The Terms for Spirit

It is perhaps surprising that translating the Greek words for "spirit" (as in Holy Spirit, *pneuma hagion*, and "evil spirit," *daimon*) would be so difficult in a culture where the supernatural invades everyday life so frequently. The difficulty lies, not in the lack of terms, but in the mismatch between the spirit world as it is known in the Bible and the spirit world of Godié culture.

2.1 Holy Spirit

To begin the search for the term for Holy Spirit, the first question is how to render the word for "spirit." If the Greek New Testament term *pneuma* has as a primary definition "supernatural beings, often impersonal, which indwell or inhabit certain places, including rivers, streams, mountains, caves, animals, and people" (Louw and Nida, 1988:141), then we are led directly to the Godié term *zlï*. But as we have seen, this term is totally unfitting for use with "Holy Spirit" since *zlï*, while sometimes good to humans, are equally evil, killing and bringing disease and misfortune. Even if we try to qualify the word with an adjective like "good" or "pure," we still arrive at a being less than God, who demands sacrifice. Anteposing the word "God," as in *Laagɔ zlï*, ("the genie of God"), really adds nothing to the term, since, of course, all genies belong to God (he has power over them). Likewise, any reference to *kuə* 'spirits of the dead,' would be inappropriate, as the Holy Spirit is not someone who has lived and died, and who continues to live on in the world of the dead.

The solution, in this case, comes from a term used to refer to the "inner nonmaterial" of a person (Loewen, 1986), in this case *zuzu* (translated alternatively as "soul," "spirit" or "shadow"). What facilitates the use of this word is the fact that every living person has a *zuzu*, and this *zuzu* can be mobile, as when a person dreams. Thus, even though Godié people do not think of God as having a *zuzu*, it is something that can be easily grasped, on analogy with the makeup of a human being. Secondly, the feature of mobility is advantageous, since the Spirit moves, descends, is sent. What is disadvantageous is that *zuzu* is, in a sense, impersonal. As we noted earlier, a person does not communicate directly with his *zuzu*, but reasons, wills, and decides in his *plɛ* 'heart.' However, this latter term is not satisfactory, since *plɛ* is only *part* of a person, not the essence of a person. *ɓuɓulɩ* 'thought,' and *wugʌ* 'soul,' are also inappropriate, the first because it is very abstract, and the second because its semantic range goes too far into the domain of "fate." Thus, for a supernatural being, "Holy Spirit," we are left with a term with human rather than divine reference.

If the term for spirit seems satisfactory, what should its qualifier be? The word for "holy" is especially difficult to render, because the Kru peoples do not always have an exact term to express "set apart" or "consecrated." In Godié there are usually two words that share some of the semantic range of "holy." One means "taboo," referring to things one does not touch, eat, or use. This word has mainly negative connotations and as such does not qualify as a good equivalent for "holy." On the other hand, there is a wider term *kplɔkplɔ*, literally "clean," and sometimes "pure." Its range is really too broad, since it can refer to clean dishes or clothes, as well as to clean in a more figurative sense. A final possibility that has been considered is *wɔlɔ* 'washed,' which is used currently in a religious sense (purified). But this term gives the connotation that something was once defiled and now is clean or purified. This last connotation excludes the possibility of its use in reference to the Holy Spirit. Thus the best solution that has been found in most Kru languages is the broader term *Zuzu kplɔkplɔ* (spirit clean/pure), or alternatively, *Laagɔ Zuzu*, "soul" or "spirit" of God. This latter term is perhaps the best expression, since it informs the hearer/reader that God, by way of analogy, has a spirit. It implies that this spirit is in some sense equal with and representative of God in the same way that man's spirit is his nonphysical essence. This expression only succeeds, however, inasmuch as the hearer/reader understands the purity and set-apartness of God himself.

2.2 Evil Spirit

In a first translation attempt, translators thought an appropriate term for evil spirit would be *zuzu nyonyu*, a somewhat literal translation meaning (spirit evil). The word *nyonyu* has a very wide semantic range, describing both physical and moral evil, thus, "ugly," "evil," and even "sinful." However, recent investigations have shown that this term may not be appropriate. The problem lies in the fact that moral qualities may be attributed to a person's *zuzu*. Thus, in describing a bad person someone may say *zuzu nyonyu ɔ kʌ* (spirit bad he has). This expression may also refer to an internal state of an individual, rather than implying that this is a state derived from the presence of a foreign entity.

Nevertheless we have seen that something close to the biblical concept of demon possession does exist in the Godié culture; it is said that a divinity or a spirit of the dead may "grab" or "fall upon" a person, causing the person to tremble, to talk in a strange voice, etc. It is obvious that the use of *kuə* 'spirit of the dead,' is excluded, because there is nothing in the biblical account allowing us to believe that evil spirits are spirits of the vengeful dead.

The other possibility would be to try to use the word *zlï* 'divinity.' But, as we have seen, these spirits appear to be ambivalent; they do both good and evil. It may be that qualifying the word, *zlï nyɛnyʌ* 'divinity evil,' will prove to be a solution. Even though all such spirits are greatly feared, there is a sense in which some are considered good and some evil.[18]

But before accepting such a term, we must pose a very important question: in adopting such a translation, are we zeroing in on a basic fear of the Godié, and thus through the Bible narrative showing how Jesus has power over these beings? Or, are we inadvertently confirming the world-view of the Godié, presupposing that there are good and bad spirits? (See Mojola, this volume, who raises a similar issue.) The answer to this question demands much thought, and testing is probably required to determine which of the two expressions, *zuzu nyonyu* or *zlï nyɛnyʌ* is the *least* misleading.

2.3 Spirit of Elijah

In places where *pneuma* has a more figurative meaning, as in Luke 1:17, the translator must move with caution. The text reads "He will go before him in the spirit and power of Elijah." If the verse is translated too literally, it will read something like "the *zuzu* and power of Elijah will be upon him." However, in the Godié (or any Kru) context, this is very likely to be interpreted as meaning that the spirit of a dead person, Elijah, will grab hold of a living person, John. This would mean that John would be in some kind of a trance, possessed by Elijah, in conformity to what actually happens in Godié culture. In this case, then, it is important to specify that it is *God's spirit*, the same that was on Elijah, which will come on John.

3. Angel

In earlier translation attempts, "angel" has also been rendered by qualifying the word *zuzu*: *Laagɔ zizi* ("God's spirits"). However, if *Laagɔ zuzu* is to be used for Holy Spirit, it is imperative to find another term for angels, since angels are not coequal with the Holy Spirit. Further, as we have seen, *zuzu* is an integral part of the person possessing it. Thus it seems inappropriate as a term to indicate beings lower than God, i.e., his creatures. An easy solution is to go for a more functional rendering: "God send-send-person" (the person element is not restricted to humans, since the same suffix is used for Lord and Savior). This messenger would be distinct from "prophet," the latter not just being sent by God, but serving as his *porte-parole* or spokesperson (*Laagɔ-nə-kʋ-ki-nyɔ* 'God-mouth-on-speak-person').

4. Devil

This term already exists in the language as a borrowing from English, *dɛvʉlv*. The fact that the borrowing is in English and not in French shows that it is quite old (since the British had contact with the Godié long before the French). Therefore, though in traditional Godié thinking there is no one being who is the chief of evil (God alone is over all beings, good, bad, or neutral), this term has become an integral part of the Godié language and its meaning is widely understood.

Conclusion

In conclusion, it is perhaps necessary to address a question raised by Wendland. Given the world-view of the community, how will they interpret its message?

There are at least two important issues. The first is: how can we encode the Biblical message so that it is taken as indicating reality and not fable? To demonstrate the problem, I include a personal anecdote. Having made friends with an elderly woman who had leprosy, I decided to practice my Godié and share some of the biblical message by telling her stories about Jesus. I came with a beautifully but simply illustrated booklet, and slowly turning the pages, told her the story of Jesus calming the storm. My friend was delighted, and she responded—not as I expected—with a question like "Who is this Jesus?" Rather, she began to tell me an elaborate tale of magical doings. The point is this: the miraculous is so common in Godié culture--talk of healings, stopping storms, and even resurrections--that the biblical message seems almost "watered down." Even with a faithful and dynamic translation, how is the *uniqueness* of the biblical account made to bear on a culture where anything is seemingly possible?

This leads to a second issue. If the miraculous stories concerning Jesus' life are not the most convincing evidence for Christianity, then what is? In studying the culture, it would seem that there are few areas in the New Testament which would immediately challenge the present belief system, thus revealing who Jesus really is and allowing people to make up their own minds concerning him. It seems to me (as Wendland notes) that we must insist on the *direct access* to Laagɔ, "God," made possible by Jesus Christ. In the case of the Godié, this would mean indicating that man does evil (a known) and is responsible to God for that evil (an unknown), and that Christ's sacrificial death is the only way to be made completely clean (an unknown but readily understandable idea in this cultural context). Secondly, this sacrifice is once and for all, and the victory of Christ proves that he is above every principality and spiritual being in high places (that is, above the terribly feared *zlï* and *kuə*[19]). It seems that it is the themes presented by Paul and the author of Hebrews that speak to the heart of the Godié belief system.

In light of these facts, it is clear that the translator, project coordinator, and to some extent, the consultant, must come to grips with the inner workings of the belief system, not only to translate correctly, but also to judge what Scripture portions will have the most effect, both as a help to the church and as a challenge to the nonbeliever. In the Godié case (and perhaps for many Kru languages), the most effective portion of Scripture to be published initially is perhaps not Mark, usually the first choice because of its easy reading style, but a selection of passages which speak to the needs of the community.[20] Indeed, it may be more effective to publish portions in a format something like "Who is Jesus?" which, while giving some details of Jesus' life, could concentrate on his *unique*, contribution, i.e., the reconciliation between God and man.

Bibliography

Alter, Robert. 1983. *The Art of Biblical Narrative*. New York: Basic Books.

Evans-Pritchard, Edward E. 1937. *Witchcraft, Oracles, and Magic Among the Azande*. London: Oxford University Press.

Greenberg, Joseph. 1966. *The Languages of Africa*. Bloomington, IN: Indiana University Press.

Hill, Harriet. ms. "Witchcraft."

Holas, Bernard. 1980. *Traditions Krou*. Poitiers: Editions Fernand Nathan.

van der Jagt, Krijn. This volume.

Loewen, Jacob A. 1986. "The translation of holy in Monkole: Solving a problem." In *The Bible Translator*. 37:2, 222-227.

Louw, Johannes P. and Eugene A. Nida, eds. 1988. *Greek-English Lexicon of the New Testament: Based on Semantic Domains*, 2 vols. New York: United Bible Societies.

Marchese, Lynell. 1979. *Atlas linguistiuqe des langues kru: essai de typologie*. Linguistique africaine 73. Abidjan: Institut de Linguistique Appliquee.

Mojola, Aloo O. This volume.

Noss, Philip. 1981. "The oral story and Bible translation." *The Bible Translator*. 32:3, 301-318.

Scott, Anna. 1858. *Day Dawn in Africa or Progress of the port Epis. Mission at Cape Palmas, West Africa*. New York: Protestant Episcopal Society for the Promotion of Evangelical Knowledge.

UBS, *Who is Jesus?*

Wendland, Ernst R. This volume.

Zogbo, Lynell Marchese. 1989. "The Kru Languages." In *The Niger-Congo Languages*. Lanham: University Press of America, Inc.

Notes

1. Information in this study comes primarily from personal interviews with Godié (in French or Godié) over a period of years, most intensively from 1972-75, and more recently in 1989. I am especially grateful to Zadi Sassi Michel for sharing his thoughts, beliefs and friendship. I benefited greatly from the input of my colleague Carol Gratrix Brinneman. Thanks also to Margaret Bohoussou, Harriet Hill, Phil Noss, Krijn van der Jagt, Ernst Wendland and Georges Zogbo for helpful discussions and comments on this paper.

2. The Kru group is defined linguistically as those people speaking Kru languages. Kru belongs to the Niger-Kordofanian language family, which groups most of the languages of sub-Saharan Africa. While it was once believed to be part of the large Kwa group to the East (Greenberg, 1966; Holas, 1980), this now seems doubtful. There is some evidence they may be more related to the Gur or Voltaic peoples to the north, but this is not universally accepted (see Zogbo, 1989). The family is subdivided into Eastern and Western Kru. Godié is an Eastern Kru language with nine dialects.

3. Contrary to Western expectations, Godié women enjoy a certain degree of autonomy. They work their own crops and have their own money. When a marriage becomes difficult, a woman just packs up her things and returns to her parents. It is left to the husband to follow her and beg for her return.

4. To my knowledge there are presently no secret societies attested in Godié or any Eastern Kru group. Holas (1980) states there are no secret societies among the Kru, but Scott (1858) noted at least one secret society in the related Grebo culture. In surrounding non-Kru groups, secret societies (including the powerful *polo*) abound, and they have apparently influenced some Western groups, including the Wobe and the Krahn.

5. While polygamy has been standard practice in the past--with economic considerations being the only limit on the number of wives taken--in more recent times it is common to have only one or two wives, the first being taken

during youth, and the second taken in old age. This custom ensures that children will continue to be born to the male when the female is too old to have offspring. It also provides the male with a sexual partner, since it is commonly believed that marital relations after menopause will lead to a fatal illness in the female.

6. *Laagɔ* also has a third meaning in both Godié and related Bete: "religion" or "denomination." This is obviously a recent semantic shift to account for the numerous cults which wax and wane in the Kru area.

7. Holas paints a similar though not identical picture of *Nyesʋa*. He is "essentially amoral, uniting numerous virtues and faults. He is an authoritarian father, respected, sometimes hated and only rarely loved" (1980:224; translation Zogbo).

8. It is clear that this is the dominant attitude throughout the Kru area. Scott, one of the first missionaries to the Grebo people in Liberia, notes:

> The Greboes have, it is true, a vague idea of a one Supreme Being, whom they call Nyesoa, and who, as they believe, is the creator of all things, but they offer him no sacrifices, and pay him no homage; on the contrary, they are continually making propitiary offerings to inferior spirits. (1858:68).

9. The practice of worshiping twins is also carried out by the Neyos, to the south, but not by the Betes, a very closely related Kru group to the northwest. This may indicate that this is not an original Kru custom but rather a borrowed one (perhaps coming from the neighboring Akan).

10. Remarkably, this description furnished to me in 1975 by Dapleu Joseph coincides with a Tepo Kru description of Hodio, a hero of oral tradition (Holas, 1980: 162). He likewise is covered with hair, the beard and eyelashes going to the waist and hair going to the ankles. Apparently hairy creatures are a feature of Bete folklore as well. These kinds of descriptions are not limited to divinities. To listen to story tellers, there are a multitude of beings that normal human eyes cannot see: dragons breathing fire in the forest, whole villages of little people on the river bottom, and "mammy-water" (mermaids) in the ocean.

11. This same kind of mixing is also attested in the Tepo complex and in the Klao culture. In Klao, even if one is worshiping a cotton silk tree or an ant hill, one will call the name of *Nyɛsoa* four times and make one's request (*Kumeh* 'personal communication'). Likewise, concerning the Tepo complex, Holas notes (1980:206):

> Il arrive couramment, . . . que le nom de *Nleswa* soit mêlé à ceux d'autres divinités, invoquées au même titre et sans discrimination . . .

12. A third kind of person who deals with the spirit world is the "fetisheur" *slʌkʌsʌnyɔ* (sacrifice take-up person), who apparently comes from outside the Godié region, usually from the northern peoples. Our understanding of this person's role in Godié society is limited and will not be treated here.

13. This story and the one concerning the man suspected of killing the 12 year old girl do not come from hearsay. I knew all the people intimately (including the two deceased) and report the events as I observed them.

14. These numbers (four for a man and three for a woman) are highly significant in Godié culture. Some suggest that combined they add up to seven, the "perfect" number. It is interesting to note that in the Klao culture, when a place is being worshiped, *Nyɛsoa* is called four times (the number of man).

15. What may be memories of human sacrifice are carried through some oral traditions. It is said, for example, that when an alliance was made between the Godié and the Dida, a young woman was sacrificed and cut in two, one part being buried in one territory, one part being buried in the other. This was to be the last blood shed between the two peoples.

16. It is difficult to know if the Godié idea of sacrifice really involves appeasement (as in the case of the Hebrew scapegoat, and later, Christ's death). Froelich (1964: 25, quoted in Holas), notes the following:

> La notion de sacrifice s'appuie sur la croyance en l'existence d'une force vitale particulièrement concentrée dans le sang des hommes et des

NOTES

animaux: par l'effusion de sang, le sacrifice *fortifie* (emphasis mine) le dieu, qui, à son tour, fortifie l'homme.

This idea of "making strong" has been observed in some of our discussions (concerning twins in the section on divinities). Scott (1858:58) notes that in the Grebo community the village priest "*feeds* . . . the public greegres and idols . . . with rice and oil every new moon." This belief has not yet been sufficiently researched to draw any conclusions.

17. This is true of Ditamari and Bariba, Gur languages spoken in Benin.

18. One person noted that people only worship good divinities and not evil ones.

19. It is not the job of the translator or project coordinator to determine if in fact the supernatural beings spoken of in the culture exist or not. The biblical message is that Christ is Lord over all powers, thus freeing people from fear. The message that *denies* a culture's world-view is not speaking to the culture but against it.

20. Though it is far from the desired goal, it is very often the case that the Gospel of Mark is the only piece of Scripture that is published and distributed before the New Testament is available (4-7 years).

Chapter 7

WOODEN SPEARS AND BROKEN POTTERY: SYMBOLS OF GBAYA FAITH

Philip A. Noss

Introduction

The Gbaya people who today live in Cameroon have experienced great changes in their way of life and in their belief system, not only during the eras of colonialism and independence, but far back into the past as well.

Changes continue to occur as the ways of the grandfathers become ever more distant and as new faiths increasingly dominate Gbaya life. But the old continues to influence the new, for as the ancestors said, "The new mat is woven over the old."

In the context of the Gbaya Christian church today, an important question is what elements of the old faith continue to speak to the Gbaya psyche? The wooden spears and broken pottery were once meaningful symbols--what do they mean to the Gbaya today?

The Gbaya in History

The Gbaya people who inhabit the central and eastern regions of the modern state of Cameroon reflect the history of migration and movement that has characterized Africa as far into the past as history can be traced.

Moving out of central Africa across the gallery forests and the savannas that lie between the rain forests of the Congo Basin to the south and the mountain ranges of the Adamawa Plateau to the north and east, the Gbaya encountered other peoples who were undergoing their own expansions, flights and migrations.

Established before their arrival around what is now Meiganga, Ngaoundere and Tibati, they found the Mbum, Adamawa peoples who themselves had moved down from the north and west at an earlier date. To the southeast were the Yaangere, an Ubangian people, who had conducted raids out of the forest as far as the southeasternmost extension of the Mbum. To the west was open land perhaps vacated under pressure of war and famine, and to the southwest the Bantoid Tikar and Mambiloid Vute (cf. Mohammadou 1979; 1986).

During the period that the Gbaya were establishing settlements on both sides of the eastern border of present-day Cameroon, Hausa and Kanuri traders were plying trade routes from the Sahel Regions of today's northern Nigeria into central Africa as far as the Congo River (Burnham 1981). Following the early trade, the Jihad or Holy War of Usman dan Fodio took place establishing the Fulbe in a position of political power at the expense of the Mbum and other Adamawa and Chadic peoples of the mountains and plateaus of eastern Nigeria and northern Cameroon (see Mohammadou 1978). Hausa merchants not only continued to sell their wares but also to teach the tenets of Islam and the language of the Qur'an.

Although one might wish to look back into the past in search of a traditional way of life that was static and coherent and uncontaminated, it is evident from the most cursory glance at what little is known of the history of Central Africa that a people such as the Gbaya has not existed in isolation. Their present-day spread from inside Nigeria to the borders of Sudan and into northern Zaire where they are known as the Ngbaka is indicative of the wide range of influences that have played on their life and thought.

The migration of the Gbaya, which was caused in part by the pressure of other movements throughout central Africa north of the Congo River, was most immediately motivated by their search for better hunting grounds and for new farm lands, for their livelihood depended on game and crops (cf. Burnham et al. 1986). They were semi-sedentary, hunting and gathering what they could from the land, and migrating to where plentiful game and empty lands beckoned.

Their life also depended on community. They were an acephalous people whose most important unifying social structure was the clan, who were ready to break up a village when disease took too deadly a toll, or when family quarrels made cohesive and constructive communal life no longer possible. Nowhere in their remembered past had their forefathers established centralized power structures either in the form of hierarchical political institutions or large population centers.

Thus, in the latter half of the nineteenth century, the Gbaya settled in the areas of Cameroon where they are today becoming increasingly urbanized, necessarily relying less and less on the fruits of hunting and gathering and more on the benefits of cash crops and salaried jobs. As the way of gaining a livelihood changes, the expression of faith which undergirds life is also undergoing change. It may be that the faith itself is changing.

The Faith of the Gbaya Fathers[1]

The Gbaya very early believed that there were beings or forces that shared their world, that were more powerful than they were, and that influenced and even determined their well-being. Perhaps this was due to the temporariness of their dwelling in any one setting, perhaps it was due to the people around them whom they saw also in movement, itinerant traders, bands of warriors seeking slaves, or the people whose abandoned pipe bowls they found in the stream beds of the land they came to occupy. Perhaps their belief was due to the unpredictability of fortune, good fortune in the hunt, or misfortune, for the hunt could indeed be *Dangá*[2] "spoiled, ruined," or to the same unpredictability in the village, for through illness or disease the village could *yáí* "fall apart."[3] Perhaps it was simply an instinctive awareness deep within the human spirit.

The Gbaya grandfathers spoke of something they called *so* and they seemed to distinguish two categories, one referring to a being for whom "So" was the name, the other referring to a class of beings that were identified with natural geographic phenomena and with the dead ancestors (see Tessmann 1937:1; Hilberth 1962:67-68).

The Ancients also spoke of someone named Gbaso, and they recounted tales of when Gbaso possessed sesame seeds which he refused to share with humankind until the Trickster, Wanto, pretending to help him sow his fields, stole some grains and thus gave the Gbaya their first seeds to plant. Gbaso also possessed and withheld the earth's water, keeping it dammed up and hidden for his own use alone, until again Wanto tricked him, discovered the dam, and pulled loose the central timber, letting the water gush forth into all the valleys, where it continues to flow for the Gbaya to use to this very day.

Both the German scholar Günter Tessmann (1934, 1937) and the Swedish missionary Jean Hilberth (1962) suggest that Gbaso may have been the Supreme God. However, other tales depict Gbaso as a monster, a dangerous and destructive creature who may be found in the darkness of the gallery forest or on hot and waterless plains. Although the Gbaya would hunt for game in the valleys and on the plains, and would cross streams and barren wasteland to reach a distant destination, neither place was deemed fit for human habitation. From his location outside human society, Gbaso would prey upon little girls who might be camping or women who had gone fishing, demanding their food and sometimes taking their lives.

Perhaps the tales seek to portray a capricious God whose ways are beyond knowing, whose will cannot be fathomed. In any case, instead of a God who created the world and all that is in it, Gbaso, whose very name "Great God" incorporates a pejorative adjective specifying something that is unnaturally huge and extraordinary, is seen as the mortal enemy of humankind. Wanto is at his heroic best when he is shown victorious over his adversary.

Tradition, which told of the *Gbo-ndaá-wesé* "the Come out of the East People," the first ancestors who were thought to have come from the East, also spoke of a *Só-e-wí* "God/Spirit put person," a God to whom humankind owed its beginning. This God was said to be a good God, for a Creator God could not be other than good. And yet, all was not good in the world that the Gbaya knew. There was life given by the Creator, but there was the very constant reality of death as well.

One account recorded by Tessmann suggests that God intended for the Gbaya to die and rise again (1937:7-8), but Chameleon, who was to bear the message of resurrection, was very slow in bringing the answer from God to the one who had sent him. The inquirer became impatient and sent Toad to ask God what was humankind's fate, and God gave the second answer, that when a person died, that was the end. Toad, a creature greatly detested by the Gbaya, hopped back with the message of death, passing the beautiful but slow Chameleon on the way. Even though Chameleon eventually arrived bearing his message of life, it was too late. Death does indeed exist, and with it illness, hunger, strife, and everything that threatens to destroy humankind and human society.

As the Gbaya traveled in their search for game or to find peace from the troubles of their last habitation, they sought to ensure that the new place would grant them what they were seeking. Tradition as memory recounts it, offered no rites to Gbaso. Nor was there a specific cult to the Creator God. If Gbaso had once been the Supreme God, he was no longer seen to be so, and he surely was not approachable by human beings. If *Só-e-wí* was the Creator God, he likewise seemed to be distant and not directly accessible to human beings for their daily bread.

There must be other powers in the land who controlled it and who might be willing for the newcomers to share in its riches. These were the *só-kao* "spirits of the land" to whom the Gbaya performed ritual prayers before establishing a new village, before hunting in new territory, each year to ensure continued peace and prosperity for the community, and at those times when calamity struck the community.[4]

The *só-kao* were thought to inhabit or at least to be associated with prominent features of nature. Whatever was nearest the proposed site of the new village, or whatever was most prominent where the hunt was to take place, there the community went to pray, whether it was the entire village, or an outing of however few hunters it might be.

The ritual might vary in detail, but it was essentially the same whenever it was performed. When it preceded the founding of a village, the father of the family that was establishing its new home would approach *Só-kao* to ask for health and good fortune in their new environment in a rite called *Dáfá-Só-kao* "worshipping the Spirit of the land."[5]

After the village had been established, the ceremony would occur annually, usually at the beginning of the dry season. The initiative for carrying out the ceremony came from the village chief, who called his people together to remind them of their good fortune during the past year, asking them when the ceremony had last been performed. In answering that it was at the beginning of the last dry season, they affirmed that the time had come for the prayers to be repeated. Then, setting the day and the time for the next ceremony, they would select one of the village elders to lead the people.

On the day of the ceremony, the appointed priest would proceed first, followed by the drummer and the ringer of the gong, the chief, and lastly the people of the village. When they arrived at the site that had been selected beforehand as the place of worship, the priest would first take off his clothes. Next he would turn to the men and ask them to hand him the wooden spears that they had cut. Gathering them in his arms carefully lest any fall to the ground, he would lay them at the foot of the shrine. He would then turn to the women and ask them to hand him the gifts they had brought. He would make a fire and cook the three eggs that the chief had offered, using the potsherds on which the women had brought fire.[6] He would mix cassava flour with water, making a paste that he would spread together with bits of egg on large leaves that had been laid out before the shrine. He would mix more flour with water, command that all lie flat on the ground, then lying on the ground himself, he would pray:

> *Só-kao*, we prayed to you last year and you gave us health, you gave us food; *kao* of the Bute and of the Mbum, give us food, help us this year again.

After the prayer, he would pour the flour-water libation over the wooden spears and over the shrine, and then all would process in reverse order back to the village. As the drum and the gong beat in honor of the chief, the women ululated, and all returned home for the beginning of the new dry season, hopeful that it would bring peace and health and many successful hunts.

When tragedy had befallen the village, the chief might also call for the rite to be performed to placate *Só-kao*. Instead of offering eggs, a chicken would be sacrificed or even a sheep.

If the rite was to prepare for a hunt, it might be performed by a father in the company of his sons. The following account was given by Reverend André Yadji, who remembered hunting with his father:[7]

> My father took his machete and went to the foot of a tree; he cleared around the foot of the tree and said we should each break a stick and hold the sticks in our hands; then we would put them at the foot of the tree before setting our traps and snares. All five of us broke sticks in our hands, and he sat at the foot of the tree and took them from us. He put them together at the foot of the tree, with some food, and said,
>
> > *Kao*, I come to you today, I come to get food for the children to eat. I set these things before you, everything, *So* at the foot of the trees, *So* beside the hills, *So* of our weapons, bless what we are going to do.
>
> Then when he had said that, he set the things there. When we went back to the house, it was he who took the first bite of food. Then he said, "Okay, children, now eat!" When we had eaten, he said, "Children, let's take our crossbows and go chase monkeys!"

When the hunt had been successful, it was also appropriate to remember *Só-kao* with gratitude. Those who had killed animals on a hunt that had been preceded by the ceremony to *Só-kao* gave either the liver or the heart to the one who had performed the rite. Taking this offering to the shrine and giving thanks, he would leave the meat for *Só-kao* and return home (Christensen 1984:154-55).

In the event of other significant answers to prayer, thanksgiving was also called for. The beneficiary of *Só-kao*'s goodness gave a chicken to an elder whom he asked to kill and clean and roast without plucking the feathers. When it was cooked, "the elder dips the tip of a *sore* branch into the chicken fat/oil, and anoints the healed person with the chicken fat" (Christensen 1984:155).[8] The chicken meat was then shared among the village children, being careful not to break any of the chicken's bones. The person giving the chicken as a thank offering ate none of the meat himself.

The rite addressed to the Spirit of the land thus opened with recognition of gratitude for past blessings, and included general requests for the good of the community. In the instance of illness and before a hunt, specific requests for alleviation of suffering or for success in the venture ahead were made. Finally, the rite concluded with thanksgiving for the blessings received in answer to the people's prayer.[9]

Gbaya Symbols and their Meanings

The rite of worshipping *Só-kao* may be described in its totality in the various contexts wherein it was performed. It was an event that united the community in a communal act of offering and petition (cf Wilson 1959). But the whole was comprised of many separate elements, all of which were of symbolic importance in their own right. The significance of each element lay in the fact that it spoke to a meaning that was greater than itself.

In an analysis of the ritual performance, we may speak of a variety of symbols. There were the obvious symbolic objects or articles, but there was also symbolism of space, place, time, participants, action, gestures, words, numbers, colors, shapes, and even quality.[10]

The symbols may all be identified in terms of meaning, but their meaning extends beyond a simple one-to-one correlation of object and representation. Eliade speaks of "multi-valency" (1988:5), and such is the nature of the Gbaya symbols. They occur not only in this rite and not only with the meaning that seems paramount in this context. As they are employed or occur within this specific ritual, they point to a larger and deeper level of meaning, at once objective and universal.

The performance of the event began with a person. In the description given above, it began with the chief of the village. On the hunt it began with the father, or the hunter who had marked out a section of land for a communal hunt. The role of the leader in each of the social structures represented is evident. Each is a caretaker responsible for the safety and security of those for whom he is responsible, the chief for the inhabitants of the village, the father for the sons hunting with him, or the lead hunter for his companions.

There may be a further relationship in that the chief of the village may be the father of the family, or the elder of the clan, for early Gbaya village structure was based on the family and the clan (cf Burnham 1980:4ff). Thus family and political structure were inherently interlinked. Responsibility before *Só-kao* provided a focal point for the two levels of social obligation. One of the rhythms beaten on the drums reminded the chief that the people were in his hand, that they looked to him for all good things. The person of the chief in the ritual represented the mutual dependence of the various ranks of society and of humankind.

Time of day, morning or evening, was determined according to practical considerations, but the time of year was significant. The beginning of the dry season represented the turning point in the annual cycle of Gbaya life. This was the time when people's attention turned from farming to hunting, from the often individual labor-intensive tasks of clearing land and planting crops to the more free time of year when the larder was full and the weather permitted long forays into the bush. With the drying of the savanna grass, the land could be burned off, depriving the animals of coverage and exposing them to the weapons of the hunters.

The chief was the first central participant in the rite, but for the performance of the ritual, he gave way to the priest chosen for the task. This person was a man selected from among the village elders, according to Burnham (1980:20), and always a member of the founding clan of the village. From the first ceremony performed by the founder before the establishment of the village throughout its annual repetitions, the continuity of the relationship first established between founder and *Só-kao* was maintained.

But of equal importance with lineage was personal character. The priest was a man of few words, who spoke well and who did not cause trouble. He represented the characteristics of a dignified and upright community living in a state of harmony and accord. Christensen observes that the entire village was to be characterized by peace and calm before the ceremony could be undertaken (1984:49-150). If there were "words" in the village, rites to re-establish peace needed to be carried out before *Só-kao* could be approached.[11] The person of the priest focused on the relationship of society to the unseen world. He was the channel, the communicative link between humankind and the world of spirits and gods. His role was one of mediation.

In addition to the community leader and the ritual leader, there were the other participants. These were all the members of the community. The presence of men, women, and children was a clear reminder that the rite belonged to the entire community. It was the duty of all to live in a responsible relationship to the Spirit of the land, it was to the benefit of all that the spirit be pleased and respond benevolently, for what was sought was not individual success or gain, but the welfare of all the community.

Space was also significant. The rite was performed outside the *saayé*, "village." The Gbaya world was divided into a dichotomy of village and bush. The village belonged to human society, it was where people had their houses, it was where they came together as community. But it was from the bush that their sustenance came, the bush was the source of their daily life. The fields were in the bush, the game was in the bush, the wood for the cooking fire was brought from the bush, the clay for the cooking pots was found in the bush, medicine was obtained from plants in the bush, it was to the bush that young men and women were taken for the training acquired through initiation, it was to the bush that children went on outings to "play house" or to learn to hunt by chasing mice and birds. It was accordingly to the bush that the community went to worship the spirit to whom they owed allegiance.

The preliminary act was the choice of the location for the ceremony. It was the village founder or the lead hunter who would select the site that would be the shrine. The place was usually characterized by some feature of nature that was remarkable or out of the ordinary. It might be a particularly large or uniquely shaped rock, a deep pool of water, a large tree, or a hill.[12] It was a normally unfrequented place, a *túú-té-fara*, "a respected, withdrawn place." Prior to the performance of the ceremony, the place would be cleared of grass and brush to make an open area where priest and people could worship.

The combined action of the people was a pilgrimage from the *saayé* "village" to the place in the bush where they could present themselves before *Só-kao*. It was a progression in which a certain order was followed, the priest first, followed by the drummer and the gong ringer, if there was one, then the chief, and finally the people themselves. The return to the village was in the reverse order. The people had departed the village following the priest, they returned to the village leading him, indicative of a fundamental change that had occurred.

The people came to the shrine bearing gifts to be left for the spirit. The men carried wooden sticks cut to represent spears. The women brought potsherds with burning charcoal, together with cassava and water. The chief offered three eggs or a chicken to be sacrificed. Other gifts that might be brought were salt, sesame or peanut oil, tobacco, and corn flour (Christensen 1984:51). Dry wood was also brought for the fire.

Each of these objects was representative of the bearer and of his way of life. The gifts also represented the mysteries of life.

The Gbaya men were hunters, and their most ancient weapon, in addition to the knife, was the spear. The largest game could be brought down by spears in the hands of courageous men. At the funeral of a respected hunter or warrior, the peers of the departed who had equaled his mighty deeds carried his spears and danced in memory and in honor of his heroic exploits. Before his death, Nyaako Banamo, a three-time initiate and hero of numerous battles and hunting expeditions, lamenting the death of the last of his generation, musingly wondered who would be worthy to carry his spears at his funeral.

The spear was not only a wooden shaft but also an iron head forged by the blacksmith's fire and shaped by the blacksmith's hammer. The power of the blacksmith and the items associated with him were thus alluded to in the presence of the spear. The spear was also a symbol in facial scarification where as a single line down the middle of the forehead it marked an only child. An only child, though a blessing to its parents, was also a mark of suffering for a lone child stood alone in the world, a lone spear did not kill a lion.

Cassava represents food, for unless a Gbaya has eaten a meal that includes cassava, he has not eaten. It is the staple of the Gbaya diet. It represents the world of the home, the nourishment prepared by the mother for her children, the sustenance of life itself. Without the mother's gardens, there can be no home and no village and accordingly no society. Food, whether it is meat or cassava, is cooked with water carried from the spring by the mother. It is prepared in a pot over fire lit with firewood brought to the village by the mother. All these items were present at the rite.

The broken pottery was not only a useful recipient for carrying hot coals, but was also representative of the woman and her duties in preparing food for her family and of the food prepared in the pot. The potsherd was a reminder that a broken pot is of no use in preserving life, for it cannot serve its function as a cooking utensil or even as a recipient to contain water. Yet even in its destruction it may still be useful for scooping water or for carrying hot coals with which new fires are lit.

Salt was a much valued commodity that was an important trade item brought by the early Hausa merchants. As stated by the proverb, "The iguana receives salt, thanks to the cane rat." The meat of the iguana was taboo for women, but having salted the prized cane rat, they would sprinkle a few grains on the meat of the iguana as well. Salt for the kitchen was therefore a highly appreciated gift. Not only is there the basic reality of life, there is the spice as well.[13]

Sesame is believed by the Gbaya to be their oldest cultivated plant. Its oil, prized for rubbing on dry skin as well as for cooking, was the first oil known to the Gbaya. Peanuts were a more recent acquisition, whose oil came to replace sesame oil in daily use. Tobacco was a luxury that was thought to be a gift from God. Its use was reserved for the elderly, both men and women, who smoked it in clay pipe bowls or occasionally chewed it.

The wood brought for the priest's fire was a solid dry block of the *gbakuá* tree. This tree is one of the hardest woods found outside the forest.[14] It is frequently left uncut in a field where it stands as a lone twisted sentinel to which the partridges fly for safety when disturbed from eating the cassava tubers. When cut, however, and when dry, the wood of the tree produces a very hot flame. A knotty chunk of the dried wood defies the sharpest axe and is therefore placed as the mainstay of a longlasting hearth fire. The three small sticks comprising the triangular platform were also of the *gbakuá* tree. The symbol then brings together the field, the wildlife that partakes of the field's produce, and the fire of the hearth into one meaning-laden whole. The *gbakuá* tree is frequently a symbol of danger, the wood evokes the nature of life. In the words of the proverb, "The dry chunk of wood that decays, how much more the human being."

The egg represented another category of offering. Often given as a gift to an honored guest, it partakes of the realm of the mysterious. Kuiso Hamadou, the younger surviving brother of Nyaako Banamo, maintains that, "As far as the Old Ones were concerned, the egg wasn't a matter of play." When asked to explain, he responded enigmatically, "It is the power of God" (Interview 10-5-89). Hidden inside its shell is the secret of life, for out of the broken shell comes forth the living chick, which is just as fragile in its early existence as the newly-born infant. In offering the egg at the shrine, the gift of life is evoked. At the same time, as with the salt, the significance of gift given and gift received in the guest-host relationship is emphasized. This is one of the central tenets of Gbaya tradition.

The chicken is also a frequently offered gift to a distinguished guest. Either given live, or preferably butchered and cooked for the visitor, it represents the fulfillment of the Gbaya belief that a guest can only be truly honored through the death of a living offering. The chicken sacrificed at the shrine was therefore life itself. In its death, blood, the essence of life, was sprinkled over the shrine.

The people's first ritual gesture was the silent progression from the village to the shrine. The priest's first gesture was that of removing his clothes, symbolizing unencumbrance before the Spirit of the land. He then placed the wooden spear and the egg that he had been carrying, if he had indeed been carrying gifts himself, at the shrine. Receiving the gifts from the people was another symbolic gesture whereby he accepted on their behalf their offerings and their petitions. The preparation of the offerings in the form of food and libation for the spirit was indication of the people's solicitousness with regard to the spirit's needs. These gifts were then offered to the spirit in the people's total silence of respect and submission. The symbolism of the people's silence is here evident in that only the words of the mediator were to be heard. These were accompanied by the gestures of humility and supplication, lying on the ground and gently clapping his hands while turning or rolling from side to side. The ritual ceremony was closed when the priest reclothed himself for the return to the village.

The prayer of thanksgiving and entreaty was itself stated in words that were both expressive and communicative. Allusion was made to past well-being and prosperity, and also to the previous inhabitants of the land, evoking them in the present inhabitants' petition for the protection and blessing of the spirit who must have cared for other peoples in the past.

A three-fold sound of an antelope horn blown by the priest was the final symbolic element. If the horn gave forth loud blasts, the people acclaimed it as evidence of the spirit's positive response to their supplication (Christensen 1984:53). But arriving in the village there might be a further act, which was the extinguishing of fire in each hearth and the lighting by the priest of a new fire before the chief's compound, to symbolize the complete break with the past year and the beginning of the new on the basis of the harmony that has been renewed between the people and the spirit of their locality.

Numbers among the Gbaya also have symbolic significance and several times in the ritual the number three appears. The number three is most often considered in relation to the number four, three being identified with men, four with women. Thus, although the one who convokes the ritual and the one who performs it are both men, the number evokes the male segment of humankind and by implication the female through the associated number four. In relationship with four, but also in its own right, three represents completeness. When the lion sees that a spear has been thrown in his direction, he waits to see whether a second spear will be thrown, for he is convinced that no one would wilfully make him their target. To afford full benefit of doubt, he waits for a third spear to come flying toward him before finally rising to defend himself from an enemy who must be intentionally seeking to do him harm.

A further symbol might be in evidence during the rite, namely, that of color (Christensen 1984:51). Before laying the men's spears before the shrine, the priest might form a platform of three sticks from the *gbakuá* tree in the shape of a triangle. The three sticks had each been colored red, black, and white.[15] Of the four basic colors named by the Gbaya, only green was missing. Each of the three colors has symbolic importance in many facets of Gbaya culture.

Red is most obviously the color of blood, it is also the color of ripeness and maturity. It represents strength and activity, it may stand for war, and here it surely evoked the sacrifice that was soon to be performed. Black and white are ambivalent colors, representing two sides of the same--light and dark, day and night. Black is associated with the goat and sorcery; at the same time it may designate the color of blackness as beauty (*kpóó-kpóó*) or as ugliness (*Bisisi*). To honor a person is to "blacken" him, while making a person feel bad is to "blacken his liver." The opposite of showing respect to someone is to "lighten, make pale," and the color of death is white. The warrior's shield is rimmed by the black and white pelt of the colobus monkey, while all three colors are significant in the boys' initiation rite known as *láBi*.[16]

From this last example may be cited symbolism of shape. The laying of the three sticks in a triangular pattern may be a practical means of keeping the offerings off the ground, but the triangle also symbolizes the three stones of the hearth or the fireplace. The woman's cooking pot stands on three stones or three termite mounds placed in the shape of a triangle, among which the fire is built. This triangle represents the mother's nurturing role in the household and when the triangle is disturbed or violated by a deliberate act, the family is in danger of disintegration. The triangle is also the central focal point of the rite performed within the family context to remember their departed ancestors.

As the symbols are seen in the rite of worshipping *Só-kao*, the participants are borne beyond themselves and the immediate meaning to the larger meaning of society and of existence. The ritual being played out before their eyes is not limited to the present, but represents the Gbaya spirit and life in its totality, including its historical depth. While each context may focus on a certain component or aspect of the symbol, the participants in the ritual are aware of the full range of valency of each symbol as they use it or see it used.

Gbaya Theology and the Christian Church

The Gbaya of present-day Cameroon first encountered Christianity through missionaries who settled in their midst in 1924. Long before then they had encountered Islam, probably first through itinerant Hausa or Kanuri traders, and from the middle of the nineteenth century through the Fulani, who exercised increasing political influence from their emirates to the northwest (cf. Christiansen 1956; Burnham 1982).

The influences extend back before the arrival of Islam and Christianity. In their earlier movements the Gbaya were in contact with other peoples in central Africa. That these people influenced their way of life is evident from Gbaya initiations, which were in a state of flux as far back as memory and tradition can be reconstructed.

It becomes difficult then today to distinguish clearly that which is truly Gbaya and that which has been adopted and adapted to the point that it has become part of Gbaya tradition. There was no Gbaya guardian of the faith. That Gbaya faith and expression of faith was influenced is certain. The term *so* seems to be Gbaya, but what it represented to the ancestors is not clear. Perhaps the ambivalence regarding "god" and "spirits" noted by early writers is evidence of the influence of Islam. The Gbaya may have incorporated the idea of "God" as distinct from "spirits," making the distinction of a "God-place-person" as the Creator God on the basis of their new knowledge of the Allah of Islam.

The Spirit of the land is associated with the previous inhabitants, as evidenced by the evocation of those people in the prayer to *Só-kao*. The word *kao* is thought by the Gbaya of Cameroon to be of Mbum origin, meaning "earth, land," and the word for the antelope horn, *fol*, is known to be Mbum. Some maintain that the rite itself was borrowed from the Mbum,[17] while others assert that the rite predates any Gbaya-Mbum contact. Hilberth, writing about the Gbaya in the Central African Republic nearly thirty years ago, identifies *kao* as "a spirit who rules over the savannahs, the forests and the rivers" (1962:9).

Clearly, however, the thanksgiving offering that Christensen describes in relation to *kao* has been influenced by Islam, including the name itself, "sacrifice-doing-thanks-to-*Só-kao*" (1984:155).[18] The custom of giving a thank offering and sharing the sacrificial food among the poor or the children of the village is Islamic and is widely known and frequently practiced among the Gbaya.

But if new influences have impinged upon the old, it is equally true that the old influences the new (cf. Taylor 1963). The new is patterned on the old, and in spite of early missionaries' efforts to purge all old beliefs and practices, the former ways have not been completely forgotten.

There may be two reasons for this. First, the old Gbaya belief system in many ways is not so different from beliefs and practices found in the Scriptures. If the rite described above is taken against the backdrop of the Old Testament, many parallels become evident, as well as some marked differences. Secondly, where there are differences, there may be relationships between the two that clarify and give meaning to the new.

Although the Gbaya did not have as clear an idea of moving toward a Promised Land as we find recorded in the story of the Exodus, there is surely a similarity in their desire for a better land, if not one flowing in milk and honey, then one blessed with plentiful game and fertile soil. Although the Gbaya do not recount having taken the land from previous dwellers, they were very aware of those who had gone before, and as we have seen, they did not hesitate to adopt practices and beliefs from those whom they encountered, which the Israelites did as well, in spite of the prophets' dire warnings.

That God's children should have built an altar for thanksgiving on crossing the Jordan, that they should have worshipped at the Sacred Oak of Mamre or sacrificed at the "high places," would have been quite in keeping with the Gbaya understanding of their responsibility to remember the spirit of the land.

That blood should be spilled in sacrifice was quite normal, and that it should be carried out by a priest as mediator was also according to the Gbaya way of worshiping. That thank offerings should be brought of the first fruits, before the meat of the chase or the harvest of the field was brought home, was also Gbaya tradition.

That a close relationship might exist between God and his people was also not foreign to Gbaya thought, for the priest addressed the spirit personally in praise and thanks and supplication on behalf of the community.[19]

But even as religious practice in Old Testament times developed from that of the nomadic patriarchs to those of the tribes in migration and settlement to the monarchy of Saul and David, aspects that may have existed all the time come into increased prominence. These aspects develop into themes that have theological import for the Israelites as well as the Gbaya.

A very common theme in the Old Testament is the offering of that which is the best. Aaron called on the Children of Israel to bring their gold earrings, from which he made the golden calf. The tabernacle was made of the finest materials, Solomon's temple even more so. Sacrifices presented to God were to be without flaw or blemish. Abraham was commanded to offer his only son.

The Gbaya, on the other hand, brought the most common and ordinary. If there are symbols, the Gbaya brought symbols of symbols, for the spears were mere sticks that represented real spears, the potsherds were broken pottery. Although possessing no gold or silver, they did have cowries and iron that were used as mediums of exchange, but money was never offered to *Só-kao*. The Chamba to the north created elaborate ritual pottery and masks, other peoples made intricate carvings for use in religious ceremonies, but the Gbaya did not. The Gbaya worshipers did not presume to be able to satisfy what might be the spirit's wishes. They tried instead to offer the gestures that would be evidence of their reverence and their supplication. There was no manipulation or magic but rather offerings made in devotion and faith.

A further aspect of the ordinary was the fact that the priest was chosen for the occasion. In the annual rite he represented the people and their chief as a mediator, but he was not of a separate class, he was not of a clan or family set apart for the task of carrying out religious duties on a professional basis. What was required was that he be of a certain character, and reminiscent of Moses' worry, a man skilled with words. On the hunt it was the leader or the eldest of the group that performed the ceremony.

The shrine likewise, if not ordinary, was natural. It was not built by human hands, it was not a temple where God dwelled, but rather a meeting place where the community would come to encounter the spirit to whom they were beholden. In the Gbaya concept of the shrine there is perhaps something of the Israelite "tent of meeting" (Exodus 33.7-11), which was also located outside the people's dwelling place.

But if there was an emphasis in the Gbaya worship, it was in doing it "according to the way." Although not all the symbols might be present at a given ritual performance, and surely the hunting ritual was less elaborate than the annual village ritual, each had to be carried out in the appropriate manner, in a spirit of devotion, reverence, and faith. The steps were not followed to manipulate the spirit, but rather to show the worshipers' attitude of dependence and trust. The importance of harmony in the village prior to the ritual performance is evidence of the people's awareness of their own attitude in approaching the divine.

In this they were not very different from the psalmist's affirmation that God wants, not sacrifices and burnt offerings, but a broken and contrite heart (Psalm 51.16-17). Ultimately, even in the Biblical tradition the sacrifices are essentially symbols of the worshiper's heart.

Conclusion

In summarizing the state of the Gbaya church, Burnham in 1982 (p. 129) asked two questions, "What *do* (author's emphasis) the Gbaya believe?" and "Will the Gbaya church be able to play an effective role in the future?" The first question is surely relevant. The second bears asking, even as it needs clarification.

The practice of worshiping *kao* is no longer carried out as it once was, but it is neither forgotten nor abandoned. In Meiganga in 1982 after a cement block fell off the upper ledges of a new cinema building during a rainstorm and killed a young boy who was waiting out the storm under the balcony below, the owner of the cinema and town elders sacrificed to *Só-kao* on the nearby mountain to restore harmony in the community. Contrary to traditional practice, this was not a public event. It was carried out by select representatives of the chief and was performed inconspicuously at night, to avoid attracting the attention and ridicule of the wider community. Following the sacrifice the episode was quietly let drop.

The community today is not as homogeneous as it once might have been. If traditional faith was a community faith, as Mbiti asserts (1970:7), the small village community is disappearing. The town today includes Muslims and Christians, both Catholic and Protestant, as well as "traditionalists." The nature of hunting is also changing from that of the spear to the gun and soon to no hunting, for there is little game remaining where the Gbaya once hunted eland, buffalo and elephant. As Monica Wilson, writing about the Nyakusa of southern Africa, posits, "This disintegration of a former coherence, and a decreasing awareness of the meaning of symbols used, are perhaps characteristic of changing societies in Africa" (1959:12).

If the purpose of faith was "utilitarian" and "practical," again in the words of Mbiti (1970:7), the needs of today are different. When tragedy strikes the city, *Só-kao* is remembered, but not for the everyday worries of salaries that may not be received or jobs that may not materialize.

Yet, the faith of the grandfathers influences even the practice of Christianity. Although Sunday offerings are remarkably meager, whether because God is pleased with a gesture or because the accounting of church finances is notoriously uncertain, the annual Harvest Festival is always a great success. At this event the entire Christian community joyously brings of its first-fruits, whether dried or raw cassava, sugar cane, corn, squash, bananas, firewood, or even a portion of one's salary. On an ordinary Sunday in the Catholic mass, when offerings are given processionally, these might include bottles of "33 Export," the modern equivalent of the traditional libation.

The elderly Gbaya evangelist laments the spirit of irreverence that he says characterizes today's Christian worship service. No more is the same care maintained in carrying out the ritual worship due to the God we worship, he says. The church leader calling on his congregation to be quiet so that he may begin the liturgy of the day compares their behavior to that of the marketplace, a far cry from the silence that characterized the worship of *Só-kao*.

Perhaps Gbaya theologians need to look more closely at tradition to seek the "seeds of the Gospel," as Aylword Shorter has written, or to paraphrase him, to look for the "Gbaya Old Testament" (1974:9,70). Christensen writes of the significance of the *sore* leaf as the Gbaya Tree of Life, which he interprets as a metaphor for the New Testament bringer of peace. "The Gbaya naming of Jesus," he calls it (1984).

The essence of the traditional rite was "fixing, preparing"; it was a worshipful act. The Christian "goes" to church or "gathers" before a God who may seem to be more distant and unresponsive than the spirit to whom the forefathers addressed their petitions. Praying was called *wórá So* from the verb "to speak." The Christian church has adopted the term *kófá So*, which means literally "to beg God." The traditional term reflected an intimate personal relationship, for the common greeting was *Wór-mo* "Let us speak." Begging was frowned upon.

When asked whether the spirits responded to petitioning, the late Banamo Nyaako affirmed that having prayed one need only go as far as that tree, and he pointed to a tree scarcely a hundred yards away, before killing an animal. But now, when asked what has happened to the spirits who are no longer remembered, he held out his hands in helpless silence (Interview 9-7-77).

"The church must find its place in living cultural traditions," Shorter asserts (1974:4), and Schreiter speaks of "local theology" that must take the local culture seriously (1985:12-16). The question is what is living in this age of change? If the practices disappear as being outmoded or no longer relevant, do the symbols survive, or the metaphors? Can the church of today retrieve from the past that which is still meaningful to the Gbaya spirit to enable the contemporary believer to interpret the Gospel within the framework of that spirit?

In sermons, traditional metaphors are often evoked and not infrequently in Scripture translation. For the sacraments the previously borrowed French terms *baptême* and *communion* have given way to *zúiá bîî* "bathing person," the metaphor of ancient purification rites, and *yongmó-kendao*, the "last meal" of Gbaya tradition. The early Gbaya spoke of covenants which were sealed by mixing and sharing a few drops of each other's blood. This rite was called "drinking blood," which is the title now given to the Old and New Testaments replacing the earlier *Alkawal* of Arabic origin.[20] But this is at the level of translation where it is normal to establish the terminology that will not only communicate the Word of God, but that will also serve the church in its understanding of the Good News and in its expression of the Christian faith.

In the realm of liturgical practice and congregational worship, however, the traditional symbols are remarkably absent, particularly in Protestant churches. In Roman Catholic chapels and churches, wood from the gallery forest may be used for the altar, or a rock from a nearby mountain. The decorative colors are sometimes the red and black and white of tradition. At the same time, while efforts have been made by both Protestant and Catholic missionaries to draw on the riches of the traditional initiation rite (Christensen 1982, Campagna 1985), this rite appears to be receding ever further into the past with all its metaphors and symbolism (cf Burnham and Noss 1982). What needs to be determined is what are truly the living cultural traditions for the Gbaya today and what will remain living tomorrow.

The new mat is being woven, but what its color and design will be is not easy to anticipate. As the ancestors said, "The drummer does not hear the rhythm of his own drum." Yet the drumming does continue as today's rhythms become those of tomorrow. If the Christian church is to continue to be the vibrant part of the Gbaya community that it is today, its theologians and translators must find the symbols and metaphors that will carry the meaning of life in the expression of tomorrow's faith.

Bibliography

Barley, Nigel. 1983. *Symbolic Structures: An Exploration of the Culture of the Dowayos*. Cambridge: Cambridge University Press.

Bodénès, Pierre. 1973. "La grande pêche gbaya." In Yves Schaller, ed. *Les Kirdi du Nord-Cameroun*. Midjivin, Cameroun: Mission Catholique. pp. 128-132.

Burnham, Philip. 1980. *Opportunity and Constraint in a Savanna Society: The Gbaya of Meiganga, Cameroun*. London: Academic Press.

———. 1981. "Notes on Gbaya History" in C. Tardits, ed. *Contibution de la recherche ethnologique à l'histoire des civilisations du Cameroun*. Paris: Centre National de Recherche Scientifique. pp. 121-130.

———. 1982. "The Gbaya and the Sudan Mission: 1924 to the Present" in Noss, pp. 115-130.

———, Elisabeth Copet-Rougier, and Philip Noss. 1986. "Gbaya et Mkako: contribution ethno-linguistique à l'histoire de l'est Cameroun" in *Paideuma* 32.87-128

Burnham, Philip and Philip Noss. 1982. "L'éducation gbaya," in Renaud Santerre and C. Mercier-Tremblay, eds. *La quête du Savoir*. Montreal: Montreal University Press. pp. 208-229.

Campagna, Marco. 1985. "Baptême Chrétien et rite d'initiation dans la tradition africaine" in *Riflessioni Rh* II.4.209-248.

Christensen, Thomas G. 1982. "La'bi, a Gbaya Initiation Rite" in Noss, pp. 173-195.

———. 1990. *An African Tree of Life*. Maryknoll, NY: Orbis Books.

————. 1984. "The Gbaya Naming of Jesus." Doctor of Theology Dissertation. Chicago: Lutheran School of Theology.

Christiansen, Ruth. 1956. *For the Heart of Africa*. Minneapolis: Augsburg Publishing House.

Eliade, Mircea. 1988. *Symbolism, the Sacred, and the Arts*. D. Apostolos-Cappadona, ed. New York: Crossroad.

Hilberth, J. 1962. *Les Gbaya*. Studia Ethnographica Upsaliensia 19. Lund: Ohlssons Boktryckeri.

Mbiti, John S. 1970. *African Religions and Philosophy*. Garden City: Anchor Books.

Mohammadou, Eldridge. 1978. *Fulbé hooseere: Les royaumes Foulbé du plateau de l'adamaoua au XIX siecle*. Tokyo: Institute for the Study of Languages and Cultures of Asia and Africa.

————. *Le peuplement de la haute bénoué*. Yaoundé: Office National de la Recherche Scientifique.

————. 1986. *Traditions d'origine des peuples du centre et de l'ouest du Cameroun*. Tokyo: Institute for the Study of Languages and Cultures of Asia and Africa.

Noss, Philip A. 1972. "An interpretation of Gbaya religious practice," in *International Review of Missions* 61:57-374.

————, ed. 1982. *Grafting Old Rootstock: Studies in Culture and Religion of the Chamba, Duru, Fula, and Gbaya of Cameroun*. Dallas: International Museum of Cultures.

Schreiter, Robert J. 1985. *Constucting Local Theologies*. Maryknoll: Orbis Books.

BIBLIOGRAPHY

Shorter, Aylward. 1974. *African Culture and the Christian Church: An Introduction to Social and Pastoral Anthropology*. Maryknoll: Orbis.

Taylor, John V. 1963. *The Primal Vision: Christian Presence amid African Religion*. Philadelphia: Fortress Press.

Tessmann, G. 1934. *Die Baja: ein Negerstamm im mittleren Sudan, Teil I, Materielle und seelische Kultur*. Stuttgart: Strecker und Schroder.

————. 1937. *Die Baja: ein Negerstamm im mittleren Sudan, Teil II, Geistige Kultur*. Stuttgart: Strecker und Schroder.

Turner, Victor. 1967. *A Forest of Symbols: Aspects of Ndembu Ritual*. Ithaca: Cornell University Press.

————. 1974. *Dramas, Fields, and Metaphors: Symbolic Action in Human Society*. Ithaca: Cornell University Press.

Wilson, Monica. 1959. *Communal Rituals of the Nyakyusa*. Oxford: Oxford University Press for the International African Institute.

Notes

1. I would express my appreciation to the many Gbaya who have shared personal knowledge and experiences in conversations over many years. I would particularly wish to mention the late Banamo Nyaako of Meidougou, the late Singmo Dua of Baina, the evangelist Daniel Sodéa, and the pastors Darman Paul and Yadji André. I am indebted to the latter for extensive notes written in 1972 depicting ritual performances that he had witnessed and performed himself. My own research notes are supplemented by additional details recorded in Christensen 1984 to whom I would also express appreciation for numerous helpful insights and comments regarding the interpretation and understanding of Gbaya theology and its significance for the church today.

2. In this essay, the implosive voiced alveolar and bilabial stops are written as *D* and *B* and the velar nasal is written as *ng*.

3. In the transcription of Gbaya terms, the acute accent represents high tone, the circumflex high-falling tone, unmarked syllables are low tone, and the cedilla is nasalization.

4. Although the Gbaya relied much more on hunting than on fishing, the rite was also performed prior to the building of a fishing platform for the annual "great fishing expedition" (cf Bodénes 1973:28-132, Christensen 1984:39-140).

5. The verb *Dáfí* literally means "to fix, repair" and is used for sacrificing, worshipping, or remembering, as in the case of the spirits of the departed ancestors.

6. If the ritual was being carried out far from the village, a fire would be lit with flint.

7. Text recorded on tapes with transcriptions deposited at Indiana Archives of Traditional Music, Indiana University, Bloomington, Indiana.

NOTES

8. The *sore* tree, Anona Senegalensis of the Anonaceae family, a common savannah tree, is very important in numerous Gbaya rites of purification and peace-making. For a detailed study of its ritual and symbolic role in Gbaya tradition, see Christensen 1984 and 1990.

9. Within the life of the Gbaya family, other *so* were also important, most notably those associated with the departed ancestors known generally as *so-dáa* "spirits of the fathers." There were the "spirits of the mothers," the "spirits of the grandmothers" and the "spirits of the grandfathers." These were remembered within the village and within the family.

10. For discussion of symbolism and for its use in studies of religion, see Turner 1967 and 1974. A helpful theoretical discussion of symbolism within the framework of a society not far to the north of the Gbaya may be found in Barley 1983.

11. Where there were "words," society was in danger of disintegrating. As a warning to someone who caused words, a person might name his dog "Wen-dong," lit. "words-behind." Whenever the dog's name was pronounced, it was a warning to avoid slander, backbiting and other forms of malicious speech. The dictum *wen dé ná* "words are bad" was seen on the edges of a French Bible, written by its Gbaya owner as a reminder of the power of words for good or evil (Personal observation in Yaoundé 23-10-88).

12. The different spirits were identified according to the object or place they were identified with and they were named accordingly, *só-gŭn-te* "spirit foot of tree," *só-dĭr-yi* "spirit pool of water," *só-kaya* "spirit hill," and *só-ta* "spirit rock."

13. In traditional use, salt seems to have been primarily used as a seasoner and not as a preservative. Prior to the arrival of salt, the Gbaya boiled plants and roots to distill a variety of salt called *Dang-tong* "bad salt."

14. The *gbakuá* is of the Combretaceae family, "terminalia dewevrei wild."

NOTES

15. Christensen identifies the coloring used as white from kaolin, black from charcoal, and red from camwood (1984:51).

16. Shorter (1974:8) notes the widespread symbolism of these three colors in African cultures.

17. Daniel Sodéa of Meiganga claims that the rite of *Dáfá kao* was borrowed from the Mbum, citing as evidence the fact that the prayers were often said in the Mbum language (Interview 10-5-89).

18. *Sadaka* "offering, sacrifice" is a borrowing from Arabic through Fulfulde, and *ósoko* "thank you" is a Fulfulde word. The Gbaya term *sîî So* "repay, propitiate God" is little used today.

19. Père Bodénès recounts accompanying the priest who periodically went to pray to *Só-kao* on behalf of the village of Djohong, who in his prayer asked the spirit's blessing on the priest and pastor and their respective communities as well.

20. Early missionaries and translators attempted to make as clear a break with the past as possible by avoiding use of any words or expressions that were associated with traditional beliefs and religious practices. They preferred instead to adopt new terms borrowed from Islam or from French. Gbaya translators during the past two decades have chosen to make maximum use of Gbaya vocabulary and expression, with less reliance on borrowed terms.

Contributors

Dr. Ernst R. Wendland is a seminary professor in Lusaka, Zambia who works extensively with the Chewa and Tonga Bible translation projects. He has a Ph.D. in African Literature from the University of Wisconsin, and is the author of several books on the cultural context of translation.

Drs. van der Jagt, Mojola, Marchese Zogbo and Noss are UBS Translation Consultants.

Dr. Krijn van der Jagt has worked in both Cameroon and Kenya and his Ph.D. from the University of Utrecht (Netherlands) was a study of Turkana religion.

Dr. Aloo O. Mojola has a Ph.D. in the Philosophy of Language from the University of Nairobi, and has also studied in Germany and the United States.

Dr. Lynell Marchese Zogbo, whose Ph.D. is in Linguistics from the University of California, Los Angeles, has written on the Kru languages of Ivory Coast and Liberia, and is known for her work in the field of discourse analysis.

Dr. Philip A. Noss, whose Ph.D was also earned at the Univeristy of Wisconsin, has written extensively on Gbaya culture and language, as well as on African literature and discourse structures.

Dr. Philip C. Stine is the UBS Translation Services Coordinator. He was formerly a UBS Translation Consultant in West Africa. His Ph.D. is in Linguistics from the University of Michigan.